Discover brown-flour baking with the
charismatic Rose Wilde—a grain geek hungry for
texture, flavor, and diversity of ingredients.

In her extraordinary debut cookbook, Rose Wilde wants you to bake with more—
more flavor, more texture, more knowledge, and more grains. From buckwheat,
barley, and brown rice to spelt, sonora, and sweet corn, *Bread and Roses* is your
comprehensive guide to rebuilding your pantry from scratch, choosing ingredients
with an impact beyond your plate, and experimenting with cakes, breads, buns,
and everything in between.

Inspired by her global travels and experience as the founder of beloved Los
Angeles bakery Red Bread, Wilde shares more than 100 unique sweet and savory
recipes, including Khorasan Grape Za'atar Sugar Buns, Durum Fried Cheese Pastry
with Juniper Gelato, and Einkorn Roasted Garlic and Leek Challah. Learn the origins and basic science behind more than fifteen ancient, heirloom, and alternative
grains; how to enhance depth of flavor by tasting for tannins, body, acidity, strength,
and hydration; and the proper way to source and preserve ingredients from local
farmers and your own backyard. The possibilities for grain-based goodies are
endless. Whether you want to rediscover your relationship with grains or grow
confidence and creativity in an eco-friendly kitchen, *Bread and Roses* is the book
you need to make your bakes blossom.

Bread
and
Roses

Bread
and
Roses

100+ Grain-Forward Recipes Featuring Global Ingredients and Botanicals

Rose Wilde

PHOTOGRAPHY BY Rebecca Stumpf
ILLUSTRATED BY Stacy Michelson

Countryman Press

An Imprint of W. W. Norton & Company
Celebrating a Century of Independent Publishing

For my mother,
the hardest worker I have ever known;
she gave me my first bread and a world full of roses

For information about permission to
reproduce selections from this book,
write to Permissions, Countryman Press,
500 Fifth Avenue, New York, NY 10110

For information about special discounts
for bulk purchases, please contact
W. W. Norton Special Sales at
specialsales@wwnorton.com or 800-233-4830

Manufacturing through Imago
Book design by Allison Chi
Production manager: Devon Zahn

Countryman Press
www.countrymanpress.com

An imprint of W. W. Norton & Company, Inc.
500 Fifth Avenue, New York, NY 10110
www.wwnorton.com

978-1-68268-743-7

10 9 8 7 6 5 4 3 2 1

This book of recipes that uses whole grains is intended as a general information resource. The author is neither a doctor nor a dietician. Consult your healthcare provider before changing your diet to include significant amounts of any new food, especially if you are diabetic or suffer from an auto-immune condition or any other health condition (and especially if you are taking any prescription drug), or if you are pregnant or nursing, or if you have food or other allergies. In particular, if you have celiac disease, non-celiac gluten sensitivity, a wheat allergy, or a similar condition, be sure to note which recipes are specifically identified as being naturally gluten-free or vegan, and which recipes require you to swap one or more ingredients in order to make that recipe gluten-free or vegan. You also should consult your doctor before introducing fermented foods into your diet. If you find yourself reacting negatively to any fermented product or any non-fermented food created from this book, stop consuming it.

This book includes directions for creating and maintaining "starters" by means of fermentation. Fermenting at home carries certain risks, including, but not limited to, contamination of foods from inadequate cleaning or sanitization of equipment, and allergic reactions to ingredients. Please be sure to read and familiarize yourself with the fermentation directions and warnings in the book. This book also discusses foraging as a means of efficiently and ethically accessing wild plants. Before you do any foraging, read and familiarize yourself with the directions and warnings in the book. In particular, make sure you can recognize poisonous plants and leaves, and do not use anything you find foraging as an ingredient unless you are absolutely sure it is okay to ingest.

Please pay careful attention to the warnings about how long you can safely store different foods in different ways (for example, in the fridge or in an airtight container) before they are no longer edible, and be sure to note the book's warnings about mold. Also, please be careful when using a blowtorch.

The commercial products that the author recommends in this book are ones that the author personally likes. You need to do your own research to find the ones that are best for you.

Any URLs displayed in this book link or refer to websites that existed as of press time. The publisher is not responsible for, and should not be deemed to endorse or recommend, any website other than its own or any app or content that it did not create. The author, also, is not responsible for any third-party material.

Contents

11 *Introduction*

15 Chapter 1.
Why Whole Grains?

17 Modern Wheats, Milling at Home, and All-Purpose Flour

18 Tasting Grain and Other Ingredients

29 Eating Root to Blossom

31 Talking to Your Farmers and Basic Gardening

32 Basics of Foraging

35 Chapter 2.
Tools, Method, Time, Temperature & Scale

37 Tools

37 How to Cookie and Tart

38 How to Pastry

40 How to Bread

52 How to Cake

56 Time Shifting: Deeper Dive in to Leaveners, Liquid Temperature, and Seed Rate

61 Chapter 3.
Ingredients, Lands & Recipes

66 ASIA: RICE, BARLEY, BUCKWHEAT

70 Brown Rice Chamomile Shortbread

73 Brown Rice Kinako Salted Cherry Blossom Cherry Crisp

74 Brown Rice Donut Bars with Genmaicha Glaze

77 Brown Rice Scallion Pancake with Chive Blossoms

80 Fried Brown Rice Pudding with Chrysanthemum Custard

82 Brown Rice Cotton Cake with Candied Sudachi Lime

84 Toasted Barley Porridge with Clotted Cream & Roasted Kumquats

87 Toasted Barley Blood Orange Caramel Thumbprint Cookies

88 Barley Miso Chocolate Chunk Cookies

91 Barley Nectarine Fritter with Lemongrass Glaze

93 Buckwheat Brown Sugar Crumble Carrot Peach Icebox Cake

96 Buckwheat Sugar Tarts with Bay Leaf Roasted Rhubarb

99 Buckwheat Soba Noodles with Cured Egg, Nukazuke Pickles & Kosho Butter Chicken

101 Buckwheat Cake with Buckwheat Milk Tea Soak, Yuzu Curd, Coconut Custard & Torched Meringue

104 EUROPE: EMMER, RYE, SONORA

109 Emmer Sourdough Pasta with Butter Parmesan Sauce & Spring Pea Tendrils

111 Emmer Pear Tarragon Honey Custard Tart

114 Emmer Maritozzo with Blistered Lavender Blackberries

117 Emmer Everything Bread: Bâtard, Boule & Grissini

120 Rye Triple Chocolate Crinkle Cookies

123 Rye Apple Onion Focaccia

125 Rye Black Bread

128 Rye Malt Ice Cream

131 Rye Chocolate Cake with Hazelnut Chocolate Custard, Sweet Woodruff Cocoa Nib Cream & German Chocolate Buttercream

133 Sonora Chocolate Custard Pie with Chicory Cream

136 Sonora Pistachio Linzer Cookies with Red Currant Violet Jam

138 Sonora Madeleines with Fennel White Chocolate Shell

141 Sonora Cheese Sticks with Arugula Blossoms, Parmesan & Fried Parsley

143 Sonora Vegetable Confetti Cake with Greengage Plum, Whipped Cheesecake & Smoky Honey Swiss Buttercream

146 AMERICAS: QUINOA, AMARANTH, CORN

151 Puffed Quinoa Brown Sugar Brownies with Persimmon

153 Quinoa Churros with Chocolate Sauce

156 Quinoa Brown Sugar Chili Buns with Hot Chocolate Drink

159 Quinoa Upside-Down Cake with Pineapple & Candied Hibiscus

162 Amaranth Marigold Buñuelos

165 Amaranth Cookie Sandwiches with Plantains, Caramelized White Chocolate & Crema Buttercream

168 Amaranth Squash Almond Butter Pancakes with Maple Syrup & Roasted Sunflower Butter

171 Amaranth & Corn Crumble with Papaya, Raspberry & Lime

172 Corn Cookies with Candied Mango & Pink Peppercorn Sugar

175 Sweet Corn Biscuits with Vanilla
 Macerated Fruit & Cultured Milk Soup

176 Corn Crust Blueberry Pie with Lilac
 Ice Cream

179 Masa Corn Nasturtium Quesadilla

182 Corn Tres Leches Honeysuckle Cake

185 Corn Cake with Lemon Verbena
 Custard, Corn Curd & Passion
 Fruit Buttercream

188 AFRICA: DURUM, TEFF,
 MILLET, OATS

193 Durum Chocolate Chunk Cookies

194 Durum Orange Blossom Overnight
 Porridge with Tamarind Syrup
 & Watermelon

197 Durum Fried Cheese Pastry with
 Juniper Gelato

198 Teff Crackers with Rooibos Olive Oil

200 Teff Sugar Moons with Peanut
 Frangipane & Marshmallow Fluff

202 Teff Anise Custard Cake

205 Millet Drop Donuts with Jasmine Sugar
 & Fermented Honey

206 Millet Cream Puffs with Coffee Custard

209 Millet Fried Sage Hand Pies with Runny
 Egg, Sweet Potato & Greens

211 Oat Walnut Cake with Banana
 Marmalade, Rose Geranium Custard
 & Sorghum Buttercream

214 Oatmeal Chocolate Chunk Cookies

217 Baked Oatmeal with Fig Bee Pollen Jam
 & Fig Leaf Oil

218 Oat Spice Crumble Biscuit Rolls

220 WESTERN ASIA &
 NORTH AFRICA: SPELT,
 KHORASAN, EINKORN

224 Spelt Mahleb Chocolate Chunk Cookies

226 Spelt Almond Rosewater Tea Cake

228 Spelt Morning Buns with Apricot Jam &
 Sumac Sugar

231 Spelt Khachapuri with Dandy Green
 Eggs

233 Khorasan Apple Halva Lattice Sheet Pie
 with Halva Custard

236 Khorasan Tahini Birdseed Muffins

239 Khorasan Grape Za'atar Sugar Buns

241 Khorasan Nigella Malawach with
 Nettle Dip

244 Einkorn Saffron Cookies with
 Pepper Sugar

247 Einkorn Blondies with Brown Butter
 Dates

248 Einkorn Labneh Dinner Rolls with
 Aleppo Butter

251 Einkorn Roasted Garlic and Leek
 Challah

254 Einkorn Bagels with Crispy Broccoli
 Rabe Borage Cream Cheese

257 Einkorn Olive Oil Cake with Roasted
 Quince in Rose Hip Custard, Poppy
 Seed Cream, Pistachio Buttercream &
 Pistachio Grass

261 Chapter 4.
Pantry & Larder

262 Salts and Sugars

264 Glazes, Sauces, Soups, and Drinks

266 Roasted, Macerated, and Candied

270 Jams and Marmalades

274 Soaks, Creams, Curds, Custards,
     and Ice Creams

281 Meringues, Marshmallow Fluff,
     and Buttercreams

284 Ferments, Spreads, Butters,
     Oils, and Spice Mixes

293 *Staying Hungry*
295 *Resources*
297 *Acknowledgments*
299 *Index*

Introduction

I grew up in a food-centric household. When I was very young, my parents ran a restaurant called The Good Earth, in St. Petersburg, Florida. My mother baked daily bread based on my grandfather's recipe and my father ran the garden and compost system in the back that dictated the menu. These models of sustainability stayed with me. I spent my earliest years in the garden, eating blossoms off new plants. I took to baking once I was tall enough to reach the counter.

Using food to build community among family, friends, and strangers was an important part of my childhood in Ecuador, and with my extended Hispanic family. In Quito, living in an international community, I learned how food can connect people of many different cultures and cross language barriers. I also learned the magic of comfort food, how to appreciate the undeniable taste of fresh produce from a bustling market, and saw firsthand the ubiquity and life-sustaining power of grains, cereals, and pulses turned into flour. From large family parties, I learned how to cook economically.

As I grew up, I continued to travel for school, for work, and for pleasure throughout Europe, Asia, and Africa. The bold flavors I encountered in various cuisines would inspire lifelong food safaris everywhere I went. Not only was I singularly obsessed with eating, I sought out kitchens with cooks and bakers in all parts of the world to teach me. In my travels, more than anything else, I was struck by how foundational and versatile breads and their grains were in otherwise radically different food cultures. Diversity of grains is what built civilization and kept the cuisines varied and interesting. But it's also the thing we have the most in common! Most babies' first food on this planet is some form of bread or porridge.

In 2011, when I was graduating from law school with a focus on international law and sustainable development, my love for food came to a head with my health. I had a gallbladder attack, ultimately having that organ removed. But it was the height of gluten phobia, so I was also told to cut dairy, gluten, and sugar from my diet. Speaking with friends, I realized that this warning was being made to nearly everyone I knew, as a "cure" for a variety of health ailments. But how could this be? I had eaten every *pain au chocolat* possible in France, packed in an embarrassing amount of *momos* in Tibet, and consumed my weight in Parmesan in Italy without a problem. And in America, I generally didn't eat a lot of these foods because, here, they were highly processed, and I didn't like the taste. When I was

finally given a test for these food allergies, they were not present. Still, I wanted to learn more about how other cultures handled a diversity of ingredients. Ultimately, this quest became a dive deep in to the traditional food practices across the world.

I returned to the kitchen armed with all the information and tastes of my travels. Eating whole foods, and forming deep relationships with farmers, was the answer—not giving up the delicious foods that helped support and grow our civilization. I knew I had to make this "global perspective"–based food accessible for everyone.

Bread and Roses is my effort to do so, combining my world experience, deep research on grains, and expertise from founding Red Bread, an award-winning and beloved Los Angeles café and bakery, to heading the pastry and bread programs at Michelin-starred Rustic Canyon, Manuela, Firehouse, Rossoblu, and Mother Wolf.

Bread and Roses illustrates how cooking and baking can be approached with reverence for all ingredients, a dedication to the pantry, and a celebration of grains around the world. It is a return to food crafted with a sense of love and abundance from farms and fields. It provides the home cook/baker and the professional with a foundational and historical understanding of grains and equips them with the tools of their own senses to be creative, and to nourish themselves and their communities.

My aim is to make you fall in love with grains and curiosity. With this book, I hope to take you on the next step on your journey to understanding whole grains as the basis of all cultural foodways: showing off singular grains and blends paired with other ingredients. For those with an allergy or related diagnosis, I have included many whole-grain recipes that are naturally gluten-free or vegan. Additionally, I note where a simple swap will make a recipe gluten-free or vegan. As for sugar, my philosophy is always "not too sweet" and as unrefined as possible.

You will learn the difference in leaveners—

including wild yeast—for more choice, depth of flavor, and control over time in your bakes. We should all consider grains with the same depth we give wine. In this book, using the tools I've developed and tested in my cooking classes, I will show you how to taste flavor, tannins, strength, activity, and hydration. I'll help you bring deep flavor to your bakes and deliver consistent results in sync with changing seasons. In time, this will allow you to develop intuition and begin to understand how to pair sweet and savory throughout the year. "Flour" should not be standardized for our planet or our plate.

Because I want these recipes to be accessible across cultures, I'll give you guidelines for how to best source grains and highlight how to make substitutions, changing out ingredients based on local and seasonal availability. Whenever possible, I include headnotes showing how and where you can adjust a recipe for time constraints, with places to stop and start to make the recipe best fit your schedule. I also make note of the shelf life of your bake so you know how long it will last. Alongside all the recipes, you will find additional illustrations showing the required tools for the recipe. This way, you will never be racing around the kitchen to find the tool you need.

Bread and Roses also provides recipes for rebuilding your pantry with a worldview, full of nourishment and variety by sourcing ingredients well and making things yourself. I aim to make you more comfortable with building relationships with farmers at local markets, the fundamentals of foraging in the wild lands that surround even urban environments, and growing your own plants. The wild is where we first found all our food, and it is where we can return for inspiration, including botanicals! Flowers have long been consumed and it's time they were brought back onto the plate with more intention and abundance. With your own senses as your guide and seasonal ingredients from your local farmers and the wild, there is an endless variety of bites that can be prepared. Food taken with context and history is the most nourishing.

It is my greatest hope that these hacks, learned from over a decade in food, make cooking and baking more efficient, more joyful, and more delicious!

Make these recipes; stain this book.

CHAPTER 1

Why Whole Grains?

The majority of people all over the world eat whole grains as the main source of calories in their daily diet. These grains come in every shape, color, and size, offering diverse flavor and in many cases as much protein per gram as meat. However, these rich, biodiverse foods are not the source of most of the "flour" we Americans see on our grocery shelves. Let's go back to the beginning.

Grain has three major components: germ, endosperm, and bran. Prior to the introduction of modern white flour in developed countries, grains were ground on stone mills powered by hand, beast, water, or wind, with the mills steadily working to crush the kernel of the grain. Because of this longer and slower process, all three components were ground into a fine, nutrient-dense brown flour with a robust flavor. This is still how grains are ground in many parts of the world. This process was far more natural than that developed to create white flour, which required laborious sifting, stripping the grain of its bran and germ, leaving behind only the white endosperm. Arising first in Europe and quickly spreading to surrounding areas, this process (and waste) was possible only for rich aristocracy. With the advent of the industrial revolution and roller milling, however, white flour and its status of affluence was suddenly available to "common" people as well. It was embraced swiftly, closing regional mills and small farms in favor of newer roller mills and consolidated monoculture. Everybody wanted the status symbol of white flour.

Roller mills utilize steel rollers instead of stone to crush grain quickly. Presoaking the grain and using a roller mill meant that the bran and the germ could be split from the endosperm in one hot, fast moment of friction. The germ burns off and the bran is sifted out, leaving isolated endosperm behind. This flour would further be bleached, bromated, and "enriched" with different vitamins for "health"—the same vitamins ironically found in the extracted and discarded bran and germ. Now, white flour is the dominate flour on the shelves of our supermarkets. This commodity flour is categorized by percentages of protein into names understood by customers—pastry flour, cake flour, and bread flour. In a commercial setting, flour is labeled by extraction amounts, or how much is lost in its processing. These percentages ultimately refer to the strength of the protein levels of the flour, and the structure it can achieve. Much of the time, the flour labeled anonymously as "whole wheat" is not whole because the delicate germ with fatty acids is burned off in the process of roller milling. Only the bran is added back, giving us whole wheat that is only two-thirds of the grain. For me, that doesn't cut it.

Thankfully, in developed countries, we have begun to slowly move back toward the agricultural product grain has been for centuries, as an increasing number of "specialty flours," made from whole grains, are gaining in popularity. We are getting back to our roots! Even better, in the last few decades, stone mills have been revived, leading to whole-grain flours that are once again whole with all three of their components intact. You can purchase these directly from your regional stone mill, supporting millers and small farmers' efforts in biodiversity. For bakers and home cooks, this instantly means more choice, more flavor, and more nutrition in our flour! These grains are also more digestible, as the different components of the grain aid one another in our body's absorption of its nutrients.

You'll notice that I've mentioned flour as both a commodity product and an agricultural product. What do I mean by this? Commodity products are standardized for consumption. Agricultural products naturally vary with changing location and seasons. This means that, like other produce, each grain is a unique reflection of how it is grown and retains its terroir. Terroir has long been discussed in terms of wine, but it actually applies to any agricultural product that retains a sense of place once harvested. This is true of grains. A drought or rainy season will be carried over into the hydration needs and behavior of the grain when it comes time to bake. The part of the grain most affected by its environment is the protein level. The protein found in most grains consists of glutenin and gliadin. Glutenin is variable, depending on the growing conditions and season. Gliadin is set in the genes of each grain. However, other grains without this paired protein are still highly affected by nature and nurture, and we'll be considering these variables in our bakes! If it seems overwhelming to learn a lot of new grains, remember when you were young and the only vegetable you knew was broccoli? It's the beginning of a new whole world of flavor and this book is your guide! It will arm you with great tools and techniques to build your confidence, knowledge, and intuition!

Now that you understand the basics, let's get in the kitchen! When working with whole grains, I am always trying to re-create the bakes I have eaten on my travels—bakes by ordinary people around the world, many based on recipes handed down through generations, and others I have created from scratch to honor the ingredients of the regions. These are all "brown flour" bakes of the people. Looking across cultures, whole grains hold together a common bond in food traditions. Utilizing these varied whole grains gives these bakes more nutrition, more diversity of texture, more flavor, and more aroma. I refer to this approach as the More Diet. I want people to bake with more.

You'll see in the recipes that follow that when you swap out flavorless, nutritionless commercial white flour, for even a small percentage of whole grains, the "bread" blossoms with flavor and nutrition. This is just the beginning of the "roses" that people deserve!

Modern Wheats, Milling at Home, and All-Purpose Flour

As you know, this book focuses on the foundational grains still consumed around the world today. It is worth noting, however, that some incredible newer grains (less than 100 years old) are being produced through traditional agricultural husbandry methods, without any genetic modifications. These modern grains are categorized by the season they grow in—spring or winter; the color of the grain—red or white; and their texture—hard or soft.

Although I do not focus on many of these in this book, it's worth understanding the terminology because it applies to older grains as well. In general,

your spring wheats will be soft white wheats ideal for delicate pastry. Or hard red spring wheats, which are slightly less strong than their winter counterparts. While there are some soft red spring wheats and hard white spring wheats, very few farmers produce them as they tend to be more finicky in the field. But demand for them is increasing!

Winter produces hard whites and hard reds best suited for bread making. Winter also gives us soft red wheats that are excellent for fall pastries, with their deep caramel notes. Likewise, some soft white winter wheats are beginning to be explored, with higher proteins than their spring counterparts.

What if I can find a grain, but not the flour? You can mill your own whole-grain flour at home! Keep in mind that milling is its own craft. Home-size stone mills cannot do the same job as a normal-size stone mill that usually takes up a whole room with stones at least 6 feet across. Crushing the grain between much smaller stones means faster and hotter. Anytime there is heat, it means nutrition is starting to burn away. To maintain the integrity of your grains, go slowly and turn your machine off and on periodically as you mill, to reduce heat. I love my NutriMill; it does the least damage to the grain via friction and heat.

While you will find many delicious 100 percent whole-grain bakes in this book, most recipes use a smaller percentage. Depending on your desired outcome, unbleached, unbromated, and enriched white flour—your own sifted whole grain—remains a useful ingredient in providing structure to bakes. Expectations of height and texture can be assisted by using percentages of all-purpose white flour. It is also useful to balance and accentuate whole grains' flavor expression. If you don't want to add any commodity flour to your bakes, add in the step of sifting to your home milling. In this way, you can make your own all-purpose flour from a whole grain! Sifting a high-protein grain, such as durum or emmer, after milling to remove the bran works great. Or if you'd like to use a modern wheat variety for accessibility and cost, I recommend a hard white winter wheat. You can use the excess bran in muffins or quick breads, such as pancakes, for added nutrition.

Many modern high-protein whole-grain flours are also available sifted or unsifted from regional mills, meant to replace commodity "all-purpose" flours. My go-to is Star, a hard white wheat, from Grist & Toll Mill in Pasadena, California. Nan Kohler mills a variety of hard whites to choose from, and other incredible grains. Most often in baking and here in this book, for accessibility and economics, I will use an unbleached, unbromated, and unenriched commodity all-purpose flour. My go-to brand is King Arthur, for reliability.

Bonus Points

Choosing whole grain has impact beyond your plate. It supports farmers growing these grains, strengthening each regional wheat shed, which leads to greater biodiversity in the field. Greater diversity in field crops means more resistance to disease and better yields, and more secure local food systems. Choosing whole grains also helps your miller. Using as little as 10 to 15 percent of whole grains sourced from stone mills in your recipes will make your local businesses sustainable and capable of providing more great ingredients to your communities. Adding such a low percentage of whole grains is scalable and easily swapped in with no adjustments necessary to all your favorite recipes. Recipes in this book already do this, with the whole grain percentage ranging from 30 to 100 percent.

Tasting Grain and Other Ingredients

Science shows us that we must try something several times and several ways before our body even establishes like or dislike. This trying of new foods is the development of a palate, and we start doing it the moment we are born. In almost every culture, grain is the first solid food babies eat. Think of this book as an opportunity to learn now as we did then, with curiosity and the engaging of all our senses.

When testing a new grain, I run it through a standard system in the kitchen. I chew it to get a sense of its strength. I make a porridge to gauge how thirsty the grain is. I sprout the grain whole, to see what sweetness can be unlocked. I begin and feed a starter with the grain to see its relative rise and strength. The acids from fermentation bring out tang and funk from the nuttiness of the grain. And finally, I make a shortbread to see how it behaves coated in fat. All along the way, we smell, taste, smell, taste, smell, and taste some more. Then, I cook or bake.

In tasting and teaching, I have found wine to be the best homology for grain as the importance of contribution of terroir is largely accepted. We have embraced the practice of tasting grapes and abstracting other analogous flavors the grapes might express postfermentation. Grain is the same in that it carries tremendous flavor from terroir; it has flavor notes reminiscent of other foods. On the next page, you will find the grain-tasting wheel, bringing you new language to tackle the wild world of grain as you taste, cook, and bake. You can think of this as a Rosetta stone translating your personal experience into the greater professional knowledge that is developing. We can use this knowledge of how to taste for flavor, tannins, body, acidity, strength, activity, and hydration to bring deeper flavor to what we make and deliver consistent results. This practice of mindful tasting can be applied to all ingredients, giving you a more nuanced perspective to use for creating unique flavor pairings. You will also find a few tests I use when I encounter a new grain or a new crop of a known grain. In bringing all this research to you, the reader, I hope you use it to leapfrog ahead into confidence and creativity.

Flour Tasting Wheel

First, the tasting wheel. This wheel breaks down major notes of taste and aroma found in whole grains.

FLOUR TASTING WHEEL

IS THIS GRAIN GOOD FOR PASTRY OR BREAD?

STICK 1 GRAIN UNDER YOUR TONGUE AND LEAVE IT FOR 10 MINUTES

→ IS IT SOFT ENOUGH TO CHEW? PASTRY!
→ IS IT STILL HARD? BREAD!

USE YOUR SENSES TO LEARN HOW TO TASTE THINGS, WITH TESTS!

FLAVOR

BITTER
- COFFEE
- NUTS
- SEED
- WINE
- DARK CHOCOLATE

DAIRY
- CREAM
- BUTTER
- MILK
- YOGURT

SOUR
- CITRUS
- VINEGAR
- PICKLES
- YEAST

SWEET
- JAM
- SUGAR
- CANDIED
- HONEY
- CARAMEL
- TOFFEE

COLOR
- RED
- WHITE
- MULTI
- BROWN

INTENSITY
- DELICATE
- HOT/SPICY
- STRONG
- MUTED
- AGGRESSIVE

ANIMAL
- FUNKY
- BARN
- MUSK

EARTH
- MUSHROOM
- SOIL
- HAY
- BRUSH
- WOOD
- OLD
- NEW

MINERAL
- SALT
- LIMESTONE
- CHALK
- SAND
- FLINT

GARDEN
- FRUIT
- VEGETAL
- ROOT
- FLORAL
- HERB
- SPICE
- COMPOST

TEXTURE
- STICKY
- SANDY
- POWDERY
- LEAN
- SOFT
- HARD
- LIGHT
- HEAVY
- DRY
- WET
- FRESH
- DRIED
- COOKED
- TOASTED

HOW WILL THIS GRAIN TASTE IN PASTRY? LET'S DO A SHORTBREAD TEST!

- MIX BUTTER, SUGAR + FLOUR
- PRESS INTO SHEET TRAY
- BAKE @ 350 DEGREES, 15-18 MINUTES TILL LIGHTLY GOLDEN BROWN
- TASTE AND USE THE WHEEL TO IDENTIFY FLAVOR

HOW WILL THIS GRAIN TASTE IN BREAD? LET'S DO A PORRIDGE TEST!

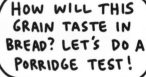

- MIX EQUAL PARTS FLOUR + WATER
- WAIT 10 MINUTES
- TASTE AND USE THE WHEEL TO IDENTIFY FLAVOR

Tasting Tests

These simple tests are quick ways to know how to use your grain, what to bake with it successfully, how much hydration it needs, how its texture changes when it's lean or enriched with fat, and most important, its flavor.

TONGUE TEST: This is a basic test to learn the strength of a whole grain.

Place a kernel of the grain under your tongue. Allow to sit for 10 minutes.

If at the end of 10 minutes you can chew the grain, it is a soft grain appropriate for pastry. If at the end of the 10 minutes the grain is still hard, it is a hard grain suitable for bread.

If you can chew it, do so. If you end up with the consistency of mush, you can confirm this is best as a pastry flour. If you end up with the consistency closer to chewing gum, you have a flour that can also act as fine bread flour. This has to do with the percentage of protein and strength of the grain.

PORRIDGE TEST: This is a basic test to learn the texture, taste, and hydration of whole grains, an excellent way to test lots of different flavor pairings and grain blends. Porridges are one of the oldest ways humans have enjoyed grains.

150 g whole-grain flour
150 g water

Combine the flour and the water in a small bowl. Vigorously mix with a spoon until combined with no lumps.

Taste; take notes as to its texture and how it tastes. Try to reach into your sense memory of other foods and smells to describe it for yourself. These are your tasting notes.

Let sit for 30 minutes. Return, use your spoon to stir it around, and taste. Take notes on any changes of taste and texture. Any change in texture will tell you how thirsty the grain will be in bakes. If it thickened, it will need more water; if it's still wet and slack, a lower hydration application may be appropriate.

Let sit for 2 hours. Return, stir, and taste again. Take notes on any changes of taste and texture. Any change will reflect the full hydration of a dough. Make a note if you will ultimately need more water for your desired application.

Next, pull at the porridge by trying to lift some with your spoon. If it's very tight or taffylike , stretching and snapping back on itself, your grain is elastic and will hold onto itself easily. If it is extending easily, is soupier or breaks, your dough is extensible and will require more agitation to build structure. Grains can be one or the other, or both. This tells you what the bake will be like when you use this flour and apply heat in the oven.

Finally, top with yogurt, honey, nuts, fruit, and enjoy! Here is where you test other ingredients and flavors that may go well with the grain!

SHORTBREAD TEST: This is a great simple bake to test finished texture and the grain in combination with fats. Whole grains love fat because it hydrates and helps amplify flavor, so a shortbread allows you to taste the full expression of an individual grain.

250 g unsalted butter, at room temperature
60 g powdered sugar, sifted
240 g whole-grain flour, plus more for dusting
2 g salt
300 g large-grain sugar, such as turbinado

In the bowl of a stand mixer fitted with the paddle attachment, mix the butter and powdered sugar on low speed until incorporated, then turn up to medium speed until light and fluffy. Turn off machine and add the flour and salt to the bowl and mix on medium until just combined.

Dump onto a lightly floured surface, divide the dough in half, and roll each into a long log 2 inches in width. Wrap in plastic wrap or parchment paper and place in the fridge to chill for 30 minutes to 1 hour. When ready, the log should feel firm to the touch.

Meanwhile, line two baking sheets with parchment paper and sprinkle the large-grain sugar over one of the prepared baking sheets. Preheat the oven to 350°F.

Pull the log from the fridge and press firmly into the sugar, rolling it so the entire outer surface is coated with the sugar. Repeat this with the second log, adding more sugar as necessary. Slice the ends off the log, and then slice off ½-inch-thick disks and place 1 inch apart on the other prepared cookie sheet.

Bake for 15 to 18 minutes, until the edges of the shortbread are golden brown.

Remove from the oven and let cool for 15 minutes on the sheets before transferring to a serving plate. Taste! Is the cookie moist and buttery or dry? Does it snap, crumble, or shatter? These cookies keep in an airtight container for a week.

✦ ✦ ✦

Note whether your grain will need more fat in the future. Test again to get your desired outcome. Note any new expressions of flavor now that more fat is present.

The variety of whole grains you will find in this book are a mix of ancient, heirloom grains and what is often poorly referred to as alternative grains. *Ancient* grains have not been heavily commodified by industry and as a result are the same or very similar as they have been for a millennium. *Heirloom*, or *heritage*, grains have been cultivated and changed slightly by traditional methods by small producers over the last two centuries. *Alternative* grains are pseudocereals that fall outside the predominantly relied-upon grass family. *Pseudocereals* are grains that come from flowering plants rather than grasses.

Make sure you source your whole grains from a farmer or miller you trust. Keep them stored in airtight containers in a cool pantry that does not receive sunlight and is not located near a heating element. It's not necessary to store them in your freezer or fridge if temperatures are cool in your region. Don't buy more than you think you'll use in six months, so start off with small amounts, particularly if you're trying something new.

Other Ingredients You Will Encounter in This Book

SUGAR: The granulated sugar in my recipes is cane sugar, not white or beet sugar. Cane sugar is an intact sugar that has not been stripped of its molasses content. When noted, dark brown sugar and large-grain sugars, such as turbinado sugar, are also used. Sugar substitutions can be made, but most substitutions will result in a sweeter taste. Reductions in sugar will impact structure and moisture of the final food product.

HONEY: Honey is a sweetener found around the world. It comes in various hues and flavors depending on what the bees have eaten. I prefer a deeply flavored honey, such as avocado or buckwheat. The robust flavor survives the heat of cooking and baking in ways a more delicate honey, such as wildflower, does not. Save those honeys for finishing glazes or buttercreams.

MOLASSES: Molasses is a syrup made from processing the sugars in various fruits, including cane fruit, down to a rich dark liquid. In this book, we use blackstrap molasses, date molasses, and pomegranate molasses, exploring all their cultural heritage and rich taste. You can find these at specialty grocery stores or online. Substitute for honey when a recipe says it can be made vegan.

MAPLE SYRUP: Maple syrup is made by tapping maple trees in winter and collecting the sap that runs out. It is then boiled down into different grades depending on color and flavor. In this book, you can use Grade A, which is lighter, or Grade B, which has a stronger taste, whichever is your preference. Maple syrup is a great substitute for honey when a recipe says it can be made vegan.

SALT: Salt is kosher fine salt. The kitchen standard is Diamond Crystal brand. Don't use iodized table salt. You will see some recipes call for fine sea salt and larger-grain flaky sea salt, such as Maldon sea salt brand. These are the preferred salts for food preservation, cooking, and baking.

FLOUR
OF THE

FUN FACTS ABOUT:

- **AGRICULTURE**– WILD GRASSES WERE FIRST CULTIVATED 55 MILLION YEARS AGO.

- **MILLS**– BERRIES WERE GROUND INTO FLOUR IN 6700 BC WITH A MORTAR + PESTLE. LATER, LARGE STONE MILLS POWERED BY LIVESTOCK WERE USED. NOW WE HAVE AUTOMATED MILLS WITH STONE OR STEEL ROLLERS.

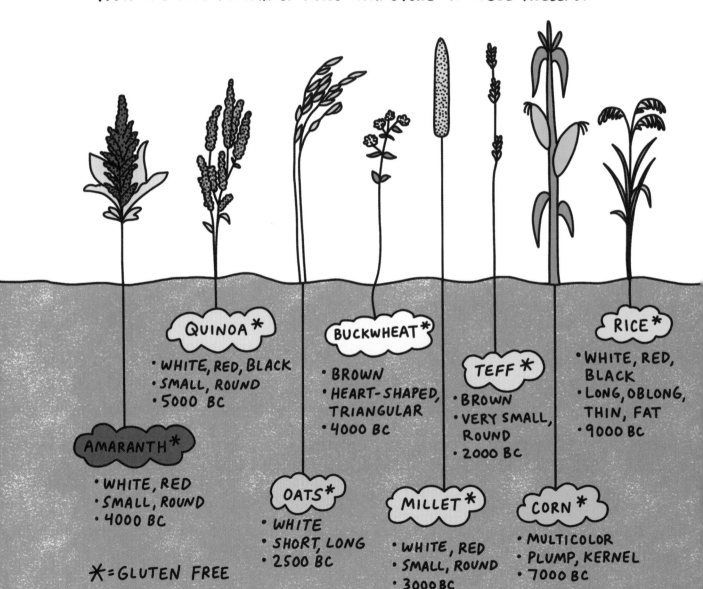

QUINOA *
- WHITE, RED, BLACK
- SMALL, ROUND
- 5000 BC

BUCKWHEAT *
- BROWN
- HEART-SHAPED, TRIANGULAR
- 4000 BC

TEFF *
- BROWN
- VERY SMALL, ROUND
- 2000 BC

RICE *
- WHITE, RED, BLACK
- LONG, OBLONG, THIN, FAT
- 9000 BC

AMARANTH *
- WHITE, RED
- SMALL, ROUND
- 4000 BC

OATS *
- WHITE
- SHORT, LONG
- 2500 BC

MILLET *
- WHITE, RED
- SMALL, ROUND
- 3000 BC

CORN *
- MULTICOLOR
- PLUMP, KERNEL
- 7000 BC

＊ = GLUTEN FREE

FAMILIES
FIELD

- **BREAD** – EGYPTIANS WERE THE FIRST TO ADD YEAST TO BREAD, AND LATER CAKE, IN 2600 BC. ANCIENT GREEKS INVENT THE ENCLOSED OVEN IN 600 BC. PRIOR TO ENCLOSURE, ALL BREADS WERE FLATBREAD, BAKED ON HOT ROCKS.

- **OVENS** – THE WORLD'S OLDEST OVEN DATES BACK TO 4000 BC, IN WHAT IS NOW CROATIA. ANCIENT ROMANS START THE FIRST BAKING GUILD AND INVENT THE POSITION OF "PASTRY CHEF" (PASTILLARIUM) IN 168 BC.

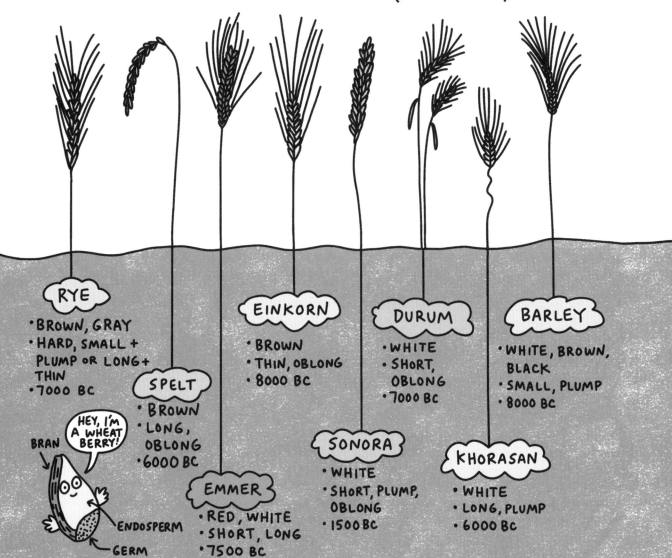

RYE
- BROWN, GRAY
- HARD, SMALL + PLUMP OR LONG + THIN
- 7000 BC

SPELT
- BROWN
- LONG, OBLONG
- 6000 BC

EMMER
- RED, WHITE
- SHORT, LONG
- 7500 BC

EINKORN
- BROWN
- THIN, OBLONG
- 8000 BC

SONORA
- WHITE
- SHORT, PLUMP, OBLONG
- 1500 BC

DURUM
- WHITE
- SHORT, OBLONG
- 7000 BC

KHORASAN
- WHITE
- LONG, PLUMP
- 6000 BC

BARLEY
- WHITE, BROWN, BLACK
- SMALL, PLUMP
- 8000 BC

HEY, I'M A WHEAT BERRY!

BRAN

ENDOSPERM

GERM

EGGS: All recipes in this book are based on large eggs sourced from a farmers' market, so there is still a slight variety in size. I often do a lot of egg math using the varied eggs I get from my own chickens! These direct sources tend to have more richly colored yolks. If you are using eggs from the supermarket, the yolk color may be lighter, resulting in less pigmentation in your bakes.

MILK: I use whole milk in my recipes. The full fat leads to a luxurious bake, which is particularly important to whole grains, as whole grains need the hydration and tenderizing capacity of dairy. You can replace with 2% milk without significant changes in the results. Skim does not have enough fat to properly hydrate a good bake.

OTHER MILK: Almond milk, oat milk, and coconut milk are present in some recipes. Opt for a full-fat, unsweetened brand so as not to change the flavor profile of the recipe. You can swap in a high-fat nut milk for dairy milk, when a recipe says it can be made vegan.

CREAM: Use heavy cream or heavy whipping cream for all recipes. The full fat of the cream is necessary for proper texture and structure. Stability comes from full-fat cream; anything else will split and curdle over time.

BUTTER: I use unsalted butter with a high fat content, ideally "European butter." These have a higher percentage of butter fat by law than do most of the butters in the American marketplace. More fat means more flavor. Do not swap out for margarine, shortening, or lard (unless called for)—butter is better. If you are looking to make something vegan, there are great vegan butters on the market right now—I love Fiore brand! But if you do this, be prepared for some changes in texture and color.

YOGURT: The best yogurt for baking is full fat and thick. I like Greek or Russian yogurts, or Lebanese labneh. If all you can find is regular yogurt, use a cheesecloth to hang and strain it suspended over a bowl overnight to remove some of the moisture, and then proceed with baking. Swap out for your favorite high-fat nut-based yogurt, where it says a recipe can be made vegan.

CHEESE: You'll find a variety of cheeses throughout this book. Always go for the full-fat version for the best flavor. Keep cheese in your fridge in airtight containers. I use a variety of hard and soft to create different textures throughout the book, including epic stretchy cheese pulls. Swap out for your favorite high-fat nut-based cheeses, where it says a recipe can be made vegan.

LEAVENERS: Leaveners may be chemical or biological. Chemical leaveners are baking powder and baking soda. Biological leaveners are yeast and wild yeast—the basis of sourdough. When a recipe calls for yeast, it refers to instant yeast or rapid-rise yeast. Either can be used successfully. Dry active and fresh yeast can be substituted with slight changes to proofing time. When substituting, you will have to adjust the amount of yeast and the time to proof. The flavor may also be affected. When using wild yeast, most recipes require an active starter, but those noted can be made with inactive starter successfully. Inactive starter can also be added to any recipe you like in small amounts to add a unique tangy flavor; 10 to 20 g (about ½ cup) is a good starting point to explore this additional flavor.

AGAR AGAR: Agar agar is a seaweed-based gelatin substitute. It is vegan and kosher. I prefer its setting power over gelatin for its soft texture, and its ability to be remelted several times to adjust your set. Agar agar also sets up at room temperature, so you know quickly whether you need to make an adjustment. It comes in powdered, flaked, and sheet form. I prefer the powdered form as it is the easiest to measure out and incorporate. It can be sourced on the internet or in local Asian grocery stores.

NUTS: Nuts used throughout this book include almonds, hazelnuts, walnuts, pine nuts, and pecans.

They are featured in recipes from the regions they originate. They can be swapped out as your flavor dreams demand. Nuts should be stored in airtight containers at room temperature in cool environments or in your fridge. Delicate oils can go off in hot temperatures, or near heat sources, such as ovens or direct sunlight. Always taste nuts to see if they have gone rancid before using in a recipe.

SEEDS: A variety of seeds are used throughout this book. Make sure you keep your seeds in an airtight container at room temperature and work through them every six months for the best taste. Toasting seeds makes the most of their flavor. Store very oily seeds in an airtight container in the fridge to prolong their shelf life.

CHOCOLATE: The recipes in this book use dark chocolate, milk chocolate, and white chocolate. When using dark chocolate, we want at least 70%; use milk chocolate ranging from 40 to 60%. Track down brands that are transparent about their sourcing and labor practices. I use couverture chocolate that comes in discs, sometimes called "feves." TCHO brand, one of my absolute favorites, named them "hexagons." Couverture chocolate is larger than the chocolate chips you find at the grocery store, and it is also a much higher quality chocolate that is meant for tempering, cooking, and baking. I like the larger size for the versatility and I can make them smaller if I want. But the biggest plus is the large pools of luscious rich chocolate it creates in the cookies you see in bakery displays, rather than just small pockets you get using chips at home. Couverture chocolate can be bought directly from chocolate companies, or sourced at specialty food and cooking stores, such as Surfas. You can also find a large selection online from companies like Thrive Market or World Wide Chocolate. Do yourself a favor and stop using grocery store chocolate chips.

COCOA POWDER: Unsweetened cocoa powder is the powdered mass left behind when processing cocoa butter. It is dry, powdered, and intensely chocolaty. I prefer to seek out a dark chocolate–based cocoa powder or Dutch processed for the most intense color and flavor.

OILS: Oils found in this book include grapeseed, coconut oil, sunflower, olive, and sesame. Oils are essential fats; they are used for moisture and building flavor. Grapeseed and sunflower are neutral oils—meaning they don't impart flavor or color. They also both have a high smoke point. The smoke point is when the oil overheats and starts to smoke. A high smoke point makes these oils versatile in the kitchen. Coconut and olive oils are much more richly flavored and colored, with lower smoke points. In all recipes that call for olive oil, extra-virgin cold pressed should be used. Sesame oil is a fantastic star in many recipes throughout this book. I use toasted sesame oil for its depth of color and flavor. For preparing baking pans, I like to use grapeseed or olive oil in a spray bottle to spray down the sides for the easy release of cakes and pies.

PASTES AND EXTRACTS: Throughout the recipes in this book, you'll use vanilla bean paste, rosewater, orange blossom water, almond extract, and spices. Keep your extracts in the fridge for the longest shelf life. Vanilla bean paste is essential and should immediately replace extract in your pantry. It is thicker, contains the whole bean, and is vastly superior in flavor. Vanilla is hard to grow, so it is very expensive; the good stuff will go farther than cheap extracts.

SPICES: Spices are best bought whole for the longest shelf life and ground when needed. Keep ground versions of your most used spices; the shelf life for ground spices is one year. Giving the container a sniff will let you know whether the spices are still good. You should be met with a strong aromatic scent; if not, time to toss and get new. Note: The reality is that a lot of the spices we use every day have a point where too much can be harmful to our bodies and overall health. Especially when consuming imitation or lower-grade spices.

Source spices from transparent companies working directly with farmers for safety and the best flavor: Diaspora Co. and Burlap & Barrel are two of my favorite brands you can order online. They provide in-depth information on all the spices they sell. A good rule with spices is "a little goes a long way," both for cost and to avoid toxicity. Research individual spices to learn more; knowing about your ingredients is part of food safety.

SEASONAL PRODUCE: I try to source all my produce from the local farmers' market, the garden, or local markets. Many of them can be ordered online and shipped direct from specialty growers. Depending on where you source from, their vibrancy of color, flavor, and texture will vary. You may have access to different produce throughout the season; feel free to make substitutions for similar fruit you have in your region.

EDIBLE BLOOMS AND HERBS: Herbs are from the local farmers' market, but all can be sourced from your local supermarket. The recipes feature edible blooms from flowers, herbs, and produce. These blooms are vital elements to the flavor of the bakes they appear in. Where possible, I have provided substitutions, but you should let your bioregion, research and creativity guide you beyond that. They are also used as decoration. Make sure to source from farmers who don't use commercial pesticides, or grow your own organically in your garden. Most flowers and herbs can grow in as little as 6 inches of soil and can thrive on a windowsill's worth of sunlight.

My Kitchen Rules

As you probably realize by now, I believe that whole grains belong in everything. I am most interested in flavor, so balance and seasoning are the keys to my recipes. However, I'm not a huge fan of sugar. I wasn't raised with a lot of sugar (or other processed foods) in the house, so I don't crave the intensely sweet flavors that dominate processed foods, especially in this country. Dessert in my house, as in many areas of the world, was bread, cheese, chocolate, or fruit with cream. My philosophy is, "Not too sweet." I like all my bakes, whether savory or a little sweet, to be punchy with acid, well salted, spiced, and loaded with botanicals. Their success depends on a few key rules in the kitchen:

YOU CAN DO ANYTHING WITH PRACTICE: It is common for people to identify as a cook or a baker and harbor some fear of the other art. But cooking and baking are two sides of the same coin, obeying the same laws of chemistry, physics, and art. Most people feel more comfortable cooking because they have, by default, cooked more in their life than they have baked—it is just a more familiar language. Your skills are transferable! Only practice will make you more familiar with both the language of cooking and baking.

MISE EN PLACE: Meaning "putting in place," this is a fancy term we use in the kitchen to mean getting all your ingredients and tools together before you begin anything. But to me, it also means reading through your whole recipe to get a sense of steps and planning for prep that fits in your schedule. Throughout the recipes, I've made suggestions for breaking up the direction steps if you cannot do everything at once. Smart prep also allows you time to make an educated substitution and be aware of the consequences instead of caught trying to catch a runaway train midbake. Just as ingredients are listed, I've added tool illustrations to help you gather everything you need for success. Mise en place is always step one.

WEIGH IT OUT FOR BEST RESULTS: In this book, ingredients are in grams and volume conversions are readily available on the internet. I cannot stress enough how much I encourage you to bake with a scale. It makes baking so much easier.

When you use cup measures and other volume measurements, the amounts can change depending on how you scoop your ingredients, how firmly they're packed, the humidity in the air, and many other factors. Even the measuring cups are often not exact or vary in consistency. These factors can radically and unpredictably change your results. On the other hand, having a scale makes your recipes repeatable and reliable. It is the number one thing I recommend to bakers to up their game. Using a scale also allows you to dramatically reduce the number of dishes you use and, to some degree, how much food you waste moving ingredients from one vessel to another. In many recipes, you can use the tare function to zero out the weight of ingredients as you add them to the same bowl. Scales are a game changer and a very economic investment.

If you do want to keep measuring in volume, here are some tips. Aerate whatever you are measuring by scooping and tossing a few times before dipping your measuring cups or spoons deeply into it. Pull straight up and use the edge of a knife to level off. Do not shake or compact. The exception is brown sugar, which should always be packed into the measuring vessel for recipes. This practice and its consistent repetition will give you the most accurate measurements working in volume. Finally, really engage your senses and memory to adjust your bake if necessary.

KEEP YOUR FOOD PREP AREA CLEAN: I know saying "clean up" is boring! But if you start organized and move things off your worktable as you go, you will find yourself far less frazzled. I like to begin any cooking or baking day by setting up my sink to receive vessels and other tools with a soaking side and a rinse side. If you don't have two compartments, simply organizing the items as you use them will make life easier come cleanup. We always

do this in the restaurant, and it is an easy hack to replicate at home. Parchment paper is also key in helping extend the life of your pans and getting better baking results.

KNOW YOUR OVEN: Every oven is different, and new is not necessarily better than old. Ovens need mass, as in weight, to hold and transfer heat effectively. Newer home ovens are made with lighter materials that don't hold heat as well. Most conventional ovens are conduction, which means they heat only from the bottom or top. By comparison, a convection oven uses a fan that circulates hot air throughout. Some ovens have both options, but either way, you want your oven to stay at an acceptable range of whatever temperature you input. If you use a convection oven, subtract 25°F from the bake temperature and check halfway through the bake time to adjust total time. In a convection oven, your recipe will be done faster than in a conduction oven. The computer readouts on the front are almost never right. Hang an analog oven thermometer from a rack in your oven for the actual internal temperature. Once again, by simply controlling a variable in baking—fine-tuning your temperature—your bakes will be far more successful and avoid the constant oven-opening (and heat-losing) game of "Is it done yet?"

MAKE MORE: My mother's best advice, in the kitchen, was to never make fewer than three of anything: one for yourself now, one for later, and one to give to an old friend or to make a new one. This is how we build community through food. So, scale up! Scaling up most of the recipes in this book will require little additional effort or time. Whether you stash the doughs in your freezer for later cravings or do a big bakeoff and share, scaling up is a great way to have treats more accessible and more often with less work.

USE IT ALL: I try to use everything, working root to blossom, in my kitchen. We throw away far too much food that still has flavor and nutrition to give.

Nothing need be wasted. I usually keep a bowl dedicated to receiving the waste as I prep any recipe. If I know I'll have a lot of one thing, I'll set aside another bowl for that. Maybe it means that if I collected a lot of beet skins, I could now dehydrate them and grind the result into powder for use in naturally coloring buttercreams and custards or simply toss them on a finished product for a dramatic effect. Or perhaps I have extra leek tops that can be infused in olive oil with a handful of other herbs. Whatever plant material you have left over after these practices is best composted into your garden, or utilize your city's composting services to help build back public soils. I also feed a lot to the chickens in our backyard, which are grateful for the varied buffet. Dairy and meat products should not be composted.

TRUST YOURSELF AND TAKE NOTES: We are working with seasonal produce and whole grains. Every crop will be unique and require your engagement and intuition. You will develop these qualities in the kitchen over time, but know you have your incredible senses to help you along the way! Smell, touch, taste, look, and listen. You've been using these senses your whole life! Although I have meticulously tested these recipes with grains from different sources around the United States, your experience will be unique, and I encourage you to trust it! Over time, you will develop your powers of observation, your culinary skills, and your intuition. These recipes are guides. Whenever you make substitutions or try something new, take notes. This will help you learn, adjust, and replicate in the future with successful results. This is also how we make recipes our own or develop new ones.

HAVE FUN: Use what you have! Experimentation and substitution are where creativity thrives. Grains are specifically paired with produce throughout this book. However, if you want to swap grains in the recipes of this book, go for it. Same goes for produce. Pay attention, take notes, and rework it to make it your own as your results will vary with any substitution. It's okay if it's not perfect. Nine times out of ten, it will still be delicious! Learning about the grains as individual ingredients will help you do this with the greatest success. Blends are superfun to work with once you understand the individual flours to achieve even more variety of flavor and texture. Using what you have already on hand is always the best place to start to make something delicious.

Eating Root to Blossom

Eating root to blossom is my answer to the nose-to-tail movement in meat. Blossoms have long been regarded to have medicinal and cultural value in our food rituals, added to dishes not just for flavor, but as a mood enhancer. In fact, many cultures consider flowers to be aphrodisiacs that highlight the intimate nature of a meal. Whole languages have developed out of giving, receiving, and eating flowers! Some blossoms are so embedded in cuisine that we forget they are the flowering parts of the plant—these include broccoli, artichoke, and cauliflower. We eat so many parts of different plants, but we still overlook other blossoms.

Blooms belong on your daily table! Flowers are obvious. But it seems we forget that anything that fruits once had a delicate bloom. All our fruits (vegetables are a botanical fallacy), culinary herbs, and wildflowers have an edible bud in its life cycle. Blossoms tend to echo the flavor of their fruiting bodies, but more delicately and aromatically.

How do we know which plants are edible? When you are sourcing flowers, ask the farmers a lot of questions about their growing practices. Use farmers who don't spray their flowers, or grow your own organically, as you don't want pesticides in or on your food. Next, learn what is nontoxic, edible, or palatable. Nontoxic generally means that eating it is not pleasant, but ingestion won't be harmful to you. Lots of dramatic flowers are nontoxic and great for showstopping decorations. Edible flowers tend to be delicate, sweet, or slightly sour in flavor; sometimes a little bitter making it unpalatable.

In this book, I make note of instances where a part of the blossom must be removed to avoid the worst of these offenses and still extract great flavor. A safe bet is if the bloom comes from an ingredient that we already eat, then we know the blossom is also edible; for example, blossoms of the sage plant are edible, as we know we already can eat the leaves of the sage plant.

Taste is subjective, so I encourage you to play and explore. The following are some examples of nontoxic and edible plants to inspire you and that I've also used throughout this book. Flowers listed for each region are nonexhaustive:

ASIA: Orchid, eucalyptus, lotus, peonies, stone fruit blossoms and branches, jasmine, hibiscus, and citrus blossoms

EUROPE: Lily of the valley, tulip, cornflower, daisy, hyacinth, lavender, hydrangea, and herbs

AMERICAS: Aster, poppy, white sage, iris, fern, hydrangea, dogwood, rhododendron, black-eyed Susan, and sunflower

AFRICA: Bird of paradise, daisy, violet, lily, protea, jasmine, Saint-John's-wort, sage, Queen Anne's lace, citrus blossom, and wandering Jew

WESTERN ASIA AND NORTH AFRICA: Roses, lotus, jasmine, anemone, cornflower, and hyacinth

To make the most of edible blooms, separate them by type and store them in an airtight container with a damp paper towel at the bottom. They will keep this way for 10 to 14 days. Or, for a different texture and long-term storage, dehydrate them overnight in a dehydrator or your oven on the lowest temperature setting. You can also press them between parchment paper and place between the pages of a heavy book, which makes for beautiful cake decorating. You can swap dried for fresh whenever fresh is unavailable. If it is a flavor component in a dish, simply increase the quantity of blossoms to get more flavor.

Talking to Your Farmers and Basic Gardening

Many countries have open markets where vendors and farmers sell their wares as the primary way to shop for goods. You'll find them throughout Europe, called *shuks* or *medinas* in Africa, and in the form of large night markets throughout Asia. Parts of the Americas also have bustling markets. Farmers' markets have become increasingly popular across the United States, which I applaud. You can find these with a quick internet search, in local papers, and even on bulletin boards in supermarkets. Frequenting your local market allows you to deepen your understanding of food seasonality through conversation and relationship with farmers. Most farmers are thrilled to answer questions about what they have grown.

In my experience, farmers are tremendously passionate people. Once you get them chatting about what's in season, it's a short conversation to what will be in the next season and the next. This will help you plan for recipes and preservation! Things to ask your farmers:

Where is your farm located?
What do you grow?
What are your farming practices?
What is your favorite thing to make with what you grow?
What are you growing just for yourself?

When I can, I make sure to bring a treat to my farmers, using the ingredients I sourced from them. I think it is important to have the people who grew the food taste the beauty you've created. This is how community is built! Don't be surprised if, next time, the berries you get handed are juicer or the citrus brighter in flavor because of your generosity.

If there is an ingredient you love and can't find in your region, consider growing it. Many crops regenerate from seeds and live roots left over from prepping—like lettuces and alliums. Place them root down in a little water so they can grow enough root strength to be transferred to soil to really take off. All culinary herbs need is 6 to 8 inches of soil to thrive, which is easily held in a windowsill planter or small pots. Generally requiring only indirect sunlight and a temperate climate, most herbs can be grown this way or even indoors.

If you have the space and ambition to set up a bigger kitchen garden, edibles need a few feet of soil to dig in their roots. This can be a great way to have greater control over your food and engage with the life cycles of plants. You'll learn and have access to a lot more edible blooms the more you grow yourself. You can also explore community gardens to inquire about plot availability. Connect with other resources, such as compost organizations, Edible Schoolyards established at public schools, or Master Gardener programs at Land Grant University Extension Schools throughout the country.

Basics of Foraging

Foraging has gained interest in the last few years here in the United States, to access wild foods not part of the industrial system. In many parts of the world and in indigenous food systems, it is the primary source of gathering food. Foraging is a new term for what we as humans have always done: gather food from our environment. I've compiled some rules for foraging safely, efficiently, and ethically from my own readings and practice.

Before you go, make sure you know generally the plants in your area and make sure you can recognize poisonous plants and leaves, for example, by reading a field guide that covers your bioregion or by taking a foraging hike with an expert. There may already be food maps in your area that have been compiled and are available online! You don't want to use anything you find foraging as an ingredient unless you are absolutely sure it is okay to eat.

Begin by exploring your environment and building relationships with plants. Go with no intention of taking; go only to learn what is in this biome and take notes to add to your research. Identify plants on your walk; take note of their state of growth, their smell, and the size of the population. Come back again for a visit a few weeks later with no intention of taking, and make notes of any changes. Any tracks of visitors, animal or human? Identify more plants. Come back again for a visit a few weeks later; take note of changes. Now, you have built relationships with some plants and are ready to forage. I've developed best practices, as follows:

- Never take from a plant that you have not built a relationship with—identify it, research it, write down uses and specific harvesting tips.
- Never take the first plant you find. This is considered the sentinel. It means you are on the right path and more friends will be nearby. Look around until you find a denser patch with a bigger population.
- Never take more than 10 percent of an individual plant, or of a grouping of plants. This ensures there is enough for others and the plant remains healthy for this season and years to come.
- Never take from a plant if it is visibly seeding. It is doing the important work of providing for the next season.
- Never take from a plant that is visibly sick. This will not serve you or the plant.
- Always respect property. If you are foraging on public lands, parks, or forests, make sure that the plants are free of pesticides, litter or pollution, or animal droppings. If you are foraging on private property or adjacent property, make sure you have permission and that the same precautions apply regarding food safety.
- Share these core values with anyone who plans to go foraging with you.

CHAPTER 2

Tools, Method, Time, Temperature & Scale

In this chapter, you will find all the tools for success and ease in the kitchen. These pages are full of pro tips on all the methods you used throughout the recipes in this book. Finally, there is a deep dive into leaveners that sets you up for making these recipes your own with an understanding of science and creativity.

IMMERSION BLENDER

COOLING RACK

RULER

SPOON

FORK

MEASURING SPOONS

MEASURING CUPS

SAUCIER

PIPING BAG

LAME

BLENDER

TONGS

SCALE

STAND MIXER

CAKE STAND

SAUCEPAN

ROLLING PIN

PIE PAN

SILICONE MAT

FISH SPATULA

MANDOLIN

THERMOMETER

LOAF PAN

CAKE PAN

PIZZA CUTTER

SCISSORS

PARING KNIFE

CHEF'S KNIFE

SHEET TRAY

WIDE POT

MICROPLANE

OFFSET SPATULA

COOKIE SCOOP

SIEVE

SILICONE SPATULA

BOWL

BENCH SCRAPER

WOODEN SPOON

WHISK

PASTRY BRUSH

Tools

I like to keep tools to a minimum, preferring to emphasize building your muscle memory in your hands for the feel and texture of food. Sensory observation empowers intuition and creativity. It also makes recipes accessible to those without a fully stocked kitchen or equipment or limited counter space.

You will need the following tools for every recipe. I encourage you to use a scale for the most accurate and reliable results. See My Kitchen Rules for best practices when measuring by volume (page 26).

Read carefully through the recipe. Some tools listed here stand in to remind you to grab something that might be slightly different. These tools are:

COOKIE SHEET: Generally a sheet tray but may also be a visual stand-in for a muffin tray or madeleine tray. Important note: Sheet tray throughout this book refers to a commercial half sheet tray or a full home sheet tray, about 18-by-13 inches.

WIDE POT: Generally a wide pot but may also be a visual stand-in for a Dutch oven when you come to the bread recipes that require a lid.

PIE PLATE: Generally a pie pan but may also be a visual stand-in for a tart pan, which is shallower.

PIZZA CUTTER: Generally a pizza cutter, but may also visually stand in for other cutters, such as a circular biscuit cutter.

A spray bottle and a tea towel are also useful tools throughout this book.

Gathering the tools you need prior to baking is just as important as gathering your ingredients. Nothing is worse than running around looking for another whisk in the middle of a bake. So, to help you succeed, you will also find these icons alongside each recipe for easily preparing yourself to accomplish each bake!

Finally, your oven and your stovetop are your greatest tools. I tested most of these recipes using gas-powered appliances. Electric stoves will take longer, and induction stoves will be faster. As I mentioned earlier, hang a thermometer inside your oven so you know the real temperature you are baking with at any time.

How to Cookie and Tart

You will find lots of recipes for cookies in this book. I love cookies. It was the first thing I learned how to make as a child. My birthday was almost always the first day of school and I was often the new kid because we moved around a bit. My mother always made sure I skipped off to the first day with a towering plate of cookies to share! I always came home with a classroom of friends to report back on. It was a very solid lesson, that the shortest route to friendship is a cookie.

I still love making them for friends, so it made sense that when I started Red Bread, cookies would be a big part of what we offered. The very first one we made won Best Cookie in Los Angeles three years in a row! You'll find the recipe for those (Oatmeal Chocolate ChunkCookies on page 214.). Over the years, I have made so many variations of cookies that it's hard to count. I am a cookie obsessive.

If you want a thinner, crispier cookie, lower the temperature and bake longer.

Resting

Some of my recipes call for resting the dough overnight. This is to ensure that all the flavors come together and that the cookie dough has enough time to hydrate. Allowing time for flavor to develop is a good practice that isn't used enough, in my opinion. Don't worry, though; most of the doughs have been formulated to allow for instant making, baking, and snacking.

How to Pastry

Pie was my very first love. It feels like a warm hug, no matter the season or the filling. My mother made lots of pies at The Good Earth, featuring items from her garden. It was the only dessert on the menu, available by the slice. You could come to the café and enjoy your lunch, while overlooking all the verdant things she was growing and see me playing between the rows. People would often ask her what

Most of the recipes in this book depend on the creaming method, which involves whipping sugar and butter together to create a fluffy, soft mixture. As you beat the two ingredients together, the sugar cuts into the butter, creating air pockets and bonding to the butter. This is the basis for the structure of the crumb of your bakes being light, airy, and tender.

Another method you will encounter when making the simpler pastries is called the sanding method. This involves combining the butter with your dry ingredients until sandy, and then adding your sugar and flavorings. This enhances the tender, crumbly nature of some cookies. This type of cookie dough is also used traditionally as a tart base.

Cookies can be frozen and bagged to bake and eat later. You can bake many things from frozen in any size batch you want, whenever the craving hits you. The baking temperatures and times in this book will give you my ideal cookie every time. But if you like a more cakelike cookie, increase the oven temperature and pull out the cookies sooner.

her favorite thing in the garden was and she would reply, "The Rose in my garden." If customers figured out it was me and not a plant, they were rewarded with a fat slice of free dessert.

FRISSAGE: I cannot recommend enough that you can—and should—scale up pastry doughs that are easier to make in a larger batch. This is because of the French technique of *frissage*, whereby you place your ingredients on your nontextured work surface or countertop and use the heel of your hand to press the butter down and away from you against your work surface. This creates thin sheets of fat that are worked into the dough. These laminated layers of fat are responsible for the puffed, flaky pastry we love. Keeping your butter cold is key, and the frissage technique reduces the heat transfer from your body to the fat.

Start by placing your dry ingredients in a bowl. Add your cubed cold butter and gently toss in the flour. Dump this onto your work surface and begin to press with the heel of your hand down and away, creating your sheets. Continue doing this until all the cubed butter is sheeted. Use a bench scraper to scrape and gather all your dough into the center of your work surface. Use the edge of the bench scraper to chop several times back and forth over the gathered dough, until all your butter pieces are the size of a nickel or smaller. Gather the dough into your original bowl, then add cold water, reserving a little. Use the bench scraper to chop the water in, evenly distributing it throughout the dough. This prevents your skin from absorbing some of the liquid from the dough. Test whether your dough is holding together by squeezing a small amount between your palm and fingers for 20 seconds. If when you release the dough, it holds together, just keep pushing your dough together. If it is really crumbly and dry, add a small amount of water. Chop it in and test again until you get the right consistency.

People can sometimes get frazzled by the need to keep ingredients cool throughout the process. The best thing you can do if you notice butter becoming shiny or melting on you, is to take a step back. Take a breath. And make a plan. The easiest one is to scrape your dough into a bowl and pop it in the fridge for a few minutes. Too often, people keep their hands in the dough, adding more heat. You can make this dough in a machine, but this, too, will add heat; you will miss out on gaining muscle memory to know a perfect dough. It is also my belief that it will never be as tender.

LAMINATING: Lamination is the final but often overlooked step in creating the flaky pastry dough of your dreams. It's a fancy term for dividing the dough and stacking the pieces on top of one another, then rerolling it. After you have brought your dough together through frissage, doing this two or three times will result in exponential layers that, once baked, will flake and crumble on your fork. Lamination is also an excellent time to add more flavor to your dough. I like to add seeds, fried herbs, nuts,

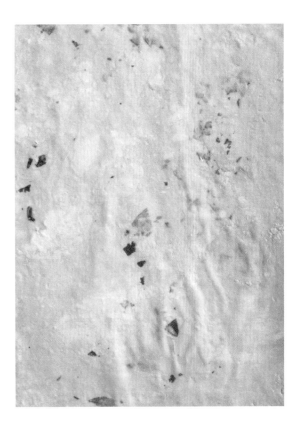

toasted whole grains, or my favorite—sprinkles—during the lamination step. A little goes a long way; the dough still needs to be able to hold together. When you are finished and you roll out the dough, you should be able to see swaths of butter and add-ins dispersed throughout the dough.

✦ ✦ ✦

Always spray your pie pan with baking spray before adding your crust. This will help you get clean slices of pie later. I like to roll up my pie dough on a rolling pin, like a scroll, to transfer it to the pie plate when making pie. A good rule, when you have a single-crust pie, is that the rim of the dough should be rolled under, coiled, and crimped. However, a double crust should be rolled over, coiled, and crimped. This helps both pie styles keep their best shape while baking. I use an egg wash, consisting of eggs or yolks with a splash of milk, and a heavy sprinkling of large-grain sugar, such as turbinado, to make pie dough sparkle out of the oven. It also gives it another textural pleasure.

Scaling up these doughs takes the same amount of time and then the extra dough can be stashed in your freezer to make single-crust, double-crust, hand or savory pies, empanadas, or more—whenever you want! Dough keeps for months, tightly wrapped, in your freezer. It can be stored in blocks or rolled out, placed between sheets of parchment paper, rerolled, and frozen. It should be thawed completely overnight in the fridge or at room temperature for an hour before being rolled out. Dough lasts for 3 to 4 days in the fridge before it begins to oxidize and turn gray.

How to Bread

Bread has become a lifelong obsession. It is what made me become a baker. Flour, water, salt, and time were all that was needed to make the most delicious magic!

Bread was discovered as a byproduct of the fermentation of a collection of bacteria. When I teach kids, I tell them to think of this bacteria community as imaginary friends who want to make great food with them! It is wild yeast or sourdough, and it leavens bread, with its carbon dioxide production aerating the dough with lots of holes we lovingly call the crumb. This same community of bacteria breaks down and predigests the larger proteins found in nutrient-rich cereals and pseudocereals, making them more accessible and digestible to the human stomach. This is essential because as complex mammals as we are, our digestive system is comparatively short and direct. We spend less time digesting than other mammals consuming the same proteins. Fermentation is a shortcut as it is digestion time outside our body, like gaining another stomach, allowing more nutrition to be released from our food sources.

This natural fermentation process can take as little as eight hours in a hot climate to as long as several days in a cooler one or in the refrigerator or a cold box. Each process favors the population density of different bacteria, producing different flavor compounds in the bread. All risen bakes were once made with sourdough prior to the introduction of commercial yeast and baking powder or baking soda. All of them can be leavened this way again! Using the sourdough process on its own is a way to recapture all its promise of flavor and nutrition of grains turned into bakes and join in an ancient craft.

These wild yeast bacteria would become captured, cultivated, and industrialized as instant yeast, rapid-rise, and fresh yeast, whose priority was a fast, consistent rise of the bread. The promise of these commercial yeast products was a rapid 2-hour rise. Although this does produce a light bouncy loaf that is aerated, the crumb is almost always tight and uniform, and it tastes of very little, especially if it is also made primarily with white flour. Flavor and nutrition are still biologically locked because there was not enough time for it to be fermented properly and released. The result is fundamentally different when you eat it, too. It can feel like a brick in your belly, instead of like nourishing food. Using commercial yeast at

HOW DO I GET STARTED?

LET'S LEARN SOME TERMS—

CULTURE/STARTER

WATER AND FLOUR THAT HAS CULTIVATED AN ECOLOGY OF YEASTS AND BACTERIA. ALSO CALLED A "MOTHER." CAN BE WET OR STIFF.

LEVAIN/LEAVEN

FRESH CULTURE FED A SPECIFIC AMOUNT FOR YOUR SPECIFIC RECIPE. CAN BE WET OR STIFF.

POOLISH/BIGA

A WET OR STIFF LEAVEN MADE WITH COMMERCIAL YEAST. INTERCHANGEABLE WITH LEAVEN/LEVAIN.

low levels, or in partnership with sourdough, is a way to regain some of the benefits of long, slow fermentation. You see this often in breads that call for the making of a levain, biga, or poolish. When you use both commercial yeast and sourdough, this is referred to as a hybrid method. If you use the hybrid method, dough can be made with active starter or inactive starter.

It tends to go on the same timeline as breads leavened only with commercial yeast, but will have much more nuanced flavor and some sourdough benefits. You can always reduce the yeast to slow down even further and favor the sourdough fermentation. This involves playing with your seed rate, which I'll go in to in depth in the next section. Changing your timing and temperature are other ways to begin to play with time shifting, a fancy way to say making something more convenient for your life, basically a bake rising slower or faster based on when you want it.

Fed, Rising, Fallen, Exhausted: Building a Liquid Starter

Sourdough terms:

- Ferment your flour and water to make a culture, or base.
- Take your culture, feed it regularly and it turns into a starter.
- Take a bit of starter, feed it once before bread-baking (usually the night before), and it becomes your leaven (optional).

Stay nonreactive! Wash your hands with simple soap and water. You'll want to use your fingers to mix because they have lots of great bacteria that will help your culture along. Flour and water don't like the antibacterial soaps and lotions we often wear today. So, keep your hands free of those when baking. Also, dough doesn't like copper or aluminum, which are reactive and don't get along with yeast. Use plastic, glass, or ceramics for fermenting.

Keep cool! Yeast (in the form of cultures, starters, or even your leaven) doesn't like freezing cold weather but perishes in hot kitchens. It also hates the hot sun and heating elements in your kitchen, so be sure to keep it in a well-protected area away from heat sources that can change temperature throughout the day.

Wrap it right! Once you are making bread, remember to always wrap it up with a towel that doesn't have texture, as you don't want piling in your dough.

Day 1: Culture

1. Place 1 to 2 tablespoons of whole-grain organic flour or all-purpose flour in a jar. Add 2 to 3 tablespoons of cool water. The best water temperature should be skin temperature, so neither hot nor cold on the inside of your wrist. Stir until the starter is the consistency of thick pancake batter or runny peanut butter. When lifted with a spoon, the starter should flow with stops and starts.
2. Place the lid on the starter jar, with a loose seal. Set on your counter out of direct sunlight, someplace dark, but within your normal routine so you can observe the life cycle.

Days 2 to 3: Starter

Over the course of days 1 through 3, you should begin to see bubbles form, due to the variance in location and your home's temperature; this can take up to 3 days. Once bubbles are present, transfer mixture to a 2- to 4-quart glass or plastic container, and begin a normal feeding schedule.

1. Repeat the feeding as described in step 1 of day 1, but now more frequently. With each feeding, your aim is to double the volume of starter. At room temperature, the average life cycle of the starter is 6 to 8 hours and it will require at least two feedings a day to remain healthy. Over the course of its life cycle, the starter will rise to double its size and fill with a honeycomb structure of bubbles, then fall and lose all structure, giving up its liquid. Feedings are best done when your starter has just begun to fall. Feeding it again now will encourage it to be voracious.

   Once you have 2 to 3 cups of starter, you are ready to make bread or you can store your starter in the fridge to feed when you want to make bread. It is a stable wild yeast culture now.

Days 4 to 5+: Making Bread and Starter Long-Term Storage

1. Make your bread (see the recipes throughout the book), ideally with the starter on the rise from a feeding or at the height of its life cycle.

2. Store your starter in the fridge: Always feed your starter before placing in the fridge. The cooler temperature slows down the fermentation but does not stop it; therefore, it is best to give it

> *Float Test!* Once you begin to see a nice rise and fall, you can check whether your starter has the stamina for bread. Fill a large, clear jar with cool water. With a spoon, grab a small amount of starter from the top and use your finger to gently slide it off the spoon and into the water. If the starter falls to the bottom, it needs to be fed and is not strong enough. If it floats at the surface or anywhere in the middle, congratulations—your starter is aerated, alive, and ready to make bread!

a good amount of food before storing. Starter stays most robust if fed 2 hours before storing, for short-term or long-term storage. To revive the starter, pull it from the fridge and give it at least two feedings as required by the room-temperature life cycle. You are ready to make bread after the second feeding. You may need to do more feedings before baking if you are making a large batch of bread, so as to have enough starter for the breads and some left over to continue your starter.

3. You can also dehydrate some of your starter assurance for later or to give away to friends. Spread active starter as thinly as possible on a clean sheet tray. Allow it to sit out for 24 hours, or until dry. It will crack away from the sheet tray. Gather up the flakes and store in a jar or bag. When rehydrating, simply place a piece of dehydrated starter, about the size of a quarter, in an 8-ounce jar. Do step 1 of day 1. Seal the jar and shake vigorously until the flake is totally dissolved. You have another starter!

Pro Tips

- Use a piece of masking or kitchen tape to mark off the starter after feeding. This will help you gauge how much it grows over its life cycle. Alternatively, you can use a rubber band wrapped around the jar.
- Use the best grain flours possible to keep your starter happy. Because you will build and use your starter often, I primarily use an all-purpose flour starter as my base. It is slightly more reliable in its life cycle of rising and falling across seasons. It is also very flexible; with a couple of feedings of your choice of whole grain, it can be changed into any starter you want. For example, I could use my all-purpose starter for a rye recipe or I can feed my all-purpose starter with rye twice and then build the recipe with matching starter. It's a choice! You don't need to keep multiple starters to be able to do all the breads and bakes in this book.

- Starters' life cycle rhythm changes with the season, faster in hot summer and slower in cold winter.
- A lidded 2-quart container is a great size for maintaining a constant starter in your home. Keep 1 to 2 cups of starter in this at any time to always have a robust starter on hand to build up for your recipes.
- If starter is left alone without feeding for a prolonged amount of time, it will take on the smell of vinegar and leach its water content. Before using, pour off the liquid and proceed with feeding as usual. The same will happen if you stash in your fridge for prolonged periods of time.
- I don't like throwing anything away! So, you won't see me saying to throw away half as you build. If you are conscious of how much sourdough starter you need for your recipes, you should not end up with excess starter or need to throw it out, which can damage pipes and cause smells in the waste bin. I always feed and build my starter in increments whereby I am doubling the total quantity. This can multiply fast, so keeping your base starter small, plus knowing when you want to bake and how much starter you need, can help you correctly determine when to start feeding.
- Sourdough starter is great for use in pancakes, pies, cookies, and cakes. Have fun! Mess around! Experiment! Embrace your environment!

Building the Dough

Building your dough always begins with liquid and flour. The minute the two meet, they start to form strong bonds that are visible as strands. In essence, no bread needs kneading because the buildup of these bonds is naturally occurring. Bread wants to happen! You are a collaborator in the magic! When you add kneading as a technique, it increases the number of bonds through additional agitation, creating more supple, elastic, and shapable doughs.

CHOOSING A LEAVENER: Which leavener you choose will set the timetable for your bake. Sourdough takes more time, but only a little active work over the course of the prep. Yeast is faster but requires more of your concentrated time. Chemical leaveners, such as baking soda and baking powder, are immediate, having their own distinctive results and textures. The recipes are written with best practices and options. The next section will teach you how to swap and switch to choose your own adventure.

MIXING THE DOUGH: The first step of making any dough is my favorite. You mix up everything until it's a shaggy mess. This is my favorite technical term. It's the point where it's just combined and hydrated but looks absolutely nothing like bread and then you stop. You let it rest. This is the most important time when the flour is hydrating with the liquids—in the professional craft, we call this the autolyse. Autolyse can be with or without leavener, but never contains salt. If the autolyse doesn't have leavening in it, you can let it hang out for a long time, slowly hydrating the dough and leading to a very supple bake. I've allowed some autolysis to go for 3 to 4 hours, creating beautiful silky results. In this book, you'll find directions for no autolyse, or short or longer autolyse. We have such an urge to get to a perfect dough right away, but this shaggy mess is my favorite; make it yours, too. Let it do its thing for a minimum of 30 minutes.

ADD SALT: Salt is a critical ingredient, enhancing the flavor of your grains as well as strengthening the formation of the protein bonds that lead to a nice, chewy loaf. Salt is also an inhibitor for yeast, and generally it should not be added at the same time. This is especially true of wild yeast or sourdough. Commercial yeast has been selected to be more robust against the shock of salt. After your autolyse, add salt dissolved in a little water. Use your fingers to grab, twist, and rip the dough all over to incorporate the salt. This should take 2 to 3 minutes and you should have another shaggy mess at the end. Let it rest for another 30 minutes.

BULK FERMENT, STRETCH, AND FOLD: The bulk ferment is the initial proof of your whole dough or the bulk of it. This is the time you are doing your stretch and folds. Stretch and fold, or slap and fold, or coiling are all methods of building dough that involve agitation and then rest. They maximize the dough's natural need for rest to hydrate and minimizes your active work time. These folds are best stretched out every 30 minutes during your 4-hour bulk ferment for sourdough, or 1-hour bulk ferment for yeast, to steadily build strength. Over the course of the next 4 hours of bulk ferment for sourdough, or 1 hour for yeast, you will be grabbing a chunk of the dough at the point farthest away from you, pulling farther away from you and then folding back toward yourself and onto the top of the dough. You will then give the bowl a quarter turn and repeat the process. Keep doing this until you have done so on the four cardinal points. If the dough feels slack, repeat again for a total of eight folds. You will see the texture and strength change with each set of folds.

For very extensible doughs, such as rye and einkorn, you can do the folds every 15 minutes to make a very wet, slack dough more manageable and give it greater height.

The coil method involves stretching the dough away from you and curling it under, continuing to stretch away and curl under until you end up with a tight coil. Rotate it 90 degrees and let it rest. Similar to the slap and fold method, if you are doing the coiling method you will repeat building a coil at least four times during the 4-hour bulk ferment for sourdough or during the 1 hour if a yeast ferment.

Whichever method you like best is the one for you. After your last set of turns or coils within your 4 hours or 1 hour for yeast, your dough needs an additional hour of proofing to build up adequate fermentation. You have some options here:

You can move it to your fridge to stay in its bulk state and finish portioning and shaping your recipe within 1 to 3 days. Or you can pull a small amount from the dough every day and finish the recipe in

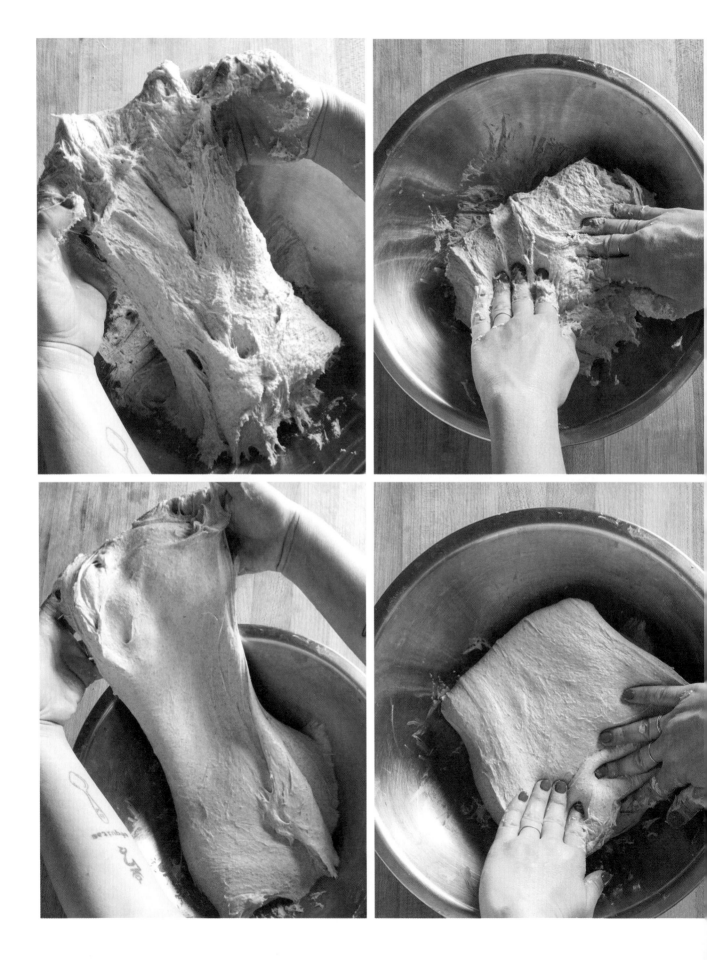

smaller batches. At the bakery, I would keep a large mother dough we could pull from for a few days, to alleviate the prep team's building the dough constantly. You can use this same practice and I point out where in each recipe! The benefit is less work and cold dough, which is naturally tighter and easier to handle.

You can also complete the final hour at room temperature. This extra hour at room temperature is useful if you want to make bread with the *direct method/hot process*—all in one day without any cold exposure—*retardation*. It is also useful during winter and in colder climates to do the extra hour before moving to your fridge to bulk ferment as above, allowing for more fermentation to be established. If you are in a hot climate or it is summer, you can and should skip this additional hour for many doughs, as the fermentation will be well established by the end of your 4-hour bulk. As always, pay attention to how it is rising in your environment and take notes!

Opposite page: The top row shows a stretch and fold at the beginning of structure building. The bottom row shows dough development by the end of the stretch and folds, when dough is ready for bulk fermentation.

SHAPING: Once your dough bulk is fermented, it's time to shape! Many of the recipes in this book can be made in another shape that will only affect the bake time. Breads shaped as *batards* or *boules* can be formed instead into breadsticks or bagels that bake more quickly. Lean doughs can be enriched with fat for a softer crumb, and you can add fixings, such as olives or raisins, to your heart's content. My rule of additions is never more than 30 percent to the weight of the dough; for instance, to 1 kg of dough, add no more than 300 g of olives. This way, the dough can still stretch around the goodies and become bread. Know that adding fats slows down fermentation and that adding sugar speeds it up. You can practice shaping by rolling and folding kitchen towels into bread shapes without any pressure to bake; this is often how I start to teach a beginner baker.

USING YOUR WORK SURFACE: Professionally, we call a work surface our bench. I prefer wood or metal, but anything with a smooth surface will work. The best way to get good at shaping is to use your work surface as another tool to help you. Sprinkle a little bit of flour on your work surface and allow the dough to stick a little. This will help you create tension. All shaping is about creating tight inner connections and solid surface tension. The technique of stretching and folding the dough into place shapes the internal crumb and dragging it against your work surface with your hands finishes the surface tension. Mastery of shaping comes with time. Build your skills with flatbreads and pan breads, such as focaccia, breadsticks, and *fougasse*. Soon, you'll be making sandwich breads, buns, and bagels.

FINAL PROOF: Once your dough is shaped, you have some options. As mentioned earlier, you can proof at room temperature or overnight in a chilled environment, such as your fridge. At room temperature, sourdoughs will take 1 to 3 hours to rise. With yeast or hybrid methods using yeast and sourdough, the dough will rise in 30 minutes to 2 hours. If you move to the fridge for the final shape, most

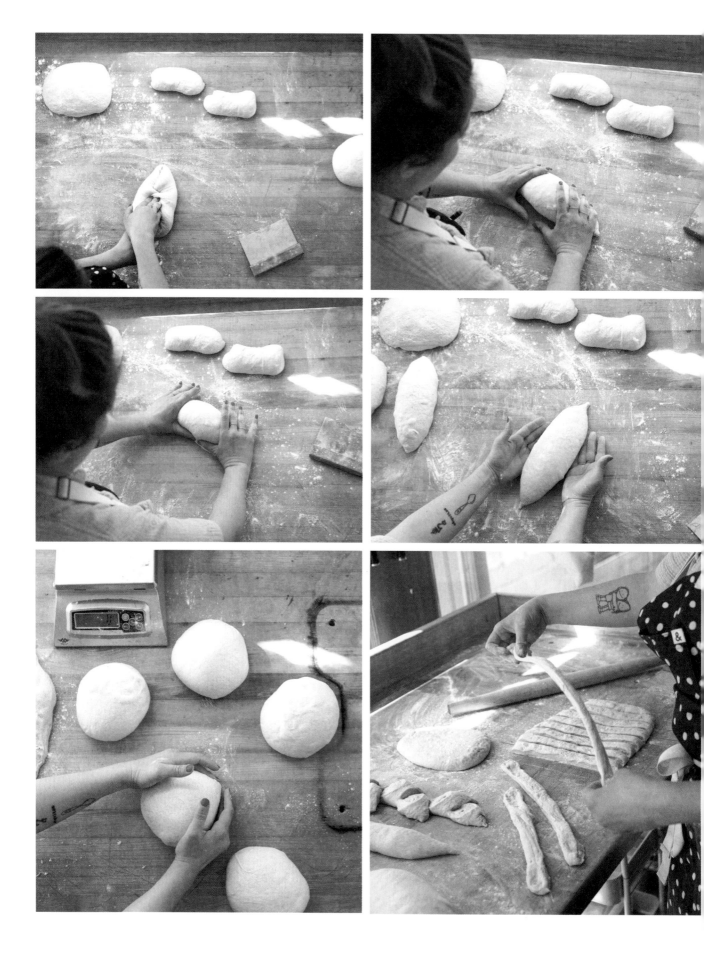

Poke test! The poke test is the best way to know whether your bread is fully proofed and ready to move to the next step, whether in bulk or final. The test involves using a well-floured finger to gently poke the dough, as you would poke a baby, not how you poke your friend you want to annoy. If it indents and immediately pops back out, the dough is still proofing and needs more time. If it indents and doesn't pop back at all, you likely overproofed it. In that case, throw the dough in the oven ASAP to get whatever height you can out of it. It may be less tall and a little less colored than a perfectly proofed dough but will still be delicious. I like to turn all overproofed doughs into focaccias by pressing them into a form and drizzling with oil. If when you poke the dough, it indents and then pops back slightly and slowly, you are right on the money!

lean doughs in this book can hang out here for 1 to 3 days before baking. Enriched doughs, those that have fat or sugar, can hold for 1 to 2 days. The longer the ferment, the less rise and more nuanced flavor. You decide when it fits your schedule and your palate. I prefer to take the chilled route to break up the process and encourage more nuanced flavors to be coaxed from the flour in the longer colder fermentation. If you are proofing in traditional wooden baskets or bannetons, make sure you line them with a clean tea towel or flour almost in excess, so the dough doesn't stick. If you are proofing in a loaf pan or on a sheet tray, spray the vessel well with baking spray

Opposite page: Doughs can be formed into many different shapes—many famous breads are named for their shape. There are many approaches to shaping dough Try all of them to find what feels the most natural and the most fun to you. Practice makes progress!

and use parchment paper overhanging on at least two sides for easier release. Whichever form you are proofing in, once the dough is in place, spray the top of the dough and drape plastic wrap on top, connecting it at the edges of the form—securely, to allow the dough to rise and not dry out during its final proof.

Baking It

SCORING AND SLASHING: Scoring the bread is an important step! Every cut is a vent for the trapped air in the bread to escape as it expands in the oven. Long ago, when towns would share one oven for weekly bakes, it was the way people could mark their dough. Each family had their mark. Don't be shy with the blade: If you don't slash deeply enough, the gas will find a way to escape. The result is blowouts on the sides of the bread or at the bottom, misshaping your loaf. Start by dusting your dough with flour before you cut. I recommend slashing with a lame at a 30- to 45-degree angle. Fewer slashes should be deeper; if you are doing a highly decorative dough with many slashes, shallower is better. If you don't have a lame, use a bread knife or kitchen scissors to score. Cold dough is easier to cut than warm dough, so if it's hot the day you are baking, popping the dough in the fridge for 10 to 15 minutes before baking will help you get cleaner cuts. The motion should come from your shoulder and swing through your elbow. Using your wrist for the motion will result in snags in the dough.

BAKING: Many of the recipes here call for baking in a cast-iron Dutch oven, which involves covering the dough for 15 minutes when it initially starts baking in the oven and then removing the lid for the remainder of the bake. This allows the bread to maintain its moisture enough for the crumb to grow and the crust to expand with it and then be cooked by the high heat. Others are baked without a cover and require adding a little steam to keep the crust flexible as the bread grows in the oven. This is achieved with a spray bottle of water. Spraying 3 minutes prior to baking and again when the bake

is placed inside the oven is the best way to achieve the mist environment for maximum rise or *oven spring* in a home oven. This oven spring happens only in the first 10 minutes of the bake; steam is not necessary beyond that and will interfere with proper baking. When spraying for steam, I aim for the walls of the oven to create the steam, avoiding the door or any glass elements.

Bread should be left to cool for at least 15 to 30 minutes after it is pulled from the oven. The bread is still cooking, with a lot of remaining water being converted into steam as the bread approaches room temperature. Cutting into the bread with a cold metal knife before it's had time to release this extra steam will cause it to condense on the crumb, giving the bread texture a glueyness despite all your good work. If you can't resist the smell of warm bread, always tear into it instead of cutting it.

Old bread that has become hard, whether a whole loaf or slices, can be easily revived in your oven. Toast is always a great usage of old bread, but if the bread is too hard to slice, all you need to do is run it under water for 30 seconds. Make sure to give the whole thing a quick rinse. Pop it into a 400°F oven for 10 minutes. The moisture from the rinse will resorb into the bread, reviving the dough as if it had just been baked. Prevent old bread by freezing portions of fresh bread, presliced and wrapped tightly, for up to 3 months.

Pro Tips

- Bread making is about being in relationship with your environment. Adjust your craft with the seasons. In winter, add extra starter and increase your water temperature to keep things moving along. Add extra fermentation time and find the warmest spot to proof. In summer, reduce the starter and lower your water temperature to control fermentation. Mix early or late in the day to avoid the hottest hours while

your bread is growing. Find cool places for it to proof and utilize long fermentations in the fridge. Be aware of changes in humidity and dryness in the air. Altitude baking will require a slight increase in hydration to account for the thinner, drier air. I often point out to people that their own experience is a good guide. Humans and the bacteria community responsible for leavening bakes evolved on the same planet and we obey the same rules. If you are hot, it's hot for the bacteria. If you are thirsty, most likely they are, too, and so on. Trust yourself.

◆ Your intuition will grow with practice. If you want to get great at bread, make a loaf a day for two months. Make three, and share, knowing it's only a little more work. This repetition will develop your intuition and your muscle memory. Also, the bacteria that helps make bread will begin to build up on your hands, because you have become an enthusiastic friend to it! Only through practice can we become better at a craft. And finally, celebrate your failures and your successes! Even wonky bread is great toasted and slathered with butter.

Baker's Math

In the bread recipes of this book, you will find an additional conversion listed—percentages. This is called baker's math. The key to baker's math is flour. Flour is always at 100 percent. The remaining ingredients are all in relation to the flour. The following salt and leavener percentages are commonly accepted amounts. For example:

100% 100 g flour
80% 80 g water
2% 2 g salt
5% (up to 25%) 5 g (up to 25 g) sourdough/yeast

In this example, we have a dough hydrated at 80 percent. Hydration ranges can go from 60 percent in a stiff dough, such as traditional bagels, to 140 percent or higher in some whole-grain loaves, such as Nordic rye breads. If you want to push your hydra-tion higher, it's good to look at your baker's math to understand the relationships. Higher hydration leads to less height and a more open crumb. It is best achieved by introducing extra water in small increments at each slap and fold turn, rather than all at once at the beginning. Your bread will have strength, instead of being soupy. Timing of water introduction makes a difference!

Baker's math also lets you scale easily. If you know how much dough you want to end up with, you can reverse-engineer your recipe by dividing your desired final dough weight by the total percentages and then multiplying by 100. Using the earlier example:

I want 100 buns at 85 g each; total dough weight: 850 g

Total dough/total percentages = flour weight
850/187 = 4.545 × 100 = 454 g flour

Now, multiplying the flour amount, by the percentages from my formula, I can figure out all my other ingredients:

454 × 0.8 = 363 g water
454 × 0.02 = 9 g salt
454 × 0.05 = 22 g leavener

From here, I can adjust my formula to fit my schedule based on water temperature, adjusting the leavener, and so on. See more on this in "Time Shifting: Deeper Dive in to Leaveners, Liquid Temperature, and Seed Rate" on page 56. Baker's math is another tool in your creative toolbox, as you gain more skills in bread making. Always remember you can make great bread with only your five senses. It's all about what works for you.

How to Cake

I am always out to convince people that cake is salad! What I mean by that seemingly outrageous claim is that even our most decadent desserts can obtain nutritional balance through produce, grain, acid, and salt. Obviously, I am not suggesting that vegetables are unnecessary, but just as salad is important, so is cake. Cake is what marks our lives with celebrations, moments remembered in custard, crumb, and buttercream. Even a simple snacking cake turns any meal into an intimate party. Breakfast cake is the best way to start a day. I've included recipes for everyday cakes, as well as showstoppers for birthdays, celebrations, anniversaries, big family reunions, anything and everything that is worth celebrating.

SNACKING CAKES: A snacking cake is a one-layer cake that is easily eaten any time of day. They will teach you skills, such as to bake a solid cake and play with a variety of decorations. Once completely cooled, this simple cake can be decorated with whipped cream, buttercream, jam, custard, caramel, chocolate drip, or a simple dusting of powdered sugar. For the final step, add seasonal fruit, herbs, and florals in bloom.

SHOWSTOPPER LAYER CAKES: There is a showstopper cake at the end of each section. These cakes build on the techniques you will encounter in the simpler recipes in this book. They feature some of my favorite flavor combinations incorporating the best ingredients of each region, with components you can swap and mix to your liking. I've included cakes made with olive oil or butter, as well as devil's food, angel, and many chiffons. A chiffon cake is my personal favorite for its stability and ability to absorb flavorful soaks.

Baking It

For the best success, make sure your oven is at the right temperature. Prepare your pans with parchment paper and baking spray. Measure out your batter equally between/among the pans. Set a timer for 5 to 10 minutes below the full bake time. Unless you smell burning, try to keep your oven shut so that the cake has the best chance for a tall rise. Cakes are generally done when you can bounce your finger gently on the center without its wobbling and the cake begins to pull from the sides of the pan. You can also use a cake tester, a thin metal probe that is inserted into the cake to check the crumb. If the cake tester pulls out clean or with a few crumbs, your cake is ready. If it's wet, allow the cake to keep baking a few more minutes. Once you see the signs that the cake is baked through, pull the cake from the oven, place the pan(s) on a cooling rack, and allow to cool completely. Run an offset spatula around each cake pan and turn the cake over to gently release. If you snag your cake while releasing it and it takes on a slumped shape, don't worry. So many things in this world can be fixed with buttercream.

Building It

Make sure all your cake layers are completely cooled and your buttercream is at room temperature. Custards and curds should be chilled for ease of use. Jam can be room temperature or cold from your fridge. A turntable is a great tool for decorating cake because it allows you to spin your 3-D sculpture for even decorating on all sides. But a cake stand or large plate works, too; just spin it manually to get similar results as you decorate. I like to work on cake boards because they are pretty and inexpensive. First, place a small amount of your buttercream on the board. Add your first layer. Now, make a moat with your buttercream; if you are using a piping bag, pipe a nice round coil. If you are using an offset spatula, put a small amount of buttercream on the center of your cake. Use your spatula to push it outward while spinning your turntable or plate. This will build up a wall on the edge of the cake. This is where you will put your delicious fillings if you are using more than buttercream. Less is more when it comes to filling; we want the cake to bond to the filling and the sides as we build. Too much filling and the cake will slip and slide as you try to put it together. If you love fillings, consider doing thinner cake layers and more of them, so you get more filling layers in your cake overall.

Use your hands to lift the next layer of cake from the cooling rack and place on top of your filling and buttercream wall, gently pressing down. Use your offset spatula to fill in any gaps between the top and bottom with buttercream, to seal the layers together. Repeat again for all the layers of your cake. You should now have a layered cake with a thin layer of buttercream around the sides; we call this the crumb coat. Now, you can check to see whether your cake is straight. If not, you can shift the layers gently by pressing on them with your finger one way or the other until it slides into place. This should fix most cakes. If you've overfilled your cake and it is still wobbly after you try to straighten it, you can then use a skewer through the center for added support to hold it in place as it chills. (Once you move it to the fridge and the buttercream has a chance to chill, you can remove the skewer and the cake will hold. For tiered cakes, skewers and straws are left in for support.) Don't worry if it leans a little; you can even this out with buttercream in the final coating.

Place the cake in the fridge to chill for at least 30 minutes, or until the crumb coat feels firm. Pull the cake from the fridge once rigid and add your final coat of buttercream with your offset spatula. Hold your bench scraper to the bottom of your turntable with the edge against your cake. Rotate the cake along the bench scraper to even out the buttercream and make sure all the sides are straight. Add buttercream where necessary. Once you have a nice final coating, use a piping bag to add details or play with your offset spatula to create organic textures. Choose your decorations.

Decorating with Blooms

Once you have the cake set with the final layer of buttercream, you are ready to decorate. I have suggested ways I like to ornament each cake, but let your creativity guide you! Some of the things I like

A word about failure. It happens to everyone. Most of the time, you (and your cake) will recover easily. Forgot the eggs in your batter and already poured it into the pans? Pour it back into your bowl, add the eggs, and put it back into the pans. Pulled the cake a little too early, or worse, the oven just shut off on you, so the edges are done but the center is wet? Pull the edges apart and serve with macerated fruit and cream for a "deconstructed" presentation. Is the cake a little cracked or went askew as you built it? Buttercream can hold the universe together and bind any break. My point is, often in failure we immediately want to be rid of the problem. But if we set it aside and come back in a few minutes with fresh eyes, we can still make it into something amazing. Cake is always delicious.

to think about are texture, height, movement, color, negative space, and centerpieces. You can pipe the buttercream for different surface textures, making dollops, ribbons, or coils. Height comes from decorating with blooms or larger deposits of buttercream. Blooms listed for each cake are my favorite from the regions of the recipes. But use whatever you have in your region in season that's edible and beautiful. I use buds, full blooms, even flowers with half of their petals that I've pulled off and strewn about the sides of the cake. Like a classic baroque Dutch still life, more variation gives the cake a sense of being alive in time and place, the sublime and revolt together. For color, I like to pick a limited palette of one to three hues or go full rainbow! I always strive for a focal point, whether a huge bloom with some petals strewn from it, or a pool of jam. This doesn't necessarily need to be

at the top or centered, but its placement will give the cake movement for the eye to follow. That's the statement moment. Finally, remember it's just cake. You can always pull off your florals, scrape off the buttercream, and start again as many times as you like until you get your dream cake.

Party Time!

An hour and a half before you want to eat cake, pull your cake from the fridge to room temperature. You want to allow adequate time for the chill to leave the cake, so the crumb softens, and your buttercream becomes luscious again before serving. You can keep your cake on the cake board to present for your party or place it on top of your cake stand for presentation. If you want to remove the cake board for aesthetic reasons, you will need two large offset spatulas and a quart container filled with

very hot water. Let the offsets sit in the hot water for 2 minutes, wipe off excess water with a kitchen towel, place one of the offsets snug against the cake board, and slide it across the full bottom of the cake to clear it from the board. The hot offset will separate the cake from the board cleanly. Now wedge both offsets in an X underneath the cake and carefully transfer to the cake stand. For slicing, you want to use this same hot water trick to get the best slices of cake. Have a chef's knife and a quart of very hot water handy, dipping the knife in hot water and wiping off excess water before cutting each slice. This will result in clean cuts of cake without any buttercream or filling drags.

Time Shifting: Deeper Dive in to Leaveners, Liquid Temperature, and Seed Rate

Time is the most precious ingredient in the kitchen. Time is also responsible for a lot of flavor! Sometimes, we don't have enough of it, and that's where "time shifting" comes in—a term for shifting the timetable of your bake and breaking up your workload, be it yeasted bread, cookies, cake, or whatever you're making, by adjusting leaveners, liquid temperature, and seed rate. We do this in a professional kitchen to balance prep, based on how many people are on hand and oven availability. I've done my best throughout the recipes of this book to show you where breaks in prep are possible to make things easier for you to fit into your schedule. Time shifting will allow you to make it even more malleable to your schedule.

Time shifting begins with what leavener we choose. Leaveners matter most in cookies, cakes, and breads. This is where we want structure via aeration, resulting in shape and height. Sourdough and commercial yeast are biological leaveners. Sourdough is the oldest leavener known to humanity. Generally, sourdough-based baked goods have a good rise, an open irregular crumb, and can take 8 to 20 hours to rise. Commercial yeast is faster, usually rising baked goods in 2 to 4 hours, and yields slightly more height than sourdough with a more uniform, tighter crumb. Chemical leaveners, baking soda, and baking powder are very modern American additions to the craft of baking that have replaced sourdough and yeast for most of our quick bakes—cakes, cookies, and so on throughout the world. They aerate immediately in the oven, produce a uniform crumb, and give great lift to bakes enriched with fat.

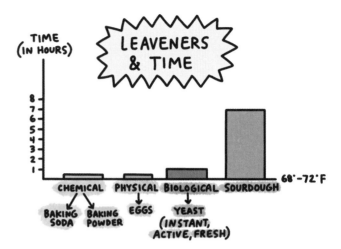

Converting between Leaveners

Converting between the leaveners allows you to choose your fighter, affecting your results and timeline.

CONVERTING BETWEEN SOURDOUGH AND YEAST: A yeast-only recipe can be converted to sourdough easily: for every 7 g of yeast, you replace the yeast with 100 g of active liquid starter and subtract 50 g of liquid from your recipe. Going the other way, for every 100 g of active liquid starter, replace with 7 g yeast and 50 g of extra liquid. Your timetable will shrink dramatically or expand. To do a hybrid method, add 1 g of yeast for every 500 g of flour in your dough or add 50 g of active or inactive liquid starter to every 500 g of flour in your dough.

CONVERTING FROM YEAST TO BAKING POWDER: Yeast and baking powder can be exchanged one for one. The result will be an

instantaneous rise in the oven but will also mean a change in texture—your bake will be generally denser and with a tighter crumb. Many batters and doughs can still be kept overnight, chilled, to make the next day without any loss in rise and texture. If you only have baking soda, you can still make the substitution for yeast, but you will also need to add acid to activate the rising power. A small splash of lemon juice or a great vinegar is enough to get the boost without changing your recipe, although the flavor may alter slightly. Always take notes when making substitutions, so you can have greater success the next time you make the recipe!

Changing Your Variables for Sourdough and Yeasted Doughs

The biggest variables in baking with sourdough and commercial yeast are the temperature of the liquids and the amount of the leavener you add—the seed rate. While manipulating these two variables is an approach used in large bakeries to juggle different bakes, it can be used on a small scale by home bakers to make baking more manageable and enjoyable.

LIQUID: The temperature of our environment is hard to change; even if we have access to air-conditioning and heating, the seasons will dictate a lot of the rise in our starter and doughs. In winter, things are slower; in summer, faster. What we can control is the temperature of the liquids we add to our doughs. Most often, this liquid is water.

Adding cold water when building doughs on hot days can stabilize rapid rising in summer. Likewise, warmer water in winter can move things along in a timelier manner. Changing your water temperature changes the speed of the rise of your dough.

Harnessing this idea, you can adjust the temperature of your liquid (within yeasts, tolerated range) to make your proof time fit in your schedule. Wild yeast proliferates in the most favorable range of water temperatures between 40° and 81°F. Commercial yeast can tolerate up to 95°F. As you change this variable, pay attention to your dough and use the poke test to guide you to successful results.

In the following illustration, you'll see how to use your body and your brain to approach this variable. Choose the right one for you! Knowing the discussed temperature ranges are helpful guidelines to adjusting your water, but if you are more the math type, there is also a formula: the desired

WHAT WATER TEMPERATURE DO I WANT?

SENSES (USE YOUR BODY)

TESTING ZONE!

WATER TEMP—
"WET" AND COOL WATER NEITHER FEELS HOT OR COLD. NO EXTREMES.

FILTERED WATER!
EVEN WITH GOOD CITY WATER TREATMENT, MANY INTELLECTUAL PROPERTY LAWS PREVENT FULL TRANSPARENCY ON CORPORATE WASTE IN WATERWAYS.

WEATHER!
- IS IT HOT? WARM? DRY? RAINY? COLD? HUMID?
- IF YOU'RE COMFORTABLE, YEAST IS COMFORTABLE!

SCIENCE + MATH (USE YOUR BRAIN)

THERMOMETERS BECOME PREVALENT IN THE EARLY 1900s FOR INDIVIDUALS.

BEFORE THAT THOUGH, THE CANDY THERMOMETER WAS PATENTED IN 1878!

DDT = DESIRED DOUGH TEMPERATURE (USUALLY 76°F)

ET = ENVIRONMENT TEMPERATURE

+ FLOUR TEMP
+ AIR TEMP
+ STARTER TEMP
+ FRICTION FACTOR (HAND = Ø, MIXER = 10-20)

YOU CAN DO IT!

TOTAL
→ LET'S DO MATH,
(DDT × 4) − (ET) = WATER TEMPERATURE

dough temperature (DDT) equation! To use this equation, you will need to pick your DDT and figure out your environmental temperature (ET), which is the combined total of the temperatures of the air, your flour, your starter, and your friction factor. This number gets subtracted from your DDT, giving you your water temperature. Once you use this formula a few times or your body sense experiences, it will become part of your intuition in bread making.

SEED RATE: In yeast and wild yeast starter, changing the amount of leavener-the seed—changes the rate of fermentation. If you increase the leavener in a recipe, the rate of fermentation will speed up. There are more bacteria present to ferment the dough, so it rises faster. If you reduce the leavener in the recipe, the rate of fermentation slows down. This is most often used with commercial yeast by bakeries wanting insurance of a rise but still wanting to develop the flavors of long fermentation. The practice involves reducing the yeast amount and adding it to a small portion of the final dough. This smaller dough portion that gets fermented longer is called a levain, biga, or poolish. This is then added to the main dough. But you can also just reduce the yeast or wild yeast starter directly in the final dough and allow it to ferment longer. Remember, bread wants to happen, but you are the guide. So, if you want to make a recipe in this book at night and sleep through the bulk to shape and bake in the morning—play with seed rate! Or if you want to make a loaf of bread fast in one day, all at room temperature—play with its seed rate!

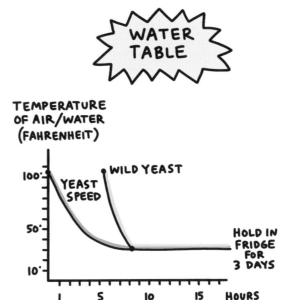

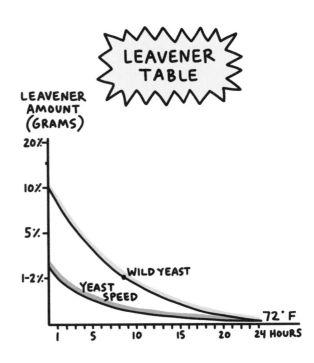

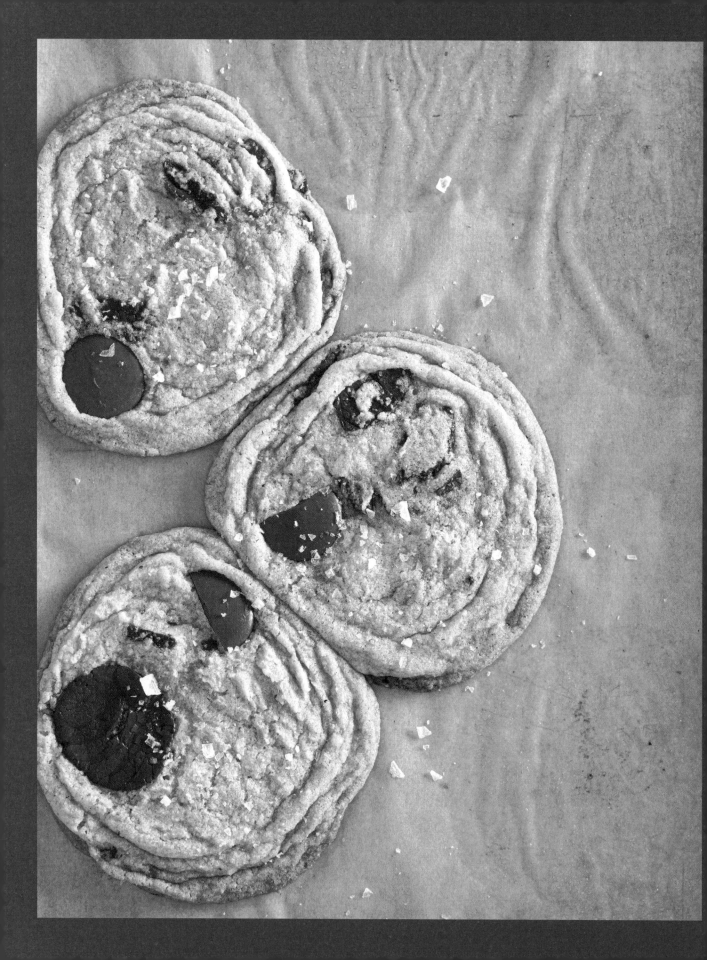

CHAPTER 3

Ingredients, Lands & Recipes

Bread and Roses is organized globally and includes a world map with dropped icons of where different whole grains and other seasonal ingredients were originally found in the wild and cultivated. These regional groupings of food resources had profound effects on the development of the complex civilizations we know today. The book seeks to show you the origins of food and celebrate how they helped build regions. I developed the recipes using produce and botanicals from the same regions, in keeping with the "What grows together, goes together" golden kitchen rule.

Some grains are dispersed over large swaths of the globe, so it was challenging in some cases to narrow down the origin. In those cases, I used the region of greatest concentration. Use this map as your quick visual guide to this book and all its recipes.

Looking to what grows in a region and in a season is a great way to begin to build flavor that feels creative, authentic, and robust. The recipes feature traditional methods as well as interpretations for the modern table. This is how I approach new cuisines, whether I have visited the regions or am making desserts in a specific tradition for a restaurant or event. I believe a deep understanding of where food is from is what makes taste come alive for us.

All recipes will focus on a minimum of 30 percent whole grains up to 100 percent, each one in its region supported by all-purpose flour. A final reminder that because whole grains are agriculture products affected by where they are sourced and their season, remember to be fully engaged as you make the recipes. Get ready to travel, explore, and celebrate our differences as well as how much in common we have at the table.

The Transformative Power of Ingredients

Some ingredients, such as cane sugar, chocolate, and some spices have had transformational power on diverse food systems since their discovery, cultivation, and distribution. Each fundamentally changed the course of food history, reshaped cultures and economies around the world, and have birthed many of the techniques contributing to modern pastry. They are also ingredients that have been historically and currently linked to slavery, mistreatment of locals, and bad farming practices. It would be difficult to make most bakes, be they savory or sweet, that we adore today without these. While other flavor pairings will be celebrating location and their match with grain, these ingredients are dispersed throughout the book. And because I love chocolate chunk cookies, there is one recipe for an instant classic in each section! So, we have broken our own rule here. A little information about these incredible foods:

Cane sugar originated in Asia, where it is thought to have been cultivated since 8000 BC.

It was spread through seafarers across the eastern Pacific and Indian oceans. India discovered the process to refine the first sugar cane, allowing for long-term storage, transport, and scaled production over 2,500 years ago. It was used to preserve other foods in one of our earliest methods of prolonging the shelf life of food. It was considered a rare, medicinal, and expensive ingredient in the Middle Ages, when its production and appreciation spread throughout Europe. It wasn't until the Portuguese colonized the "New World" in Brazil and established slave-based plantations that its mass production and availability to the common person began. The growth of this practice spread to the Caribbean in the mid-1600s, leading to a sugar craze in Europe. This was the beginning of the transatlantic slave trade that was active until 1834. In many regions where sugar is grown today, these problems persist in some forms. Sugar still holds its power over us for its preservation capacity, ability to impart long-term moisture, structure building in baking, and flavor. You'll find the recipes in this book meet my personal baking philosophy of "Not too sweet." We want sugar, but we want it balanced with salt, acid, and produce.

Chocolate's history begins in 2000 BC, when it was used by people native to the Americas as a drink in medicinal practices and cultural rituals. When Europeans landed in the "New World," they were met with vast empires that had variations on this drink served thick and foaming, involving spices and cornmeal. It was first transported back to Spain in 1528, where it was enjoyed only by the elite who mixed it with sugar and honey to counter the bitter taste. The Spanish did their best to keep chocolate a secret from neighboring countries; it was 100 years before neighboring France knew of its existence. Not until the late 1600s was dairy added by the Swiss, and chocolate didn't make its way back to the Americas as something to purchase until 1755. Again, the rise of slave-based plantations began as demand increased. The invention of the chocolate press in 1828 as part of the industrial revolution made this producible for people beyond the elite of European courts. The British made the first chocolate bar in the 1830s. And Hershey set off the craze in America that is still alive today in the candy aisle. Chocolate has never let up its hold on people across the globe. Everyone has their favorite type and visceral memories associated with this very special ingredient. The recipes in this book use a mix of different chocolates for sublime taste.

Spices such as cinnamon, mace, nutmeg, and cloves come to us by way of Indonesia and Asia. The subcontinent of India is to thank for peppercorns we season our food with. Spices can come from roots, rhizomes, seeds, stems, fruits, leaves, bark, and flowers. The spice trade started 4,000 years ago with merchants hiding their sources and spinning fantastic tales of fighting off beasts or climbing trees growing in midair to gather spices. Cinnamon was the spice that started the craze—I prefer Ceylon to cassia for its intense flavor. Direct access to the lucrative spice trail was a major motivating factor in European exploration. Europeans were looking for this direct route when they encountered the New World, resulting in devastation of civilizations that had existed on these lands for thousands of years. These traumas to indigenous populations continue to shape the world. Spices are still sourced from areas of the world where slave labor and other human rights abuses persist.

The best way to engage with these special ingredients is to seek out companies and farmers who are transparent about their treatment of their environment, the communities in the region, and their workers. These companies, thankfully, do exist and are worth celebrating! Find many of them listed in Resources (page 295).

FOOD MAP

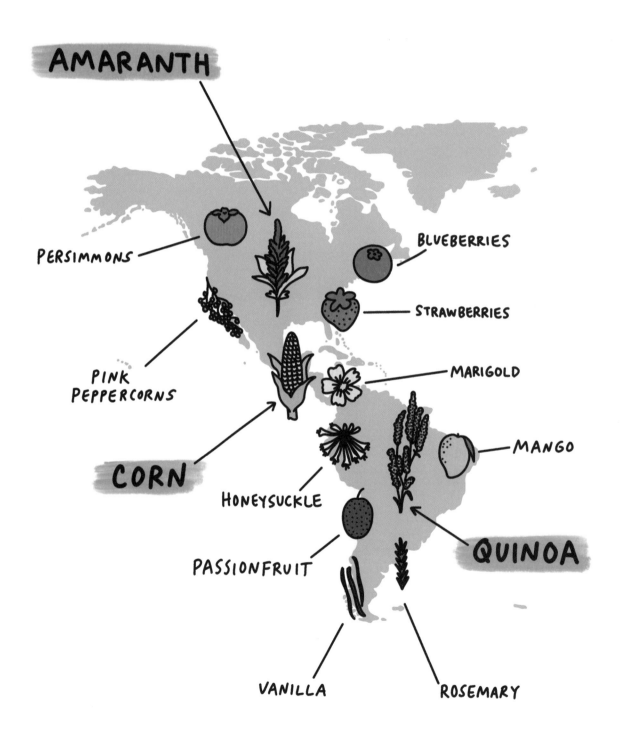

AMARANTH

PERSIMMONS

BLUEBERRIES

STRAWBERRIES

PINK PEPPERCORNS

MARIGOLD

MANGO

CORN

HONEYSUCKLE

QUINOA

PASSIONFRUIT

VANILLA

ROSEMARY

OF THE WORLD

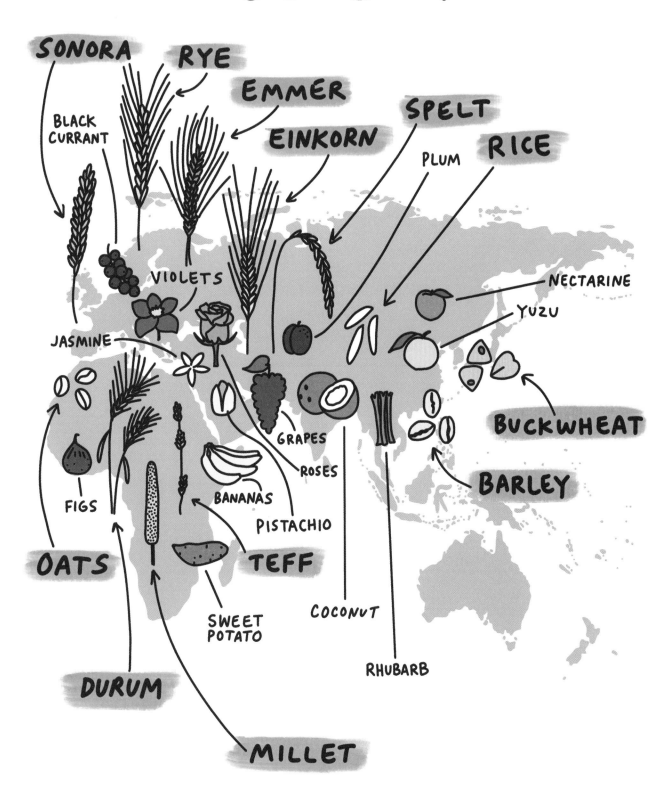

SONORA

RYE

EMMER

EINKORN

SPELT

RICE

BLACK CURRANT

PLUM

NECTARINE

YUZU

VIOLETS

JASMINE

BUCKWHEAT

GRAPES

ROSES

BARLEY

FIGS

BANANAS

PISTACHIO

OATS

TEFF

SWEET POTATO

COCONUT

DURUM

RHUBARB

MILLET

ASIA

RICE   BARLEY   BUCKWHEAT

70   Brown Rice Chamomile Shortbread

73   Brown Rice Kinako Salted Cherry Blossom Cherry Crisp

74   Brown Rice Donut Bars with Genmaicha Glaze

77   Brown Rice Scallion Pancake with Chive Blossoms

80   Fried Brown Rice Pudding with Chrysanthemum Custard

82   Brown Rice Cotton Cake with Candied Sudachi Lime

84   Toasted Barley Porridge with Clotted Cream
     & Roasted Kumquats

87   Toasted Barley Blood Orange Caramel Thumbprint Cookies

88   Barley Miso Chocolate Chunk Cookies

91   Barley Nectarine Fritter with Lemongrass Glaze

93   Buckwheat Brown Sugar Crumble Carrot Peach Icebox Cake

96   Buckwheat Sugar Tarts with Bay Leaf Roasted Rhubarb

99   Buckwheat Soba Noodles with Cured Egg, Nukazuke Pickles
     & Kosho Butter Chicken

101 Buckwheat Cake with Buckwheat Milk Tea Soak, Yuzu Curd,
     Coconut Custard & Torched Meringue

The Grains of Asia

RICE: A thin, oblong grain usually categorized by its length—long, medium, short—and that comes in many colors. An ancient grain, it is a member of the grass family. Rice comes primarily from Asia; it swept across the continent through India into Africa. From there, it was carried to Europe and brought to the New World, where it thrived. It is one of the most consumed grains in the world. In this book, we will primarily work with brown rice as our whole grain—but wild rice, black rice, and purple rice are all whole grains worth exploring.

Flavor notes: Sweet, milk, jasmine, white tea.

How it is sourced: Rice is found primarily as whole grain or flour.

How it is used: Rice is used in savory and sweet cooking preparations and brewing. It has become foundational to cuisines the world over, from Spanish paella, to Iranian *tahdig*, to Japanese sushi and sticky rice. As a grain, it has a starchy body that sticks together when cooked. As a flour, it is sandy and lends a crumbly texture to bakes.

BARLEY: A small, plump grain. It can be white, black, or purple. Barley is also a member of the grass family and an ancient grain. It is incredibly nutritionally dense; in ancient Rome, gladiators were often called "barley men" because it formed a huge part of their diet. Barley is adaptable, with a short growing season. It has found a home growing all over the world. Barley is a main component in brewery operations. Three barley grains placed end to end were used to define the length of an inch under King Edward II in England. I prefer black and purple barleys.

Flavor notes: Earthy, chocolaty, black sesame seeds, smoky, sweet.

How it is sourced: Barley is often found whole, hulled, flaked, pearled, or as flour.

How it is used: Barley is used for porridge as a grain and as a flour. It is a stable of the Tibetan Plateau in the form of *tsampa*. It is often toasted to deepen its flavor. Barley grain in cooking maintains its shape without much sticking together, making it perfect for salads. Pearled barley releases some starch and is a good option for risottos. Barley as flour in bakes is very creamy, producing a dense but soft crumb.

BUCKWHEAT: A small, brown triangular pseudo-cereal in the same family as rhubarb. It has been prized in Asia for millennia, later in Europe, and most recently in the Americas. It is famously used for noodles, crepes, pasta, and griddle cakes. Buckwheat is one of the oldest cultivated crops and a rare complete protein. It grows in poor-quality soil and is very adaptable. It is often used as a cover crop, preventing weeds and providing nutrition back to the soil.

Flavor notes: Sour, earthy, sorrel, wine, tea, cherry blossoms.

How it is sourced: Buckwheat can be found in groats or as flour.

How it is used: The groats are great toasted, often called kasha in this state, and made into a tea. They are great eaten out of hand as well! Or hydrated overnight for a healthy muesli in the morning. As flour, buckwheat is sandy and gray. It is very thirsty and very extensible.

The Blossoms

- Orchid, eucalyptus, lotus, peony, chamomile, chrysanthemum
- Stone fruit blossoms and branches, herb blossoms
- Jasmine, hibiscus, citrus blossoms, osmanthus

Brown Rice Chamomile Shortbread

Shortbread is one of my favorite cookies. As an avid tea lover, one of my favorite cookies to have in the morning or before bed. Great with all grains, it's particularly lovely with brown rice. The flavor of the brown rice adds depth to the butter and the most delicate crumb that will melt in your mouth. Press the dough very firmly into the pan prior to baking and cut with a very sharp knife while still warm, for the cleanest edges. If you want more flower flavor, feel free to up the chamomile. These are also incredible with jasmine flowers. Serve with green tea or coffee for a morning breakfast or an after-dinner treat. Keeps for 2 weeks in an airtight container at room temperature.

MAKES A SHEET TRAY, 24 TO 28 COOKIES

Sift together the flours and starch into a medium bowl. Set aside.

In a stand mixer fitted with the paddle attachment, beat together the butter and granulated sugar starting on low speed and increasing once incorporated to medium speed until light and fluffy, 3 to 6 minutes. Add the salt and chamomile, and beat for another 2 minutes on medium speed.

Reduce to low, and pour in the flours and starch. Increase the speed to medium and mix until a dough forms. Wrap in plastic and chill the dough 30 minutes.

Meanwhile, preheat the oven to 325°F. Line a sheet tray with parchment paper and spray lightly with baking spray.

Remove plastic and dump your dough onto the prepared sheet tray. Place a fresh sheet of parchment paper on top and use your hands to gently press the dough down and out to fill the prepared pan. Peel off and discard the top parchment. Bake for 25 to 30 minutes, until the shortbread is lightly golden at the edges.

Pull the shortbread from the oven. While still in the pan, use a sharp knife to trim the edges and cut into 3-inch square portions. Let cool completely in the pan, then lift cookies out of pan and decorate with powdered sugar and more chamomile.

540 g unsalted butter, at room temperature

140 g granulated sugar

5 g kosher salt

25 g dried chamomile flowers, ground and sifted, plus more for garnish

150 g brown rice flour

400 g all-purpose flour

50 g tapioca starch

Baking spray

Powdered sugar for garnish

Brown Rice Kinako Salted Cherry Blossom Cherry Crisp

Stone fruit is often paired with nuts to highlight the almond flavor its seed contains within its hard shell and imparts to the fruit. *Kinako* is toasted soybean flour, a great source of protein. Its taste reminds me of toasted honey. It is warm, nutty, and slightly sweet. It is a popular garnish for Japanese bakes and ice creams. Kinako plays the role of nuts in flavor layering here with ripe, sweet cherries, in this classic simple crumble. If you can't find cherry blossoms, substitute a pinch more of salt. The crumble topping comes together in minutes; it is great scaled up and stashed in your freezer for quick dessert any day. The crumble topping keeps, in an airtight container, for 3 months in your freezer. Serve fully baked crumble warm with whipped cream or ice cream. It keeps at room temperature for 3 days and in your fridge for a week. Replace the all-purpose flour completely with brown rice flour to make it gluten-free.

MAKES ONE 9-INCH CRUMBLE

Preheat the oven to 350°F.

Prepare the cherry filling: Mix all the filling ingredients together in a medium bowl, tossing thoroughly to coat everything.

Prepare the topping: In another bowl, mix together all the crumble ingredients, using your fingertips to work the butter into the dry ingredients.

Pour the filling into a 9-inch pie pan. Top generously with the crumble. Place on a sheet tray lined with parchment paper to catch any excess juices. Bake for 30 to 40 minutes, until the juices are thick and bubbling and the crumble is golden brown.

Enjoy warm or cold.

CHERRY FILLING

750 g cherries, pitted and halved

1 lemon, cut in half vertically and sliced thinly horizontally, seeds removed

180 g granulated sugar

16 g cornstarch

5 g salt

BROWN RICE CRUMBLE TOPPING

150 g brown rice flour

150 g all-purpose flour

50 g kinako flour

250 g dark brown sugar

250 g unsalted butter, melted

10 g Salted Cherry Blossoms (page 262), stems removed and discarded, minced

Pinch of salt

The easiest method to pit cherries is to place them on a sheet tray with parchment paper. Put another sheet tray on top, and stomp on it a few times. Lift the top tray and easily remove the pits.

Brown Rice Donut Bars
WITH GENMAICHA GLAZE

My favorite donut, hands down, is an old-fashioned donut. I love how substantial yet tender crumbed it is. I love the feeling that it's really just fried cake, and what could be better than that?! Our friend brown rice makes this donut delicate and toasty. A delicious treat with just a simple glaze, it becomes a showstopper when paired with *genmaicha*. Genmaicha is a blend of green tea and broken brown rice, both "unfit" for market alone but, combined, a revelation. The rice gives a deep green brew with a very nutty finish. It is called the people's tea, drunk by many making the most of their resources—tea leaves and whole grain together. Grain-based teas are very popular in many Asian countries and make great glazes to pair with this donut! For brighter color, look for a higher-end blend that contains matcha powder, and get frying. This green stunner is begging to be your weekend breakfast. The donut dough keeps in the fridge for 2 days or in the freezer for 1 month. Fried donuts are best eaten the same day, but I enjoy them day-old as well.

MAKES 12 TO 15 DONUTS

Use a whisk to mix together the flours, baking powder, and salt in a medium bowl.

In a stand mixer fitted with the paddle attachment, beat together the butter and sugar on medium speed for 2 minutes, or until combined. Add the yolks, in two batches of three yolks each, and mix to combine, making sure that the yolks disappear into the dough before adding the second set.

Turn off the mixer, scrape down all the sides, and turn the mixer back on to medium speed. Add the vinegar and yogurt, and mix on medium until combined.

Add the dry mixture slowly and mix until just combined. Line a sheet tray with parchment paper and dust lightly with all-purpose flour. Dump the dough onto the prepared sheet tray and press down with your hands or a rolling pin to 1 inch thick. Lightly dust the top with flour and wrap with plastic wrap. Place the dough in the fridge to chill for 1 hour or overnight.

CONTINUES ▶

200 g brown rice flour

475 g all-purpose flour, plus more for dusting

15 g baking powder

5 g salt

40 g unsalted butter, at room temperature

250 g sugar

6 large egg yolks

15 g rice vinegar

400 g thick yogurt

Neutral oil for frying

Genmaicha Glaze (page 265)

Heat 2 inches of oil in a large wide pot to 350°F. Place the dough on a flat work surface and cut out 2-by-3-inch logs. Working in batches of three to four depending on the size of your pot, slip logs into the hot oil and fry for 2 minutes on each side. Use a sieve to transfer to a cooling rack set over a sheet tray.

Fry all the donuts. While still slightly warm, dip the donuts *halfway* into the genmaicha glaze, shake to remove any excess, flip over, and place back on the cooling rack to allow any excess to drip away.

Brown Rice Scallion Pancake
WITH CHIVE BLOSSOMS

Scallion pancakes are my favorite item on a Chinese food menu! Flaky and oniony with a crisp outside and a soft, layered inside, they are great for stuffing with meat and vegetables or snacking on their own. This classic dish is easy to make and comes together quickly. Using chive blossoms adds beautiful color and another flavor dimension of allium to the flatbread. If blossoms aren't in season, add more chives or scallions. Preparing the pancakes involves laminating twice with sesame oil to create many flaky layers; if you want even more flaky layers, you can add a third lamination. The dough may tear a little, but you will be rewarded. Unbaked flatbreads can be frozen for up to 3 months. Frying from frozen or very cold yields the best layers.

MAKES 8 PANCAKES

Bring the water to a boil in a saucepan, add the ginger, and steep for 2 minutes. Remove the ginger. In the bowl of a stand mixer fitted with the dough hook attachment, combine the flours. With the mixer running on low speed, drizzle in the boiling ginger water, add salt, and process for 15 to 20 seconds. Knead the dough on medium speed for 5 to 7 minutes, until a smooth dough forms. Cover and let rest for 30 minutes at room temperature.

Divide the dough into eight equal portions. Let rest for 30 minutes. Use a rolling pin to roll out one portion to an 8-inch circle, then use your fingers to smear butter over the entire dough disk. Roll up lengthwise and coil. Do this to all the portions. Let rest for 15 minutes. Starting with the first portion you coiled, roll out flat again to 8 inches in diameter, between sheets of parchment paper. Brush generously with sesame oil, then sprinkle with some scallions, sesame seeds, and chive blossoms. Roll up lengthwise and coil. Let rest for 30 minutes and roll out flat again to 8 inches in diameter, between sheets of parchment paper. Place on a sheet tray lined with parchment paper. Repeat the process with remaining dough, stacking the pancakes on the sheet tray with parchment paper between them. Chill for 1 hour in the freezer or overnight in the fridge, to get very chilled and firm.

CONTINUES ▶

456 g water

40 g sliced and crushed fresh ginger

80 g brown rice flour

420 g all-purpose flour

3 g salt

60 g unsalted butter, at room temperature

80 g sesame oil

2 bunches scallions, sliced thinly

Sesame seeds

Chive blossoms

Grapeseed oil for cooking

Heat ¼ inch of grapeseed oil in a large saucepan over medium heat until it shimmers. Slip a pancake into the oil, using tongs to swirl gently, and fry for 2 minutes on each side. Pull from the oil and transfer to plate lined with paper towels to drain. Fry the remaining pancakes. Cut into wedges and serve immediately with soy sauce or your favorite dipping sauce.

Cooking pancakes from frozen is convenient and gives you the flakiest layers!

Note: I love throwing inactive starter into these for increased tang and nutrition!

Fried Brown Rice Pudding

WITH CHRYSANTHEMUM CUSTARD

Sweet rice desserts are very popular in Asia; often paired with coconut milk or dairy, they are always barely sweet and very custardy. Shaping custard into balls and frying them gives this "bowl" dessert a whole new life. They are perfect as party appetizers or plated up for a substantial dessert with a fun crunch! I love serving the fried balls warm in cold custard infused with chrysanthemum flowers, to make the dessert even creamier. Chrysanthemum blossoms lend a floral, honey, and buttery note to the custard. If you can't find them, stir in a couple of tablespoons of wildflower honey to your custard at the end. Rolled pudding balls and custard keep for 1 week in your fridge. You can also freeze the rice balls, prior to frying, for up to 3 months. You can fry the balls from frozen, only requiring a little longer in the oil. Fried balls should be eaten the same day. Replace the panko bread crumbs with rice flour for a gluten-free version.

MAKES 6 TO 8 BALLS

Prepare the pudding balls: Combine the milk, rice, water, lemon zest, sugar, and salt in a small pot. Cook, stirring a couple of times until the rice is done; this will take about 20 minutes over medium-high heat and then 20 minutes over low heat. Remove from the heat, press plastic wrap directly onto the surface, and place in the fridge. Let cool completely.

Scoop 1-ounce portions. A cookie scooper is great for this. Use your hands to roll each portion into a ball but don't fuss, it doesn't need to be perfect. Set balls an inch apart on a sheet tray lined with parchment paper.

Prepare the coating: Set up a dipping station by whisking the eggs in one bowl and whisking together the rice flour and bread crumbs in another. One at a time, dip the rice pudding balls into the eggs and then into the flour mixture. Place back on the lined sheet tray until ready to fry. Finish coating all the rice pudding balls.

Bring 2 inches of oil to 350°F in a large wide pot. Working in batches, drop the rice balls into the oil and fry for 4 to 6 minutes, until golden brown. Remove from the oil with sieve and transfer to a plate lined with paper towels. Serve with chrysanthemum custard légère.

RICE PUDDING BALLS

600 g whole milk

500 g uncooked short-grain rice

Zest of 2 lemons

600 g water

125 g sugar

3 g salt

COATING

3 large eggs

200 g rice flour

100 g panko bread crumbs

Chrysanthemum Custard Légère (page 275)

Brown Rice Cotton Cake
WITH CANDIED SUDACHI LIME

Cotton cake is a Japanese version of cheesecake stabilized with a little grain, so it doesn't need to be baked in a water bath. It has a lovely bouncy texture and is light and creamy, like a sweet cotton cloud. My favorite topping for a creamy dessert is tart citrus. Sudachi limes are small, yellow-skinned limes that are intensely floral and very tart. If you can't find Sudachi limes, Key limes will do the trick, or kumquats are a great option. Make the candied citrus ahead of time; the syrup and rind only get softer and tastier the next day. The candied citrus keeps for 2 weeks in your fridge. Cotton cake keeps in the fridge for 2 to 3 days. This is naturally gluten-free.

MAKES ONE 10-INCH CAKE OR THREE 6-INCH CAKES

Preheat the oven to 325°F. Prepare one 10-inch or three 6-inch spring-form pans by lightly spraying cooking spray on the bottom and sides. Put a larger round of parchment on the bottom and attach the pan's collar over it. Inside this add a parchment collar.

In a stand mixer fitted with the whisk attachment, beat the egg whites on medium-high speed until bubbly. Add the cream of tartar and increase the speed to high. Gently rain 50 g of the sugar into the egg whites and continue to beat until soft peaks form, about 3 minutes. Scrape into another bowl.

In your stand mixer bowl, still using the whisk attachment, beat the cream cheese and milk together on low speed. Add the butter, remaining 50 g of sugar, and the vinegar, and increase the speed to medium. Beat for 2 minutes, or until combined.

In a separate bowl, mix together the rice flour and starch. Add to the butter mixture in the mixer bowl and mix until combined on medium. Add the five yolks and mix for another minute on medium. Strain the mixture through a sieve until it's very smooth.

Use a spatula to very gently fold the beaten egg whites into the mixture until incorporated. Scrape the spatula against the sides of the bowl and bring through to the center. Continue until the mixture is uniform, being careful to maintain as much air as possible.

Baking spray

5 large eggs, separated

4 g cream of tartar

100 g sugar

226 g cream cheese, at room temperature

113 g whole milk, at room temperature

12 g rice vinegar

40 g brown rice flour

15 g tapioca starch

55 g unsalted butter

3 g salt

Candied Sudachi Limes (page 267)

Pour the batter into the prepared pan(s). Bake for 40 to 60 minutes; the center should be puffed, very jiggly, and lightly golden. Turn off the oven and leave the cake(s) inside, with the door ajar to cool, for another hour. Transfer to the fridge to chill for 4 hours. Remove from the pan(s) and transfer to a serving dish. Serve with the candied Suda-chi limes and their syrup on top.

Toasted Barley Porridge WITH CLOTTED CREAM & ROASTED KUMQUATS

Toasted barley porridge, or tsampa, is a dietary staple in Tibet. When I spent almost a year there, most meals involved tsampa in some form, depending on how much liquid was added to the grain base. My favorite was the loose morning porridge version with some yak yogurt, earthy and tart. When I returned home, I still craved this satisfying dish, and when I opened my first restaurant, we had it on the menu with sweetened cream and seasonal roasted fruit. Here is one of my favorite winter variations, featuring kumquats! Roasting fruit is a wonderful quick way to deepen flavors, mellow acids, and caramelize fruits' natural sugars. Roasted fruit keeps for 2 to 3 days in the fridge. It can be used as a topping for ice cream or baked into pies. Clotted cream keeps for 2 weeks in the fridge. Roasted flour can be made up to a month in advance and kept in an airtight container. Porridge can be made fast and should be eaten the same day. When serving, omit the clotted cream and replace the honey with pure maple syrup for a vegan version. Delicious with a nut-based cream drizzled on top!

MAKES 4 PORTIONS

Preheat the oven to 350°F. Spread the barley flour on a dry sheet tray. Bake for 5 to 10 minutes, until toasted and fragrant. Remove from the oven and let cool completely.

Mix together the barley flour, hot water, and honey in a medium heatproof bowl. The porridge should be smooth and soft set when picked up with a spoon. Add more water or flour to change the consistency as desired. Top with clotted cream, roasted kumquats, and a sprinkle of large-grain sugar.

150 g barley flour

800 g very hot water, 150 to 170°F

40 g honey

Pinch of salt

Clotted Cream (page 274)

Roasted Kumquats (page 266)

Large-grain sugar, such as turbinado, for sprinkling

Roast kumquats until they take on some color and expel some juices. Geat for snacking!

Toasted Barley Blood Orange Caramel Thumbprint Cookies

Barley is a very earthy, tannic grain with a sweetness that reminds me of cooked sugar. Blood orange juice makes for a beautiful amber-colored caramel to top these very shareable cookies. Easily made, these cookies benefit from being rolled evenly into balls for a while in your hands. The contact with your body heat helps the thirsty grain absorb the fat, keeping it hydrated and malleable when you place the balls on your sheet tray and push your thumb into them for their namesake imprint. If they crack or break, just reroll until supple. Make sure to bake until you see a slight golden brown, for a nice snap on your cookies. Unfilled cookies keep in an airtight container for a week at room temperature. Caramel keeps for a week at room temperature. Fill the cookies right before serving for a runny caramel bite, or let them sit, once filled, for an hour to allow the caramel to air dry and tighten slightly for a chewier bite. Filled cookies should be eaten in one to three days.

MAKES 30 TO 36 COOKIES

Preheat the oven to 350°F. Spread the barley flour on a dry sheet tray. Bake for 5 to 10 minutes, until toasted and fragrant. Remove from the oven and let cool completely.

In a stand mixer fitted with the paddle attachment, combine the toasted barley flour, all-purpose flour, egg yolks, powdered sugar, blood orange zest, and thyme leaves on low speed, then bring up to medium speed to mix together. The mixture will initially look like sand; add in butter and continue to mix on medium until a cohesive dough forms.

Pinch off a tablespoon-size portion of dough, about 25 g, then roll in your hands to warm the dough and form a ball. Set on a parchment-lined sheet tray. Dimple the center of each dough ball deeply with your thumb and place them about 1 inch apart on the prepared sheet tray. Place the large-grain sugar in a small bowl. Lightly brush the rim of the dough portions with cream and dip into the large-grain sugar to coat each rim.

Bake for 15 to 18 minutes, until lightly golden. Remove from the oven and let cool completely on the sheet tray. Use a piping bag or teaspoon to fill the centers with blood orange caramel. Chill for 5 minutes in the fridge to set the caramel. Sprinkle with sea salt, crushing it between your fingers as it falls on the cookies.

180 g barley flour

180 g all-purpose flour

3 large egg yolks

120 g powdered sugar

300 g unsalted butter, cold, cubed

Zest of 2 blood oranges

Leaves from 3 to 4 thyme sprigs

Heavy cream for brushing

Large-grain sugar, such as turbinado, for dipping

Blood Orange Caramel (page 267)

Flaky sea salt

Barley Miso Chocolate Chunk Cookies

I first made these cookies for a pop-up in Los Angeles in partnership with a small, curated grocery shop in Chinatown called Sesame LA. I wanted to create a signature chocolate chunk cookie that honored the shop in some way. Sesame and barley are both nutty, a natural match. Miso is a ferment of soybeans, sometimes combined with rice or barley, and used extensively in savory cooking, but is fantastic in desserts—like salt but with tons of umami. You can use any color miso you like, but my favorite is red, for its intense flavor. I make my own, but store-bought is fine! The addition of miso to these cookies makes them instantly craveable. I like to dip the cookies halfway in seeds to achieve a two-toned look, but if you are a seed lover, feel free to roll the entire cookie in sesame seeds; it will add extra crunch. The cookie dough lasts for 2 weeks in the fridge or 3 months in the freezer. Baked cookies keep for 2 weeks at room temperature in an airtight container.

MAKES 24 TO 30 LARGE COOKIES

Preheat the oven to 325°F. Line two sheet trays with parchment paper. Set aside.

In a stand mixer fitted with the paddle attachment, cream the butter, miso, brown sugar, and salt on medium speed until light and fluffy. You'll see the color lighten as well; this process will take 5 to 7 minutes.

Meanwhile, in a separate bowl, whisk together the flours, granulated sugar, baking powder, and baking soda. Set aside.

Add the eggs, one at a time, to the butter mixture, beating on medium until completely incorporated. Scrape down the sides completely between each addition.

Add the dry mixture to the wet mixture and mix on low until combined.

Add the dark and milk chocolate and mix for another minute on medium. Place the sesame seeds in a bowl.

Scoop about 2-ounce portions to form cookies. Roll half of each cookie in sesame seeds. Place the seed-covered balls 3 inches apart on the prepared sheet tray, about six total on each pan. Bake for 10 minutes, then open the oven and quickly lift each sheet tray 1 inch off its rack and let it drop back down. Bake for another 5 to 6 minutes, until golden brown.

550 g unsalted butter, at room temperature

150 g red miso

500 g dark brown sugar

8 g salt

150 g barley flour

650 g all-purpose flour

350 g granulated sugar

12 g baking powder

8 g baking soda

200 g dark chocolate discs

350 g milk chocolate discs

3 large eggs

300 g or more sesame seeds for rolling

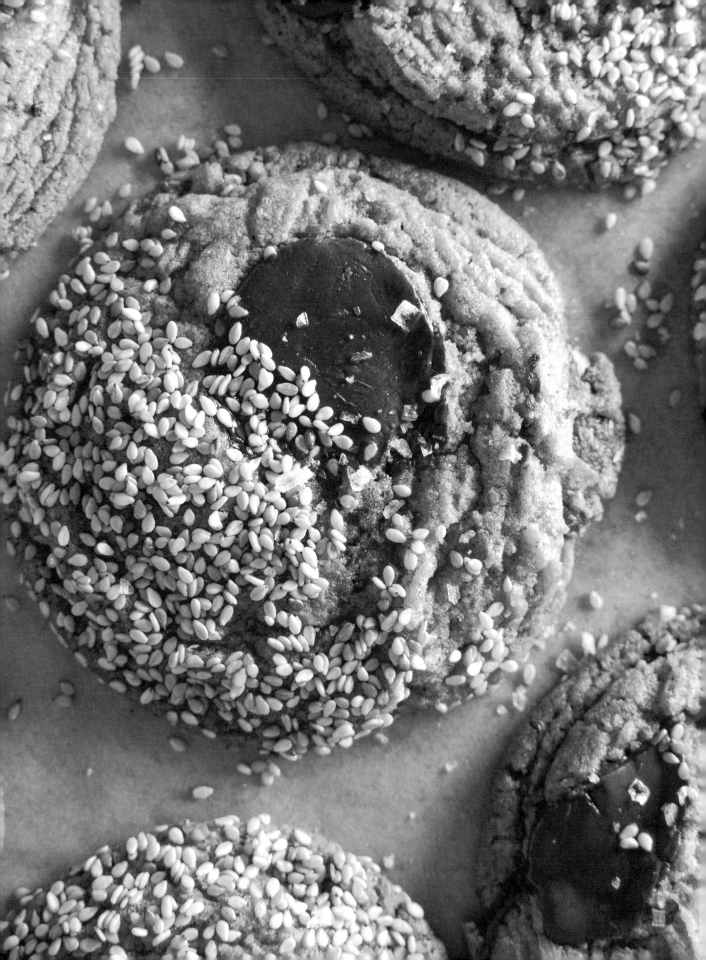

Barley Nectarine Fritter WITH LEMONGRASS GLAZE

2%	10 g yeast
5%	30 g active starter
18%	90 g (5 large) egg yolks
69%	350 g whole milk
18%	95 g barley flour
81%	410 g all-purpose flour
15%	80 g sugar
1%	3 g salt
16%	80 g unsalted butter

Total Formula: 225%

2 to 3 nectarines, chopped into 1-inch cubes

Baking spray

Neutral oil for frying

Lemongrass Glaze (page 265)

Fritters are an underrated member of the donut family. They are a favorite of mine from childhood, for all the nooks and crannies that hold on to the glaze. I love finding the fruit folded in the knots of dough. Making them is equally delightful, because the shaping is so forgiving. They should be weird looking! The best fritters are fried dark, and when done, should look as if you made a great plate of fried chicken. How long the fritter dough takes to make and proof will depend on the biological leavening agent you pick—yeast or sourdough. The dough can be held in the fridge for 2 days before shaping and frying. I love the flavors of nectarine and lemongrass paired here. Both are bright, floral, and herby. Dip the donuts in the glaze for full coverage or paint like Jackson Pollock for a more dynamic look. Make extra tea when making your lemongrass glaze; it is an excellent drink for pairing with these donuts on a lazy morning.

MAKES 12 LARGE FRITTERS

In a stand mixer fitted with the dough hook attachment, add the yeast, starter, egg yolks, and milk and mix on medium. In a separate bowl, combine the flours, sugar, and salt. Add the dry mix to your stand mixer on low speed until incorporated, then increase the speed to medium and mix for 10 minutes to build strength. Cover the bowl and let rest for 15 minutes.

Turn on the mixer at medium speed and add the butter slowly until fully incorporated. Then, beat for another 2 minutes for extra strength.

Clear the dough from the hook and tuck the edges of the dough against the inside of the bowl. Cover with a damp, clean kitchen towel or plastic wrap and let rise until double in volume—2 hours for yeast-only or the hybrid method, 6 to 8 hours for sourdough.

Roll out the dough to a 9-by-18-inch rectangle and sprinkle with chopped nectarines. Fold the dough like a letter and use a rolling pin to press on the dough to seal and extend lengthwise to 24 inches. Use a bench scraper to make rough chops about three-fourths through the dough down and then the length of the dough. Go back and cut 12 equal portions all the way through the dough. Tuck any escaping fruit into the fritter folds. Cut the same number of parchment paper squares. Transfer each portion onto a parchment square and arrange about 3 inches apart on sheet trays, to proof. Lightly spray the tops

CONTINUES ▶

of the fritters with baking spray and cover with plastic wrap. Proof until they are doubled in volume and pass the poke test, 1 to 2 hours for yeast-only or the hybrid method, or 4 to 6 hours for sourdough.

Heat 3 inches of oil in a large wide pot to 350°F. Working in batches is key; you want your fritters to have plenty of room between them to fry properly. Don't overcrowd your pan by frying more than three to four, depending on the size of your pot. Slip each of the fritters into the oil with the parchment paper attached. As it fries, the parchment paper will slip off and you can pull it from the oil with tongs. Fry in the hot oil for 2 to 3 minutes on each side. Use a wide sieve, tongs, or a fish spatula to transfer to a cooling rack set over a sheet tray.

While still slightly warm, splash with glaze over cooling rack or dip each fritter fully into the glaze and place back on the cooling rack to allow any excess to drip away.

Note: If you use the hybrid method, dough can be made with active starter or inactive starter.

Buckwheat Brown Sugar Crumble Carrot Peach Icebox Cake

This is one of my favorite recipes. It was on the menu when I was the pastry chef at Rustic Canyon in Los Angeles. Carrots are my love language; they are sweet, earthy, brightly colored, and a vegetable we eat for dessert! This icebox cake takes all the great vibes of carrot cake and transforms it into a 1950s ice cream dream that comes together without churning in a few minutes and freezes in a matter of hours. Buckwheat, a flower transformed into flour, is dark and a little spicy. Brown sugar highlights these elements with its added molasses content. Eat sliced plain or jazz it up with fresh peaches tossed in peach verbena jam and a swoosh of carrot sauce for a high-end presentation. Peaches and carrots share a late spring sweetness and make a great pairing. Make this for a dessert that you can always have stashed in your freezer for last-minute guests or late-night cravings. Keeps for 2 months, tightly wrapped, in the freezer. Replace all-purpose flour with all buckwheat flour to make a gluten-free version.

MAKES 2 ICEBOX LOAVES

Preheat the oven to 350°F. Line two sheet pans with parchment paper.

Prepare the crumble: Combine the flours, brown sugar, baking powder, and salt in a bowl. Work in the butter with your hands, using your fingers to crumble the mixture as you go and to bring it together. Spread the crumble on the prepared sheet pans. Bake for 25 to 30 minutes, stirring once at about the 15-minute mark. Remove from the oven when golden brown, let cool completely on the pans, and break up with your hands to form large crumbles.

Prepare the ice cream: In the bowl of a stand mixer fitted with the whisk attachment, whip the cream on medium-high until it forms medium peaks. Wrap a towel around the top of your stand mixer if to catch any splashing. Pour in the condensed milk and whip to combine. Add carrot puree and salt; continue to whip on medium-high until the mixture comes back together and medium peaks form.

Line two 9-by-5-inch loaf pans completely with plastic wrap. Sprinkle the bottom of both lined pans with a ½-inch layer of crumble and press into the form. Split half of the carrot cream equally between the two pans. Add another ½-inch layer of crumble, gently pressing into the cream. Add the remaining carrot cream split equally between the two pans, then top with the remaining crumble. Cover with plastic wrap, gently pressing down on the top.

CONTINUES ▶

CRUMBLE
200 g buckwheat flour

260 g all-purpose flour

200 g dark brown sugar

450 g unsalted butter, cold

10 g baking powder

10 g salt

ICE CREAM
1.2 kg heavy whipping cream

800 g sweetened condensed milk

450 g boiled, drained, and blended carrots (10 to 12 carrots)

3 g salt

Carrot Sauce (page 265)

2 fresh peaches, chopped into 1-inch cubes

Ground cherries, cut in half

Peach Jam (page 272)

Tulip petals for serving

Place in the freezer for 4 hours.

To serve: Use a spoon to drop a little carrot sauce on an individual serving plate, then use the back of the spoon to create a smear. Remove one of the icebox cakes from the freezer and unwrap completely. Get a sharp knife and a quart of very hot water. Dip the knife into the water for 2 minutes, wipe off excess water with a kitchen towel, and cut cake into 1-inch-thick slices. Lay each slice flat on the plate on top of the carrot sauce. In a small bowl, toss the fresh peaches with 2 to 3 tablespoons of peach jam. Top each serving of icebox cake with some of the peach mixture, ground cherries, and petals. Serve immediately or temper for 10 minutes for a semifreddo texture.

Buckwheat Sugar Tarts
WITH BAY LEAF ROASTED RHUBARB

Buckwheat flour is made from the seeds of a bushy plant. It is often eaten as porridge. These sugar cookie tarts are like my favorite porridge that can be eaten out of hand. Buckwheat and rhubarb are members of the same plant family! Their close biological relation makes for natural flavor pairing, both tart and floral. Rhubarb has enchanted humans for a long time and has always been eaten with a healthy amount of sugar, turning a very tart celery-like plant into pink jammy goodness. Roasting it with bay leaf keeps some of those initial tannic savory notes to the rhubarb as it bakes out sweet, creating beautiful balance to the cookie. Undecorated cut cookie dough keeps for 3 months in the freezer. Baked cookies keep for 2 to 3 days at room temperature or a week in the fridge, softening over time.

MAKES EIGHTEEN 3-INCH SQUARE COOKIES

In a stand mixer fitted with the paddle attachment, cream the butter and granulated sugar on medium speed, then add the salt and beat until light and fluffy, 5 to 7 minutes. The color will lighten as well. Scrape down the sides occasionally to make sure the ingredients get mixed well.

Continuing to mix on medium speed, add the eggs one at a time. Scrape down between each addition to make sure the eggs combine well.

In a separate bowl, whisk together the flours. Add the flour mixture to the butter mixture and beat until just combined. Scrape down the sides and bottom of the bowl and beat for 30 more seconds.

Dump the dough onto a sheet of parchment paper and top with another piece of parchment. Use a rolling pin to roll out to a ¼-inch-thick rectangle. Transfer to a sheet tray and place in the fridge to chill completely.

Preheat the oven to 325°F. Line two sheet trays with parchment paper.

Pull the dough from the fridge and use a ruler and a wheel cutter to cut it into 3-inch squares.

Place 1 inch apart on the prepared sheet trays. If the dough sticks, use a bench scraper or fish spatula to lift and transfer it to the pans. Arrange the roasted rhubarb on top in a shingle pattern, then sprinkle generously with large-grain sugar. Bake for 30 to 35 minutes, until golden brown on the edges.

340 g unsalted butter

130 g granulated sugar

10 g salt

2 large eggs

500 g rhubarb, cut into 3-inch lengths and then into thirds vertically

180 g buckwheat flour

380 g all-purpose flour

Bay Leaf Sugar (page 262)

Juice of 1 lemon

Large-grain sugar, such as turbinado, for sprinkling

Buckwheat Soba Noodles
WITH CURED EGG, NUKAZUKE PICKLES & KOSHO BUTTER CHICKEN

Soba noodles are a great lunch or dinner. Packed with flavor and nutrition, it's endless what they can be paired with to create a meal. Often, you see a protein, fresh vegetables, and pickles. Soba shops are popular throughout Japan and people dedicate their lives to becoming master noodle makers. This recipe involves a little all-purpose flour to make this traditionally 100 percent buckwheat noodle easier to handle. Make the dough by working slowly and purposefully. Roll out as thinly as possible and cut very narrow noodles. Usually, soba noodles are cut with a special knife, but you can use any knife that has a flat bottom. The buckwheat expands quite a bit when hydrated in boiling water; a thick noodle is a lot to chew, but a thin noodle divine. Here, I've made my favorite way to eat it with citrus-heavy, spicy *kosho* roasted chicken plus *nukazuke* pickles, cured egg yolks, and crunchy flowers. It's sour, earthy, full of umami, and very filling. The noodles keep, uncooked, in an airtight container in your fridge for 1 week or in the freezer for 3 months. With a little practice, you can attempt the traditional gluten-free version, by substituting buckwheat flour for the all-purpose flour.

MAKES 4 PORTIONS

Combine the flours and cold water in a large bowl. Use your hand to massage the flours and water together until the mixture forms a cohesive dough. Transfer the dough to a clean, smooth work surface. Use the heel of your hand to knead the dough in a circular pattern for 8 to 10 minutes, creating petals. When dough is smooth and cohesive, roll into a cone by placing one hand with your thumb facing the ceiling against the side of the dough. Your other hand should be at an angle with the side on your work bench; tilt your hand over the dough. Hold this position and roll back and forth until the dough forms a cone. Put the dough point side down onto the work bench and then press down into a flat disk with no cracks. The dough should be soft and smooth when you are done.

Sprinkle your work surface with cornstarch. Roll the dough into a 12-by-20-inch rectangle that is a scant $\frac{1}{16}$ inch thick. Sprinkle with cornstarch and fold up first lengthwise and then widthwise, so it is now folded into fourths.

Use a knife at the short nonfolded side of your dough to cut very thin noodles. Shaking off any excess cornstarch, place on a parchment paper–lined sheet tray, and cover lightly with plastic wrap or a kitchen towel until ready to boil.

440 g buckwheat flour

180 g all-purpose flour

350 g cold water

Cornstarch for dusting

1 roast chicken, cooled, boned, and shredded

Kosho Oil (page 286)

Sesame oil for tossing

Nukazuke Pickles (page 286)

Cured Egg Yolks (page 286)

Osmanthus or begonia flowers

CONTINUES ▶

Place the shredded chicken in a bowl, toss with 2 tablespoons of kosho oil. Taste to adjust seasoning with more kosho oil or salt; set aside.

Bring a large saucepot of water to a boil over medium-high heat. Lower the heat to medium and drop half of the noodles into the water. Cook the noodles for 90 seconds, then transfer from the heat into an ice-filled bowl to stop the cooking. Drain the cooked noodles. Toss with the sesame oil. Repeat with the remaining noodles.

Serve the noodles cold or at room temperature with bowls of the nukazuke pickles, shaved cured egg yolks, osmanthus flowers, and kosho-roasted chicken so everyone can build their perfect plate at the table.

When kneading soba, you work by folding the dough into petals pulled onto itself, working around the circle to create a chrysanthemum. This helps create a smooth strong dough.

It is essential to cut soba noodle thin, as they expand greatly in water when cooked.

Buckwheat Cake WITH BUCKWHEAT MILK TEA SOAK, YUZU CURD, COCONUT CUSTARD & TORCHED MERINGUE

Milk teas are very popular as a drink in many Asian countries and are paired with some of my favorite fruits in this showstopper cake. The semi-angel cake base is sturdy enough to absorb lots of the delicious soak and still provide structure. The coconut custard has a lot of chunky coconut flakes for texture, in contrast to the tart, silky curd. Yuzu is an incredible floral and tart Japanese citrus. If you can't find yuzu, any lemon variety will do. Torched meringue is the quickest and most stunning cake frosting there is. The drama comes from every individual and unique swoop highlighted by fire. I like a hard torching so that the meringue puffs a little like a marshmallow and takes on a variety of satisfying scorched colors. The cake layers can be baked two to three days ahead. Keep baked cake layers wrapped tightly in plastic and in your fridge until ready to fill and frost. Built cake keeps in the freezer for 1 week. Frosted cake keeps in the fridge for four to five days, but it will be devoured long before that.

MAKES ONE 8-INCH THREE-LAYER CAKE

Preheat the oven to 350°F. Line three 8-inch round cake pans with parchment paper and spray with baking spray.

Combine the egg yolks, half of the sugar, and the milk, flours, baking powder, and salt in a medium bowl and whisk together.

In the bowl of a stand mixer fitted with the whisk attachment, whisk the egg whites and remaining sugar on high speed until you get a meringue with medium peaks. Use a spatula to fold the egg whites into the yolk mixture—working slowly to scrape the bowl, pull the batter through the center of the egg whites and fold under. Continue to do this until the mixture looks uniform, being careful not to deflate.

Portion the cake batter equally into the three prepared pans. Bake for 20 to 25 minutes, until puffed and slightly golden brown. Remove from the oven, turn pans upside-down, and place on a cooling rack. Let each cake cool completely in its pan.

Build your cake: Line an 8-inch cake pan with parchment paper on the bottom and a parchment collar along the sides. Run an offset spatula between the edge of your cake and your pans to release cake onto cooling rack. Poke a lot of holes in all the cakes with the tip of a knife. Place the first layer of cake all the way down into the prepared pan. Use a brush to paint the cake with a couple of passes of the buckwheat milk soak.

Baking spray

8 large eggs, separated

320 g sugar

80 g buckwheat flour

184 g all-purpose flour

11 g baking powder

6 g salt

120 g whole milk

Buckwheat Milk Soak (page 275)

Coconut Custard (page 275)

Yuzu Curd (page 276)

Torched Meringue, not yet torched (page 281)

Citrus, citrus blossoms, and peonies

CONTINUES ▶

Top with a thin layer of yuzu curd. Now, add the second cake layer and press down very gently to seal. Repeat the milk soak process on the second cake. Top with a thin layer of coconut custard and then the final cake. Press down to seal. Brush with the milk soak. Transfer the entire cake to the freezer to set for 2 to 4 hours.

Remove the cake from the freezer and unmold from the pan by briefly passing a kitchen torch over the bottom and sides of the cake pan or rubbing the pan with a hot, wet towel. Peel away all the parchment. Place directly on a plate or cake stand; do not use a cake board as it is a fire hazard.

Working quickly, use a spatula to cover the entire cake generously with meringue in big swoops. Then, use a kitchen torch to burn and set the meringue all around. Decorate with citrus, leaves and blossoms, and peonies. If serving immediately, the inside of the cake will defrost in about 30 minutes at room temperature. It can also be kept chilled in the fridge until ready to serve. See Party Time (page 55) for best cutting practices.

Serve slices of cake with extra citrus for a zesty lift!

EMMER RYE SONORA

109   Emmer Sourdough Pasta with Butter Parmesan Sauce & Spring Pea Tendrils

111   Emmer Pear Tarragon Honey Custard Tart

114   Emmer Maritozzo with Blistered Lavender Blackberries

117   Emmer Everything Bread: Bâtard, Boule & Grissini

120   Rye Triple Chocolate Crinkle Cookies

123   Rye Apple Onion Focaccia

125   Rye Black Bread

128   Rye Malt Ice Cream

131   Rye Chocolate Cake with Hazelnut Chocolate Custard, Sweet Woodruff Cocoa Nib Cream & German Chocolate Buttercream

133   Sonora Chocolate Custard Pie with Chicory Cream

136   Sonora Pistachio Linzer Cookies with Red Currant Violet Jam

138   Sonora Madeleines with Fennel White Chocolate Shell

141   Sonora Cheese Sticks with Arugula Blossoms, Parmesan & Fried Parsley

143   Sonora Vegetable Confetti Cake with Greengage Plum, Whipped Cheesecake & Smoky Honey Swiss Buttercream

The Grains of Europe

EMMER: Also known as farro, emmer can be found short and long, and its descendent grains are categorized as red or white. Emmer is an ancient grain and a member of the grass/wheat family. Cultivated first in the Fertile Crescent of western Asia, North Africa and Asia, it quickly spread, and eventually was the main fuel that built the Roman Empire. Hundreds of years later in the Americas, many of the original colonies were called bread colonies for the immigrants from Germany, Spain, and Britain who grew varietals of this wheat.

Flavor notes: Caramel, sweet, cream, clay.

How it is sourced: Emmer is found as whole grain or as flour.

How it is used: Emmer is a relative of most modern wheats; it can be used in every application. I like it best in hearty breads, pastas, and pizzas. It is very chewy and beloved in Mediterranean cuisine.

RYE: A grayish-brown grain. Small and hard, it is a member of the grass/wheat family. Rye also hails from the Fertile Crescent. It was one of the later cultivated grass grains and is known for rebuilding the soil in which it is planted. Often grown as a cover crop, it is rich in nutrition and flavor. Rye is low gluten and high fiber.

Flavor notes: Malt, soil, chocolate, whiskey, sour.

How it is sourced: Rye is found as whole grain, flakes, or as flour.

How it is used: As a grain, rye is used as the mash in beer, whiskeys, and some vodkas. As a flour, rye is very extensible but not very elastic; it is used for bread, crackers, and pastries. Rye is the basis for popular food preparations in Nordic, eastern European, and traditional Ashkenazi Jewish cuisine. It has been richly tied to these cultures for a thousand years.

SONORA: A soft white wheat. It is small and blond in color. An heirloom grain descended from emmer, sonora was brought from the Old World to the New World by Spain during conquest. California, my home state, is having an incredible revival of sonora through the efforts of the Tehachapi Heritage Grain Project under the stewardship of Sherry Mandell and Alex Weiser of Weiser Family Farms only a couple hundred miles outside Los Angeles. I am so grateful for the fresh, local, whole-grain flours they bring to the market every Wednesday.

Flavor notes: Fresh milk, clotted cream, cut grass.

How it is sourced: Sonora is found whole or as flour.

How it is used: As a grain, sonora makes a great overnight porridge. As a flour, it expresses itself best in pastry, tender and light. It can be swapped in equal parts, or at a 1:1 ratio, for any all-purpose recipe you love, resulting in a golden-hued, tender bake with an incredible buttery flavor. Sonora flour became integral to the Sonora region of Mexico and the West Coast for tortilla production.

The Blossoms

- Lily of the valley, tulip, cornflower, daisy, pea tendrils
- Lavender, hydrangea, blossoming herbs, daisy
- Fennel flowers, hyacinth

Emmer Sourdough Pasta

WITH BUTTER PARMESAN SAUCE & SPRING PEA TENDRILS

I learned the beauty of simple pasta dishes while sharing the pastry room at Rossoblu in Los Angeles with Francesco Allegro from Puglia, Italy. In between making beautiful pastas of every shape, he would occasionally cook up a simple dish to share. I bribed him with ice cream to make these feasts more frequent. They were always unfussy and delicious. Here is a dish with the same ideas. A few ingredients make a great-tasting, nourishing pasta, matched with a sauce of butter and Parmesan that all ages will love and finished with one of spring's best treats—pea tendrils. If you can't find pea tendrils, any tender green is beautiful folded in here. I like to top mine off with a little lemon zest at the table, for a hit of floral acid.

MAKES 4 PORTIONS

Place the flour on a clean, flat surface. Make a well in the center.

Crack the eggs into the center and add the sourdough starter. Use a fork to whisk the eggs and starter together. Start to incorporate the flour by grabbing from the walls of your well as you continue to mix the egg and starter. Slowly incorporate more flour as you go around the well in circles. Once you've incorporated half of the flour, use the edge of the fork to cut the remaining flour into the eggs until combined. Once you have a shaggy mess, switch to using your hands.

Knead the dough, using the heel of your hand to push the top of the dough away from you, fold in half toward you, give it a quarter turn, and repeat. Continue to knead in this way for 10 to 12 minutes, until the dough is soft, supple, and doesn't crack. Cover the dough with a tea towel and let rest for 30 minutes to an hour.

Lightly sprinkle some flour on the surface of the dough. Roll out the pasta dough to $1/16$ inch thick with a rolling pin or with a pasta machine at its thinnest setting. If using a machine, follow the manufacturer's instructions. Once the pasta is rolled out, sprinkle with more flour and allow to dry out slightly for 30 minutes, covered with a clean tea towel. This will make cutting it easier as it will be less likely to stick to itself. Sprinkle with more flour and fold into quarters, widthwise. Cut either 1 inch thick for pappardelle or $1/4$ inch thick for tagliatelle. Use your fingers to pinch up a bunch of noodles and transfer to parchment-lined sheet tray, twisting the noodles into a nest as you set them down. Allow the nests to dry out completely over 24 hours at room temperature, freeze for 3 months, or cook right away.

CONTINUES ▶

400 g emmer flour, plus more for dusting

4 large eggs

20 g active starter

110 g unsalted butter

170 g Parmesan, plus more for sprinkling

1 bunch pea tendrils

Freshly ground black pepper

To cook, bring a large pot of water to a boil. Salt the water liberally. Boil the pasta until tender, only a minute or more for fresh, longer for dried or frozen. In another pan, melt the butter over medium heat. Drain the pasta, reserving ¼ cup of the pasta water. Add the cooked pasta and the pasta water to the butter, then sprinkle in the Parmesan steadily as you use tongs to stir the pasta in the butter. Once the sauce thickens slightly, remove from the heat and fold in pea tendrils. Transfer to plates and top with delicate blossoms and more tendrils. Serve warm with extra Parmesan and cracks of black pepper.

Twirling pasta into nests allows the pasta to dry out well for longer term storage. Nests take about 48 hours to dry out at room temperature. Dried pasta nests keep for 2 weeks in an airtight container.

Note: Pasta dough can be made with active starter or inactive starter.

Emmer Pear Tarragon Honey Custard Tart

Custard tarts topped with syrup-glazed fruit are a classic French pastry. You can find versions topped with different ornamentation of produce throughout the year, big or small. They were my mother's favorite, and her request for every birthday instead of a cake. She loved pears and honey, as they are a natural match. I imagine she would adore this tart, and I think you will, too. Make sure your tart shell is completely cooled, the custard is chilled, and the pears are well drained for greatest stability. The tart dough can be scaled up, mixed together, wrapped tightly, and kept frozen for 3 months. The pears keep for 2 weeks in their poaching liquid in an airtight container in your fridge. Built, the tart keeps in your fridge for 1 to 2 days. Serve cold, cutting wedges with a sharp knife.

MAKES TWO 10-INCH TART SHELLS

In a stand mixer fitted with the paddle attachment, cream together the butter, sugar, and salt on medium speed until light and fluffy. You'll see the color lighten as well; this process will take 5 to 7 minutes. Scrape down the sides occasionally to make sure the ingredients are well mixed.

Continuing to mix on medium speed, add the eggs. Continue mixing to bring the dough together.

In a separate bowl, whisk together the flours. Add the flour mixture to the butter mixture and beat until just combined. Scrape down the sides and bottom of the bowl and beat for 30 more seconds.

Dump the dough onto a sheet of parchment paper and top with another piece of parchment. Use a rolling pin to roll out to ¼ inch thick, 14-inch circle. Transfer to a sheet tray and place in the fridge to chill completely.

Preheat the oven to 325°F. Line a sheet tray with parchment paper.

Pull the dough from the fridge and roll out into an 11-inch circle, about a ¼ inch thick between parchment paper. Transfer to a 10-inch tart pan and press into the pan bottom and sides, letting any of the extra dough hang off the rim. Gently press down on this excess against the rim to trim the dough and perfectly fill your tart pan.

Place on the prepared sheet tray. Use a fork to prick all over. Bake for 20 to 25 minutes, until golden brown on the edges. Remove from the oven and let cool completely.

340 g unsalted butter

130 g sugar

5 g salt

2 large eggs

220 g emmer flour

340 g all-purpose flour

Salty Honey Custard (page 276)

Tarragon Poached Pears (page 267)

Fresh tarragon for sprinkling

CONTINUES ▶

Fill with the custard. Chill for 4 hours. Remove the pears from their syrup and cut into ¼-inch-thick slices. Place on paper towels to absorb any excess syrup and allow to dry out slightly. Arrange the poached pear slices, overlapping in a circle pattern, on top of the baked crust; garnish with more tarragon. Serve chilled.

Fanning fruit is a beautiful and classic way to decorate a tart.

Emmer Maritozzo
WITH BLISTERED LAVENDER BLACKBERRIES

Maritozzo is a delicious Roman dessert dating back to the medieval times. Traditionally, maritozzi are baked and given by men to women they intended to marry or had recently married. Soft brioche buns stuffed with fruit and filled with cream, they are at once light and indulgent. This version shows off emmer, a mother wheat, whose tannic notes pair with the blistered blackberries. Baking in lavender enhances blackberries' fragrance and flavor. Really stuff these with cream and use a spatula to level off. The buns can be made a day ahead and kept at room temperature in an airtight container until filled. Once filled, maritozzo is best eaten on the same day.

MAKES 24 BUNS

In a small bowl, dissolve your yeast in the warm water for a couple of minutes.

In a stand mixer fitted with the dough hook attachment, combine the flours, granulated sugar, and salt. Next, add the yeast water, starter mixture, egg yolks, and milk, and mix on medium speed for 10 minutes. Cover the bowl and let rest for 15 minutes.

Turn on the mixer to medium speed and add the butter slowly until fully incorporated. Then, beat for another 2 minutes for extra strength.

Clear the dough from the hook and tuck the edges of the dough against the inside of the bowl. Cover with a clean, damp kitchen towel or plastic wrap and let rise until double in volume, 2 hours for yeast-only or the hybrid method, 6 to 8 hours for sourdough .

Line two sheet trays with parchment paper.

Divide the dough into 18 to 24 portions, 85 g (3 ounces) each. Using your hand to cup each ball of dough, keeping the edges of your hand tight to the work service and your palm vaulted over the dough, move your hand in large circles to tighten the dough underneath. Or moving clockwise, tuck the outside edges to the center of the dough on top, stretching slightly as you go until you have a round ball. Place the dough balls, seam side down and 3 inches apart, on the prepared sheet trays to proof. Lightly spray the tops of the buns with baking spray and cover with plastic wrap. Proof until they double in volume, 1 to 2 hours for yeast-only or the hybrid method, 6 to 8 hours for sourdough.

6%	50 g warm water (see pages 57–58)
2%	16 g yeast
35%	300 g emmer flour
65%	550 g all-purpose flour
9%	80 g granulated sugar
3%	20 g salt
30%	250 g active starter
13%	108 g (6 large) egg yolks
45%	380 g whole milk
21%	180 g unsalted butter, at room temperature

Total Formula: 229%

Baking spray

1 egg for egg wash

Splash of milk

Blistered Berries (page 267)

Sweet Cream (page 276)

Powdered sugar for sprinkling

Lavender flowers for decoration

CONTINUES ▶

When the buns are fully proofed, make an egg wash by combining the egg with a splash of milk in a small bowl and beating with a fork until uniform. Use a pastry brush to lightly paint all the buns, going all the way to the parchment paper. Make sure to do so lightly, to not deflate the buns and to not leave a lot of egg wash on the sheet tray.

Bake the buns for 16 to 18 minutes, until golden brown and with an internal temperature of 200°F. Pull the buns from the oven and let cool completely.

Cut a wedge out of the top of each bun, then use your finger to poke a deeper hole inside the bun on either side of this wedge. Stuff the buns with blistered berries, then top with sweet cream, using a spatula to follow the shape of the bun. Dust with powdered sugar, then top with more lavender flowers.

Blackberries need only a moment under the broiler to blister beautifully.

Notes: Putting the dough in the fridge for 30 minutes before the shaping steps will help make the dough less sticky and easier to handle. The dough can also proof overnight at either proofing stage, and bake directly from the fridge. If you use the hybrid method, dough can be made with active starter or inactive starter.

Emmer Everything Bread:
BÂTARD, BOULE & GRISSINI

This is my go-to dough to make just about everything bread. In a large-scale bakery, usually the process is to have a master dough that is shaped into various shapes for sale. The bread can be stuffed with cheese, olives, nuts, and dried fruit. Its lower hydration makes it accessible to all levels of bread making and sturdy to any adjustments. Make sure your sourdough starter is very ripe and active for this recipe. The dough can be held in your fridge for 3 days before baking, after which time its structure breaks down and it is best used as focaccia or another flatbread. Adding 100 g of butter to the recipe on the turn after the salt will result in a great sandwich bread variation when baked in a loaf pan at 350°F. The baked bread keeps for a week on your counter wrapped in a clean tea cloth. Toast and enjoy. Unless you add butter, this recipe is naturally vegan.

MAKES 2 BÂTARDS OR BOULES, OR 24 TO 36 GRISSINI

Use your hands to mix the flours with the 700 g of water in a large bowl until you have a shaggy mess. Allow to rest or autolyse for 1 hour for the dough to hydrate and relax.

Use your hands to break up the dough and mix in the starter mixture. Rest for 30 minutes.

Mix the salt with the 50 g of water. Use your hands again to rip and break up the dough while adding the salt water. Let rest for another 30 minutes.

Starting at the edge farthest from you, stretch the dough up and away, then fold over and back toward you. Give the bowl a quarter turn and repeat. Do another quarter turn and repeat, then another quarter turn and repeat. Repeat another full cycle of quarter turns (four more turns for a total of eight turns). Let rest for 30 minutes.

Repeat the stretch and fold method, going twice around, for a total of eight turns. Let rest another 30 minutes. Repeat process two more times, including rests.

Repeat stretch and fold method, going twice around, for a total of eight turns. Let rest 1 hour. Transfer the bowl to the fridge.

Choose your shape: For boules, dump the dough onto a well-floured clean table and split it into three equal portions. Grab the top corner of each portion of dough and fold to the center, then work your way

70%	700 g all-purpose flour, plus more for dusting
30%	300 g emmer flour
70%	700 g warm water (see pages 57–58)
20%	200 g active starter
2%	20 g salt
5%	50 g water to mix with the salt

Total Formula: 197%

Olive oil and flaky sea salt for sprinkling grissini (optional)

Baking spray (optional)

CONTINUES ▶

around the dough, folding all four corners to the center similar to how you were building in bulk. Flip the dough over so the seams are on your work bench. Use the edges of your hands, pressed firmly against your table, to drag the dough toward you, tightening the surface and sealing the dough underneath. Transfer to a bread form or a bowl lined with a clean tea towel and dust liberally with flour. Cover the top with a large, clean tea towel and allow to proof for 1 to 2 hours, depending on the ambient temperature.

For bâtards, dump the dough onto a well-floured clean table and split the dough into three equal portions. Grab the top of each portion and stretch and fold to the center. Grab the points on either side of this fold and fold them into the center as well. Roll the dough over itself, then push the dough away from you, pushing your hands firmly against the table, to tighten into a football shape. Transfer to a sturdy, clean cloth to proof; the sides of the cloth should be able to hold up the bread. Canvas is a good option. Cover with a large, clean tea towel and allow to proof for 1 to 2 hours, depending on the ambient temperature.

For *grissini*, dump the dough onto well-floured, clean table and use your hands to flatten to an inch-thick rectangle. Use a bench scraper to cut dough into ½- to 1-inch-thick sticks. Pick up each stick, gently stretching it, then transfer them all to a lightly sprayed parchment-lined sheet tray to proof. Cover with a clean tea towel and allow to proof for 1 to 2 hours, depending on the ambient temperature.

Preheat the oven, with a Dutch oven inside it, to 450°F for at least 30 minutes to 1 hour.

Turn out the boules or bâtards onto parchment paper, then slash with a serrated knife or a lame with your choice of pattern. Transfer to the Dutch oven and cover. Bake for 15 minutes. Remove the cover and bake for another 20 minutes, or until golden brown and they sound hollow inside.

For grissini, fill a spray bottle with cold water, brush tops lightly with olive oil, and sprinkle with flaky sea salt. Open the oven and spray the sides with water—avoiding glass and heating elements—to create steam. Bake on the sheet tray for 15 minutes, or until golden brown. Serve immediately.

Note: If you use the hybrid method, dough can be made with active starter or inactive starter.

Rye Triple Chocolate Crinkle Cookies

Variations of the crinkle cookie are found the world over. Visually, they are so appealing, with the snow-covered crispy shell cracked deeply by a soft cookie underneath. I've made these a million times and I am still obsessed with their crunch and fudgy center. Rye and chocolate are fast friends in this one. It's a quick cookie to put together and will satisfy any chocolate lover's sweet tooth year-round. You can scoop the dough and keep in the freezer for up to 3 months. Allow to thaw to room temperature and dry out, rolling in powdered sugar only right before baking, for best results. Baked cookies keep for 2 weeks in an airtight container. Replace the butter with olive oil to make recipe vegan. A perfect cookie for bake sales and holiday tins!

MAKES 30 TO 36 SMALL COOKIES

Preheat the oven to 325°F. Line a sheet tray with parchment paper.

Use a double boiler or fill a small saucepot with 2 inches of water; heat over medium heat and place a medium heatproof bowl on top. Make sure the water in the lower vessel does not touch the upper pot/bowl. Add the butter and the 60 g of dark chocolate to the upper vessel and heat until melted. Set aside.

In the bowl of a stand mixer fitted with the paddle attachment, mix together the eggs, brown sugar, and vanilla on medium speed. Beat in the cooled melted chocolate mixture.

In another bowl, whisk together the flours, cocoa powder, baking powder, baking soda, and salt. Add the flour mixture to the chocolate mixture on low speed; beat until just combined. Add the dark and milk chocolate and mix for another minute. Let the batter rest for 30 minutes.

Scoop 1-ounce portions and use your hands to gently roll into a ball. Roll in powdered sugar, flatten slightly, and then place 2 inches apart on the prepared sheet tray. Bake for 10 minutes, or until puffed and cracked.

60 g unsalted butter, at room temperature

60 g dark chocolate for melting

3 large eggs

300 g dark brown sugar

5 g vanilla bean paste

140 g rye flour

130 g all-purpose flour

100 g unsweetened cocoa powder

8 g baking powder

10 g baking soda

8 g salt

50 g dark chocolate discs

50 g milk chocolate discs

Powdered sugar for rolling

Rye Apple Onion Focaccia

I started making this rye focaccia while leading the Pastry and Bread program at Rossoblu in Los Angeles. I wanted the bread program to reflect the whole-grain heritage of Italy, and I loved making seasonal variations with fruit. Focaccia is also known as a salt cake, and I love cake with fruit. Here, we are celebrating a classic autumn variation of apples and onions, with some lemons to brighten the whole affair. Feel free to change out the toppings as the seasons change! This dough is extremely forgiving and a great place to build shaping confidence. Focaccia is great served warm alongside dinner or enjoyed cold as the ultimate sandwich bread stuffed with your choice of fillings. I also love it sliced thick and grilled with olive oil. Keeps for a week at room temperature, wrapped in a tea towel. Replace the honey with molasses to make the recipe vegan.

MAKES 1 FULL SHEET TRAY OR THREE 8-INCH ROUNDS

Toss the cut apples, onion, and lemon in the 10 g of olive oil in a medium bowl and set aside.

With a stand mixer fitted with the dough hook attachment, set to low speed, combine the starter, 675 g of the warm water, flours, and yeast, if using the hybrid method. Continue to mix for 5 minutes.

In a separate bowl, whisk together the remaining 75 g of the water, olive oil, honey, and salt. Add to the dough while still mixing on low speed. Raise the speed to medium and let mix for 10 minutes, or until the dough is smooth and silky. Dip your fingers into some water and drag them down the hook to clear the dough. Cover with a clean, damp kitchen towel or plastic wrap. Adjust for the ambient temperature according to the season: If you have a cool kitchen, leave the dough out for 1 hour at room temperature, then shape onto a sheet tray and transfer to the fridge (shaping instructions follow); if your kitchen is warm, shape on a sheet tray and transfer to the fridge immediately (shaping instructions follow).

Oil a sheet tray or three 8-inch round cake pans with olive oil: 3 tablespoons for a sheet tray, 1 tablespoon per pan for cake pans. To shape the focaccia, dust a clean, flat work surface with a small amount of flour.

For a sheet tray, dump the dough onto the surface and flatten it into a rough square. Grab each corner and pull it to touch the center of the dough. Once all the corners are tucked into the center, flip the dough over, press the sides of your hands against the work surface, and drag the dough toward you to tighten. Do this a few times until you have good tension. Let rest for 20 minutes.

Ingredients

- 2 apples, cored, sliced ¼ inch thick vertically
- 1 onion, halved vertically and sliced ¼ inch thick vertically
- 1 lemon, halved vertically and sliced ¼ inch thick horizontally, seeds removed
- 10 g extra-virgin olive oil for tossing apple, onion, and lemon
- 180 g active starter
- 750 g warm water (see pages 57–58)
- 200 g rye flour
- 825 g all-purpose flour, plus more for dusting
- 4 g yeast
- 225 g extra-virgin olive oil, plus more for pan(s)
- 120 g honey, plus more for drizzling
- 15 g salt
- Baking spray
- Flaky sea salt

CONTINUES ▶

Oil your fingers well before dimpling the dough all over. Don't be shy: the dimples should be deep and plenty!

Pick up the dough with the sides of your hands and place on your prepared sheet tray. Top the dough with another 3 tablespoons of olive oil, gently spreading it over the top with the palm of your hand, patting gently down and not out until the dough stretches to fill the sheet tray or pans. Wrap lightly with plastic wrap; lightly spraying the top with baking spray will keep it from sticking as it proofs. Place in the fridge to final proof overnight or proof at room temperature for 2 hours.

For three 8-inch round cakes, dump the dough onto the surface and flatten it into a rough square. Divide dough into three equal parts. Grab each corner of each portion and pull it to touch the center of the dough. Once all the corners are tucked into the center, flip the dough over, press the sides of your hands against the work surface, and drag the dough toward you to tighten. Do this a few times until you have good tension. Do this for all portions and let rest for 20 minutes.

Pick up the doughs with the sides of your hands and transfer them into your cake pans. Top each dough with another tablespoon of olive oil, gently spreading it over the top with the palm of your hand, patting gently down and not out until the dough stretches to fill the sheet tray or pans. Wrap lightly with plastic wrap; lightly spraying the top with baking spray will keep it from sticking as it proofs. Place in the fridge to final proof overnight or proof at room temperature for 2 hours.

Preheat the oven to 375°F. Fill a small spray bottle with cold water. Pull the focaccia from the fridge or, if room temperature, do a few quick dimples in the dough. Spread your fingers wide and poke the dough all over, about three-quarters deep into the dough. Pop any huge bubbles, by pinching between your fingers but let little ones remain. Use a small spray bottle to spray the oven walls with cold water to create steam as you add the dough. Bake the focaccia for 15 minutes. Working quickly, scatter the apple mixture over the top of the focaccia. Sprinkle with sea salt and return to the oven. Bake for another 30 to 40 minutes, until golden brown and the internal temperature reads over 200°F. Use an offset spatula to clear bread from the edges of your sheet tray or cake pans. Remove bread to a cooling rack and drizzle the top with a little extra honey while still warm.

Note: If you use the hybrid method, dough can be made with active starter or inactive starter.

Rye Black Bread

This was one of the first breads I developed that turned out just how I wanted. It's a rich, superdark pumpernickel mimicking the dense breads of eastern Europe and Russia. At my first restaurant, it was on the daily bread menu and always sold out, even before it was voted Best Bread in Los Angeles by the *LA Times*. I saved that paper, but my favorite memory is the long line of happy bread lovers that wound around the block each day. In the kitchen, we'd cube and griddle it in a cast-iron skillet in butter with sea salt and thyme, plop a sunny-side-up egg on top, and serve it alongside a big salad of leafy greens—a recipe by way of my mother's time in the USSR when she was a young woman. After she passed away, I found comfort when I read a similar meal prep in Anya Von Bremzen's stunning memoir *Mastering the Art of Soviet Cooking*. I'd always catch one of my sous chefs, Lisa Beck, cutting it thick, slathering it with butter, and heaping chopped fresh dill on top to munch on during break. Whichever way you do it, the bread is rich, tasty, and a meal in itself. This recipe makes three loaves, one for now, one for later, and one to make a friend—my mom's rule for bread to keep the gift going. You won't see much rise throughout the proofs, but the pop in the oven is unrivaled. This recipe is naturally vegan.

MAKES 3 LOAVES

Dissolve the starter in the 400 g of water in a large bowl. Add the molasses and brewed coffee and whisk to combine. Set aside.

In another large bowl, combine all three flours with the cocoa powder, ground espresso, and ground fennel seeds.

Pour starter mixture into the dry mixture and move around rapidly with your hands to fully hydrate all the dry ingredients; stop when you have a shaggy mess. Allow to rest for 1 hour.

Mix the salt with the remaining 100 g of water. Pour over the dough and break it apart with your hands to incorporate fully. Allow to rest for 1 hour.

Grab the part of the dough ball farthest away from you; pull up to stretch and fold under. Grab the next part of the dough and continue to stretch and fold the dough under itself, creating a coil with the seams facing down. Rotate 90 degrees. Allow to rest 30 minutes. Repeat coil four times, with 30-minute rests in between for a total of 3 hours. Allow to rest for 1 hour after the final coil.

CONTINUES ▶

- 100 g active starter
- 400 g water
- 50 g blackstrap molasses
- 300 g brewed coffee, cooled
- 240 g rye flour
- 278 g emmer flour
- 500 g all-purpose flour, plus more for dusting
- 25 g unsweetened cocoa powder
- 40 g ground espresso coffee
- 3 g ground fennel seeds,
- 24 g salt
- 100 g water to mix with the salt

Lightly flour your clean work surface, then dump the dough onto the surface. Divide into three portions, 700 g each. Gently flatten each portion of dough with the palm of your hand to 1 inch thick and roll it toward you. Use the side of your hands to seal together the edges at the end.

For free-form loaves, place in an oval wooden bread form or a clean sturdy clothlike canvas, seam side up, to final proof overnight in the fridge.

For a sandwich loaf, place dough seam sides down directly into a 8-by-4-inch loaf pan prepared with baking spray and a parchment sling. Wrap with plastic and move to the fridge for final proof. This dough does not rise a lot in the final proof but has a huge spring once in the oven.

For free-form loaves, the next day preheat the oven with a Dutch oven inside it to 450°F for at least 30 minutes to 1 hour. Turn free-form loaves onto parchment paper, dust with flour, then slash with a serrated knife or a lame with your choice of pattern. Transfer to the Dutch oven and cover. Bake for 15 minutes. Remove the cover and bake for another 20 minutes, until deep brown and they sound hollow inside. Internal temperature should be over 200°F.

For sandwich loaves, the next day preheat the oven to 400°F and pull the dough from the fridge. Dust the top of the loaves with flour, then use a lame to cut one slit down the center. Each slit should be 1 inch deep at a 45-degree angle. Fill a small spray bottle with cold water. Place the pans in the oven and spray the walls with water. Bake for 10 minutes. Spray the sides of the oven with the spray bottle to create steam. Bake for an additional 40 minutes, or until the bread has puffed and is deep brown. The internal temperature should be over 200°F, and when tapped, the bread should sound hollow.

Remove from the oven and allow to cool for at least 30 minutes before breaking the bread.

Rye Malt Ice Cream

Bakeries always end up with a glut of extra bread. Either it is loaves that weren't sold or heels from sandwiches made throughout the day. This ice cream was born out of the need to create less bread waste. I have offered a bread-based ice cream at every restaurant where I have run the pastry program. I got the idea from loving ice cream and having too much bread on hand. Use any bread as the base flavor to infuse into your custard, but I particularly like using the dark rye from the previous recipe to impart a lot of color and flavor. If you use a Jewish or Scandinavian rye, expect your ice cream to be paler. The addition of malt gives it an old-fashioned diner vibe. Either way, you will end up with a delicious, thick, and toasty ice cream. Serve on slices of bread for a real "ice cream sandwich."

MAKES 1 QUART

Preheat the oven to 350°F. Toast the bread cubes on a sheet tray for 10 to 15 minutes, until completely dried out. Remove from the oven and set aside.

Place the egg yolks and granulated sugar in a medium bowl and whisk to combine. Set aside.

Place the toasted bread cubes, milk, cream, malt powder, and brown sugar in a small saucepot and bring to a simmer over medium heat. Remove the mixture from the heat, then strain through a very fine mesh strainer, reserving the liquid. Slowly whisk the liquid into the yolk mixture. Return the yolk mixture to the pot in which you heated the bread mixture and place over low heat. Cook for a minute, stirring constantly with a whisk, until thickened slightly. Dip a wooden spoon into the mixture; it should coat the whisk, and when you run your finger through it, the mixture should hold the edges of your tracks. Remove from the heat, strain again, and transfer to the fridge to chill 4 hours or overnight.

Follow your ice cream maker's instructions to transform the mixture into ice cream.

Crush some of your bread cubes to great crumbs of varying sizes. Sprinkle over the top of your ice cream.

120 g cubed Rye Black Bread (page 125; cut into 1-inch cubes), plus more for garnish

6 large egg yolks

80 g granulated sugar

720 g whole milk

600 g heavy whipping cream

50 g malt powder

100 g dark brown sugar

Rye Chocolate Cake WITH HAZELNUT CHOCOLATE CUSTARD, SWEET WOODRUFF COCOA NIB CREAM & GERMAN CHOCOLATE BUTTERCREAM

56 g rye flour

Baking spray

100 g unsweetened cocoa powder, plus more for dusting

510 g granulated sugar

225 g all-purpose flour

7 g baking powder

6 g baking soda

23 g malt powder

5 g salt

255 g boiling water

113 g grapeseed oil

255 g whole milk

2 large eggs

1 large egg yolk

11 g freshly squeezed lemon juice

German Chocolate Buttercream (page 281)

Hazelnut Chocolate Custard (page 277)

Sweet Woodruff Cocoa Nib Cream (page 277)

Sweet woodruff, tulips, and hyacinth

This is my chocolate cake of dreams: deeply rich and chocolaty but lightened with a cream filling that balances it perfectly. The devil's food is a dream, as the boiling water allows the cocoa powder to blossom to its darkest color and richest flavor. The custard is a sublime homemade Nutella. But the star for me is the German chocolate buttercream; less well known than the Swiss and Italian preparation, it is very deserving of your time and attention. Rather than having a meringue base, it starts off as a custard to which butter is added. The result is the silkiest, darkest, richest, most chocolaty buttercream you have ever tasted. It's also incredibly stable at room temperature for hours. Fun hack: Because it's a custard-based buttercream, I have had success reducing kitchen waste by beating butter into leftover pastry creams with a paddle attachment in a stand mixer on medium, to make a variety of different German buttercreams. The cakes can be made a day ahead, wrapped tightly in plastic wrap, in your fridge until you are ready to use them. Once baked and frosted, it keeps for 3 to 4 days in your fridge. Enjoy with my favorite cake accompaniment—a tall glass of milk.

MAKES ONE 8-INCH THREE-LAYER CAKE

Preheat the oven to 325°F. Spread the rye flour on a sheet tray. Toast for 10 minutes, or until golden and fragrant. Remove from the oven and let cool completely.

Line three 8-inch round cake pans with parchment paper and spray with baking spray. Sprinkle lightly with cocoa powder. Set aside.

Whisk together the cocoa powder, sugar, toasted rye flour, all-purpose flour, baking powder, baking soda, malt powder, and salt in a large bowl. Make a well in the center and add the boiling water and oil. Whisk together and let sit for 3 minutes to cool a little. Add the milk, eggs, egg yolk, and lemon juice and whisk until the mixture is combined. Divide evenly among the three prepared pans. Bake for 30 minutes, or until the top is springy to the touch.

Pull the cakes from the oven and let cool completely in their pans on a cooling rack before running an offset spatula around the edges and turning upside down to release the cakes. Trim off any domed portion of the cakes until each is a level layer.

CONTINUES ▶

Build your cake: Put the first layer of cake on a cake board or a large plate. If you have a turntable, use it, but a cake stand will do. Load your buttercream into a piping bag and pipe a ring along the outside edge of your cake layer. Fill with a thin layer of hazelnut chocolate custard. Place a second cake on top and press gently to seal the edges. Use an offset spatula to add more buttercream to seal where the cake layers join. Pipe another buttercream ring and fill with the sweet woodruff cocoa nib cream. Stack the final cake layer on top and use an offset spatula with extra buttercream to seal. Use your offset spatula to add more buttercream to coat the cake in a thin primary layer. Transfer to the fridge to chill for 30 minutes, or until the buttercream is firm.

Pull the cake from the fridge and add more buttercream to create a final layer. Use a bench scraper while turning your cake stand to create smooth sides. Use Ateco piping tip #127, or a pastry bag cut to have a circular opening, and then a small vertical slit to the top to create ruffles with your buttercream. Decorate with sweet woodruff, tulips, and hyacinth.

Keep in the fridge until an hour before you want to cut and serve. See Party Time (page 55) for best cutting practices.

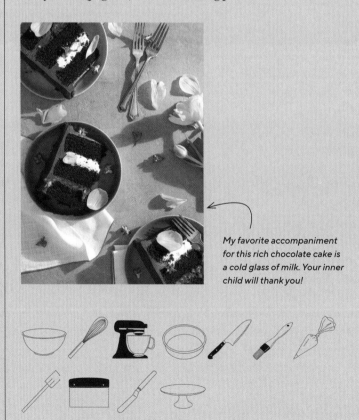

My favorite accompaniment for this rich chocolate cake is a cold glass of milk. Your inner child will thank you!

Sonora Chocolate Custard Pie
WITH CHICORY CREAM

CRUST

30 g active starter

325 g cold water

440 g sonora flour

640 g all-purpose flour

150 g dark brown sugar

600 g unsalted butter, cold, cubed

10 g salt

FILLING

120 g unsalted butter, melted

110 g dark chocolate discs

30 g unsweetened cocoa powder

175 g heavy whipping cream

3 large eggs

420 g sugar

5 g salt

Uncooked rice to use as pie weights

1 egg for egg wash

Splash of milk for egg wash

Large-grain sugar, such as turbinado, for sprinkling

TO SERVE

Chicory Cream (page 277)

This is the recipe that I made for a tasting before I was hired as the pastry chef at Manuela. When I served it to the executive chef, his eyes teared up and he told me about his grandmother. Food can move us across time, and this pie seems to always bring up a strong feeling for people. This fudge custard is baked into a flaky all-butter sonora crust. You can't go wrong. I love serving it with softly whipped chicory cream. Chicory is a plant that, when processed and ground, resembles the flavor of coffee in many ways—in fact, during past wartime shortages, it was what most people drank instead of coffee. It's very delicious and a beautiful complement to the chocolate. The pie will puff quite dramatically while baking and then fall, creating its signature large cracks. The pie dough is scaled up so you have some for the next time you crave pie; a smaller batch is actually harder to pull together. Embrace scale! The dough keeps, unbaked and unfilled, wrapped tightly in the fridge for 1 week or in the freezer for 3 months. Filled and baked pie keeps in the fridge for one week or room temperature for 2 to 3 days.

MAKES TWO 9-INCH DOUBLE CRUSTS, OR FOUR 9-INCH SINGLE CRUSTS; FILLING MAKES 1 PIE

In a small bowl, dissolve the starter in the cold water. Set aside.

Prepare the crust: Combine the flours and brown sugar in a medium bowl. Whisk vigorously to mix and break up any lumps in the sugar. Add the butter to the flour mixture and gently coat by tossing quickly.

Dump onto a clean work surface. Use the heel of your hand to press the butter down against the work surface and away from you, creating thin sheets. Do this to all the butter. When you've touched every piece of butter, use a bench scraper to scrape everything off the work surface and back together.

Make a well in the center and add half of the starter mixture, using your bench scraper to cut it into the flour. Add the rest of the starter mixture and continue to cut it into the dough with your bench scraper. Once you have a chunky mass, use your hands to pull the mass together. Press it down flat and cut into three sections. Stack these sections on top of one another and press down flat again. Cut in half and stack once more, pressing down flat. Divide the dough into four equal portions. Wrap the doughs in plastic wrap and place in the fridge to rest for 30 minutes or overnight.

CONTINUES ▶

Make the filling: Place the butter, chocolate, and cocoa powder in a medium heatproof bowl set atop a small saucepot filled with 2 inches of water. Heating over medium-high heat, use a whisk to stir everything together until melted. Remove from the heat and set aside to cool slightly.

In a separate bowl, whisk together the cream, three of the eggs, and the granulated sugar and salt. Whisking vigorously, pour the chocolate into the egg mixture. Set aside.

Pull one dough portion from the fridge and, starting from the center, roll out dough in all directions until it is 2 inches bigger all around than your pie pan. Use your rolling pin to gather the dough onto it like a scroll, then lift and set it into the pie pan. Roll the edges under to form a coil and crimp all around. Chill the pie dough for 30 minutes or overnight. Move extra dough into the freezer for the next time you have a craving for pie.

Preheat the oven to 350°F. Prick the bottom of the crust with a fork, cover with parchment, and fill with uncooked rice. Bake for 20 minutes, remove the rice and parchment, return the crust to the oven, and bake for another 5 minutes. Make an egg wash by combining the remaining egg with a splash of milk and whisking vigorously. Pull the crust from the oven. Brush the edges with egg wash and sprinkle with large-grain sugar. Pour in the filling and return the pan to the oven. Bake for 40 to 45 minutes, until the custard is puffed and jiggly. As the pie cools, the filling will fall and shatter. Serve at room temperature or cold with chicory cream on the side.

Notes: You can also use sugar as a pie weight! Repeated baking of the sugar will toast it and gently caramelize it. This becomes a yummy fun ingredient you can use in your pantry. You can use active starter or inactive here, as the pie dough's structure is not coming from the starter. We are adding flavor and nutrition!

Sonora Pistachio Linzer Cookies WITH RED CURRANT VIOLET JAM

Linzer cookies are my all-time favorite cookie. There is so much fun to be had with different fillings and different shapes. They are the ultimate holiday cookie, in my mind. I love the flavor pairing but also the color play of the green and red of pistachio and red currant. Sonora is the perfect swap for almost all pastry preparations. Small and soft, it always yields a soft crumb. These cookies are soft and nutty. The jam is tart and sweet. If you can't find red currants, swamp for another bright red jam, such as raspberry or strawberry. Linzers are best after they have been sandwiched together for a few hours, as the cookies soften and attach to the jam, creating a tender sweet dream. The dough can be kept for 3 months in the freezer. Unfilled, the cookies keep for 1 week in an airtight container at room temperature. Once filled, the cookies should be eaten in 1 to 2 days.

MAKES 9 TO 12 LARGE LINZER COOKIES

Preheat the oven to 350°F.

In a stand mixer fitted with the paddle attachment, beat the granulated sugar and butter together for 3 to 5 minutes on medium speed. Add all the flours, powdered sugar, baking powder, salt, and egg and mix on low speed until combined, turning the machine off a few times while mixing, to scrape down the sides and to ensure even distribution of the ingredients.

Place a sheet of parchment paper on your work surface. Dump the dough onto the parchment. Place another piece of parchment paper on top of the dough. Use a rolling pin to roll out dough to the length and width of the parchment sheets, about 1/4 inch thick. Place in the fridge to firm up for 30 minutes.

Remove the dough from the fridge, remove the top parchment paper, and cut out your desired shapes (I like to make circles 2 to 3 inches in diameter); use your largest biscuit cutter or in a pinch you can use a jar lid or cup. Make sure you have an even number for cookie sandwiches. I like to punch out fun peekaboo holes in the cookie that will go on top (be sure to keep count and cut holes in only half of the total number of cookie dough shapes). Place the cut shapes about 1/2 inch apart on sheet tray lined with fresh parchment paper. Bake for 12 to 14 minutes, until baked through and slightly golden on the edges. Remove from the oven and let cool completely on the sheet trays.

100 g granulated sugar

225 g unsalted butter, at room temperature

300 g sonora flour

160 g pistachio flour

125 g powdered sugar, plus more for dusting

3 g baking powder

3 g salt

1 large egg

Red Currant Violet Jam (page 273)

Flip your bottom cookies over, to have a flat surface on top, and fill the center with a heaping tablespoon of jam. Place a cutout cookie on top of the jam, holding the edges, and gently press down to spread the jam evenly. Once all cookies are filled, use a sieve to dust the tops lightly with powdered sugar.

Sonora Madeleines

WITH FENNEL WHITE CHOCOLATE SHELL

Madeleines are such a great little cookie, but they are actually little cakes! These play with sonora's flavor of butter and hay, by pairing brown butter in the dough. The signature bump on the back comes from a long, cold rest once the dough is piped into the form, and although pressing them into a white chocolate shell is a little extra work, it raises this little treat to the sublime. Pressing fennel or flowers into the chocolate creates a gorgeous look that can become the centerpiece of a casual gathering. These are great with tea. Madeleines keep for a week in an airtight container at room temperature.

MAKES 24

Melt the butter in a small saucepan over medium-low heat and allow to brown, 5 to 8 minutes. Set aside to cool.

Sift the flours, baking powder, and salt together into a small bowl. Set aside.

In a stand mixer fitted with the whisk attachment, beat the eggs and sugar on high speed until light and fluffy. You will see the color lighten as well. Reduce speed to medium; drizzle in the milk until combined.

Remove the bowl of the egg mixture from the stand mixer. Lightly dust half of the flour mixture over your egg mixture and use a spatula to fold until just combined. Folding is a gentle method of combining ingredients, involving scraping the spatula against the sides of the bowl and bringing it through to the center of the batter. Dust remaining flour and finish folding. Finally, fold in brown butter slowly until incorporated. Transfer the dough to an airtight container or piping bag. Chill the dough in the fridge for 2 hours or overnight, the colder the better.

Preheat the oven to 400°F. Prepare madeleine pans by lightly spraying the entire pan with baking spray and adding an even dusting of flour. Turn the pan over and knock off any excess flour. Scoop a tablespoon of batter into a madeleine divot or pipe the dough divot of your pan; make sure you are filling only halfway. Bake the madeleines for 8 to 10 minutes, until golden. Remove from the oven and let cool completely.

In a double boiler, warm the white chocolate until it begins to melt. Gently stir, then pull from the heat when the chocolate looks 80 percent melted. Continue to stir off the heat until smooth. Sprinkle and stir in the fennel pollen.

130 g unsalted butter

70 g sonora flour

60 g all-purpose flour, plus more for dusting

10 g baking powder

3 g salt

2 large eggs

120 g sugar

40 g whole milk

Baking spray

White chocolate discs for shell

1 g fennel pollen

Fennel fronds

Spray clean madeleine pans with baking spray. Lay the fennel fronds into the molds. Add a tablespoon of melted chocolate to each mold and gently press a madeleine into the chocolate, spreading the chocolate out beneath it. Chill in the fridge for 15 minutes to set the chocolate. Pop the madeleines out of the mold by gentle pushing on the edges to release them.

Sonora Cheese Sticks

WITH ARUGULA BLOSSOMS, PARMESAN & FRIED PARSLEY

Laminated pastries are excellent canvases for whole grains because whole grains love fat; it helps soften their bran and express their flavor better. We add even more flavor through fried herbs, sprouted flowers, cheese, and spices. More flavor, more fun! This sonora is laminated with spring blossoms from bolted winter arugula, plus grated Parmesan. Arugula flowers are very peppery, bringing a floral *cacio e pepe* vibe to this cracker. If you can't source arugula flowers, swap out for the soft blossom of any herb or member of the brassica family. Frying the parsley removes the moisture and keeps it green, crispy, and delicious. A savory cracker using the pastry technique, this is the perfect cheesy snack before or after dinner. Use any flowers you like and feel free to sub another hard cheese. These are infinitely variable. They keep, in an airtight container, for 1 week at room temperature.

MAKES 18 TO 24

Heat 2 inches of neutral oil in a large saucepot to 350°F. Drop in the parsley and immediately stand back; the oil will sputter. Fry for 20 to 30 seconds, then transfer to a plate lined with paper towels to drain any excess oil. Parsley should be vibrant and translucent. Sprinkle with salt. Set aside.

In a small bowl, dissolve the starter in the cold water; set aside.

Combine the salt and flours in a bowl and mix with your hand. Add the cold butter and toss to cover.

Dump onto a clean counter, then use the heel of your hand to smoosh the butter down and away from you, creating a sheet. Sheet out all the butter with the heel of your hands. Use a bench scraper to pull up the butter and dough together from the table. Once regathered, use the bench scraper to chop up any butter pieces larger than a dime. Gently toss in three-quarters of the fried parsley, arugula flowers, and cheese, remembering to reserve some of each for garnish.

Make a well in the center of the mixture and add half of the starter mixture. Use your fingers to toss some of the dough on top of the water mixture to absorb, then use the bench scraper to cut the rest of the starter mixture into the dough. Chop the dough until it pulls together. Press together with your hands until you have a shaggy disk. Cut the dough into thirds and stack. Use the heels of your hands to compress down to 1 inch. Repeat cutting into thirds, stacking, and compressing.

Neutral oil for frying

Leaves from 1 bunch parsley

10 g salt, plus more for sprinkling parsley

50 g active starter

200 g cold water

240 g sonora flour

360 g all-purpose flour, plus more for dusting

325 g unsalted butter, cold, cubed

1 bunch arugula flowers

100 g Parmesan, plus more for garnish

1 large egg

Splash of milk

Flaky sea salt for garnish

CONTINUES ▶

Gather into a disk. Wrap tightly with plastic wrap and place in the fridge for at least 30 minutes.

Preheat the oven to 350°F and line a sheet tray with parchment paper. Lightly dust the work surface with flour. Roll out the dough to a ¼-inch-thick, 8-by-13-inch rectangle. Use a pizza cutter to cut 1-inch-thick ribbons. Arrange them in a single layer on the prepared sheet tray. If the pastry has become warm, allow to chill in the fridge for 30 minutes at this point.

Make an egg wash by combining the egg with a splash of milk in a small bowl and mixing thoroughly. Brush the entire surface of the ribbons with egg wash, then sprinkle each generously with flaky sea salt and extra Parmesan.

Bake for 25 to 30 minutes, until golden and aromatic. Allow to cool completely on the sheet tray. Pile high in a bowl and top with remaining fried parsley to serve.

Note: You can use active or inactive starter here, as the cracker's structure is not coming from the starter. We are adding flavor and nutrition!

Sonora Vegetable Confetti Cake

WITH GREENGAGE PLUM, WHIPPED CHEESECAKE & SMOKY HONEY SWISS BUTTERCREAM

I first made this cake for a vegetable series while working as the pastry chef at Rustic Canyon under Jeremy Fox. I wanted to call to mind the confetti cakes of childhood, using the rainbow of vegetables available at the Santa Monica Farmers Market in Los Angeles. Many herbs are sweet and vegetables are actually all fruit, both begging for use in dessert! If you can't find rainbow carrots, sub in some beets to keep the rainbow effect. This cake is based on a vintage silver cake batter, and its white bake really lets the colors of the vegetable pop. The smoky honey buttercream is a personal favorite that I pair with loads of flavors throughout the year. It is lovely here alongside whipped cheesecake and greengage plum jam whose flavor is like eating an emerald—bright, juicy, tannic, sweet. If you can't find these beauties, use any plum for the jam. The key to a perfect dome is to chill it often and to add the final layer of buttercream slowly. Gently heating your offset spatula in hot water and drying it off before you run it across the buttercream will create a very smooth finish. The cake layers can be made a day ahead. Keep the assembled cake in the fridge for up to 3 days. Pull from the fridge an hour before serving.

MAKES TWO 8-INCH CAKE LAYERS AND ONE 6-INCH CAKE LAYER

Preheat the oven to 350°F. Line cake pans with parchment paper and spray with baking spray. Set aside.

In the bowl of a stand mixer fitted with the paddle attachment, beat the butter and sugar together on medium speed until light and fluffy.

In a separate bowl, combine the flours, baking powder, and salt. Add one-third of the flour mixture to the butter mixture while on low speed. Add one-third (100 g) of the cold water. Continue alternating adding the dry and water additions until everything is combined.

In another large bowl, using a handheld mixer, whisk the egg whites until medium peaks form. Remove cake batter bowl from the stand mixer and fold in the egg whites. Fold in the parsley, carrot, and lemon peel "sprinkles." Portion equally into two 8-inch round cake pans as well as into one 6-inch round cake pan.

Bake for 20 to 25 minutes, until the cakes are springy to the touch in the center. Remove from the oven and let cool completely in the pans.

CONTINUES ▶

Ingredients

- 187 g unsalted butter, at room temperature
- 375 g sugar
- 125 g sonora flour
- 231 g all-purpose flour
- 10 g baking powder
- 6 g salt
- 300 g cold water
- 5 large egg whites
- 63 g minced parsley sprigs, leaves removed
- 100 g minced carrot (5 or 6 carrots), different colors
- Peel from 2 lemons, minced
- Greengage Jam (page 273)
- Whipped Cheesecake (page 277)
- Smoky Honey Swiss Buttercream (page 282)
- Rainbow edible florals

Build your cake: Use an offset spatula to run along the edge of each cake and overturn to release. Put the one 8-inch cake on a cake board or a large plate. If you have a turntable, use it, but a cake stand will do. Load your buttercream into a piping bag and pipe a ring along the outside edge of your cake layer. Fill with a thin layer of whipped cheesecake. Place the second 8-inch cake on top and press gently to seal the edges. Use an offset spatula to add more buttercream to seal where the cake layers join. Pipe another buttercream ring about an inch inside the circle and fill with greengage jam. Press the 6-inch cake on top and use the offset spatula with extra buttercream to seal. Use your offset spatula to add more buttercream to coat the cake in a thin primary layer. You will need to fill the space between the 8-inch and 6-inch cakes with buttercream and create a slope. Transfer to the fridge to chill for 30 minutes, or until the buttercream is firm.

Pull the cake from the fridge and add more buttercream to create a final layer. Use a bench scraper or offset spatula while turning your cake stand to create smooth sides. Use Ateco piping tip #803 or a pastry bag cut to have a circular opening to create clouds or bloops over the surface. Decorate with colorful edible flowers such as hydrangea, blossoming herbs and cornflowers. Keep in the fridge until an hour before you want to cut and serve. See Party Time (page 55) for best cutting practices.

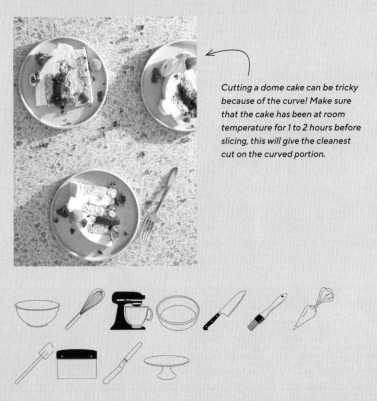

Cutting a dome cake can be tricky because of the curve! Make sure that the cake has been at room temperature for 1 to 2 hours before slicing, this will give the cleanest cut on the curved portion.

AMERICAS

QUINOA AMARANTH CORN

151   Puffed Quinoa Brown Sugar Brownies with Persimmon

153   Quinoa Churros with Chocolate Sauce

156   Quinoa Brown Sugar Chili Buns with Hot Chocolate Drink

159   Quinoa Upside-Down Cake with Pineapple &
Candied Hibiscus

162   Amaranth Marigold Buñuelos

165   Amaranth Cookie Sandwiches with Plantains, Caramelized
White Chocolate & Crema Buttercream

168   Amaranth Squash Almond Butter Pancakes with Maple
Syrup & Roasted Sunflower Butter

171   Amaranth & Corn Crumble with Papaya, Raspberry & Lime

172   Corn Cookies with Candied Mango & Pink Peppercorn Sugar

175   Sweet Corn Biscuits with Vanilla Macerated Fruit
& Cultured Milk Soup

176   Corn Crust Blueberry Pie with Lilac Ice Cream

179   Masa Corn Nasturtium Quesadilla

182   Corn Tres Leches Honeysuckle Cake

185   Corn Cake with Lemon Verbena Custard, Corn Curd
& Passion Fruit Buttercream

The Grains of the Americas

QUINOA: A small, round pseudocereal that comes in many colors, originating from the Andean mountains of South America. High in protein and nutrients, quinoa was the main source of food for those living in the Americas for millennia. It was considered the mother grain of this area of the world, by the Quechua people who called it *kinwa*. It is a member of a flowering plant family that includes spinach and amaranth. Quinoa is naturally gluten-free.

Flavor notes: Nutty, floral, green tea, sour cream, black beans.

How it is sourced: Quinoa is usually found whole or as a flour.

How it is used: This is a fast-cooking grain! It is valued for its great texture; when boiled, it is light and bouncy; and when fried, it takes on a great crisp. It is still the dominant grain in cuisines of South America, for both sweet and savory dishes.

AMARANTH: A tiny, round pseudocereal that is mostly sourced in red and white variations. It is an heirloom grain in the same family of quinoa and from the same area. It is smaller and more intensely flavored than its kin. Its popularity spread throughout the Americas and its use is tied to religious celebrations to this day. Amaranth is naturally gluten-free.

Flavor notes: Grass, sour, lemon pith, fermented.

How it is sourced: Amaranth is found in whole grain and as flour.

How it is used: Amaranth is prized for its seed and for its leaves, which are common in savory preparations of the region. Whole, it has a crunchy, popping texture, and its sour flavor balances well with high-sugar candy making. Cooking it mellows the sometimes intense sour flavor of some crops, and it is particularly great lightly roasted in a pan prior to using.

CORN: An ancient grain of the New World. It is a plump kernel found in a multitude of colors, sizes, and varieties. Corn is a member of the grass family. One of the first grains cultivated by humanity in all its forms, it is so versatile, dried or fresh. Corn was domesticated in what is now modern-day North and Central America. It was the main crop for the many complex civilizations of the Americas and vital to cultural and religious practices of its indigenous people. Corn is naturally gluten-free.

Flavor notes: Sweet, starchy, buttery, whole milk, juicy.

How it is sourced: Corn is primarily found as a kernel, large-grain flour (polenta, grits, etc.), fine flour, or cornstarch.

How it is used: Corn can be tender, crumbly, and crunchy. Corn is consumed in every way you can imagine—polenta, popcorn, tea, tortillas, and so on. I think it expresses itself best as pastry and flatbreads, giving great bite and crunch to your food. It gains even more powers when cooked or nixtamalized (soaked in an alkaline solution) for masa tortillas. Throw in a little corn whenever you want to add extra texture and sweet flavor.

The Blossoms

- Aster, poppy, white sage, iris, marigold, honeysuckle
- Fern, hydrangea, dogwood, rhododendron
- Black-eyed Susan, sunflower, herb blossoms, hibiscus

Puffed Quinoa Brown Sugar Brownies
WITH PERSIMMON

While I was growing up in Ecuador, quinoa was everywhere in every color. It was my mother's favorite grain to cook. So, it turned up in salads, puddings, and often in my school lunches even after we'd moved back to the United States, where there was always a curious person asking me, "What's that?!" Its mild and nutty flavor goes great with almost anything. It's easy to cook and puff, because it releases its outer shell when ready, giving you an easy visual cue that it's done. I think its nuttiness pairs beautifully with chocolate, another prized ingredient from South America. Quinoa, being gluten-free, is perfect for brownies that don't require structure from grain to work. Puffed quinoa is so crunchy and gives these brownies their signature look like stars splashed against a dark sky. Store-bought works well if you want these brownies fast. The brownies keep for 1 week at room temperature, or freeze for up to 3 months.

MAKES 1 SHEET TRAY

Fill a small saucepot with ½ inch of neutral oil and bring to 350°F. Drop in the quinoa flour and allow to puff for 15 to 30 seconds. Remove with a strainer and place on a paper towel to drain and cool. Set aside.

Preheat the oven to 350°F.

Fill a small saucepot with 2 inches of water and set a medium heatproof bowl on top to create a double boiler. Add the butter and chocolate to the bowl, then place over medium heat until melted. Remove from the heat and set aside.

In a stand mixer fitted with the whisk attachment, combine the eggs, brown sugar, and salt. Beat on high speed for 5 to 6 minutes, until light, fluffy, and the sugar has dissolved.

Remove the bowl from the stand mixer and use a spatula to gently fold in the chocolate mixture until incorporated. Scrape the spatula against the sides of the bowl and bring through to the center of the batter.

Next, lightly dust half the quinoa flour over your mixture and fold it in. Dust the remaining flour into the mixture and finish folding.

CONTINUES ▶

Neutral oil, such as grapeseed

140 g quinoa flour

285 g unsalted butter

750 g dark chocolate discs

8 large eggs

675 g dark brown sugar

6 g salt

Baking spray

4 to 6 persimmons, very ripe

200 g puffed quinoa

Flaky sea salt for sprinkling

Line a sheet tray with parchment paper and lightly spray with baking spray. Pour the quinoa mixture onto the prepared pan, spreading it into an even layer. Scoop the persimmon flesh and dollop all over the quinoa mixture. Sprinkle with the puffed quinoa.

Bake for 30 to 35 minutes, until the center is just set. Sprinkle with sea salt. Remove from the oven, let cool to room temperature, then slice and serve.

Every square is delicious but an edge slice is always my first pick! The center pieces are extra gooey from the persimmon.

Quinoa Churros WITH CHOCOLATE SAUCE

These churros combine so many of my favorite memories from childhood. Churros are an ultimate street or festival food. I love them in small logs, long sticks, or hooped together. You decide what your favorite shape is. Plain or stuffed, churros are always delicious! Once fried, they are paired with ground coriander, which when combined with sugar, tastes like Froot Loops and balances out the tart elements of quinoa. Finally, we'll dip them in a thick chocolate sauce that will become your most beloved fudge syrup for all kinds of treats. Make sure when you're piping to double bag your batter, so you don't have any blowouts. Fry until golden brown, for the best crunch. Churros should be eaten the same day as made. You can also pipe and cut dough onto a parchment paper–lined sheet tray and freeze for up to 3 months.

MAKES 24 TO 36 SMALL CHURROS

Combine the flours in a medium bowl. Set aside.

Combine the water, butter, sugar, scraped vanilla bean, and salt in a small saucepan and bring to a simmer, gently stirring together with a wooden spoon. Remove vanilla bean pod. Add the flour mixture and continue to stir, vigorously scraping the bottom as you go for another 2 minutes, or until a thin skin forms on the bottom of the pot.

Dump the dough into the bowl of a stand mixer fitted with the paddle attachment. Beat on medium-high speed until the bowl has cooled completely.

Crack three of your eggs into a separate bowl; do not beat together. With the mixer still running, tilt your egg bowl to slip one egg at a time into your dough, allowing each egg to fully incorporate before you add another.

Check the consistency. Stop the machine and pull the paddle from the dough. The dough should be thick and break in a smooth consistency with a pointed end. If it is dry, add the fourth egg.

Transfer the dough into a piping bag fitted with a closed star tip, such as Ateco 849 or Ateco 855. Chill the dough for 30 minutes or up to two days. You can pipe directly into oil for very organic shapes, or onto a parchment-lined sheet tray; and place in your freezer overnight for consistent shapes.

70 g quinoa flour

200 g all-purpose flour

340 g water

170 g unsalted butter

20 g granulated sugar

1 vanilla bean, split in half and scraped

8 g salt

4 large eggs

Grapeseed oil for frying

Coriander Sugar (page 262)

Chocolate Sauce (page 265)

CONTINUES ▶

Bring at least 2 inches of grapeseed oil in a large saucepot to 375°F. Fry chilled dough for 2 minutes on each side, or until puffed and golden brown. Fry frozen dough straight from the freezer for 3 minutes on each side, until puffed and golden brown. Use a sieve to transfer to a cooling rack and let cool slightly.

Toss the churros in coriander sugar. Serve with chocolate sauce for dipping.

Eat the churros as is or dip in chocolate sauce. Dulce de leche, or cajeta, is another amazing sauce for dipping.

Quinoa Brown Sugar Chili Buns WITH HOT CHOCOLATE DRINK

As a child growing up in Ecuador, breakfast was my favorite meal—a cup of hot chocolate and a soft sweet bun. I would rip the bun in pieces and dip it in the chocolate, the pillowy dough absorbing the milk until it was heavy and dripping, and then plop it in my mouth, letting the chocolate gush. These buns are my reimagining of these meals I had as a kid. My mother loved to add rosemary to the traditional hot chocolate drink preparation. It's an herb that's good for you and adds a lovely scent as you stir and sip. These buns are delicious with butter and jam or alongside a bigger dinner meal. Their slight heat complements so many dishes. Hot Chocolate Drink (page 266) keeps in your fridge for 3 to 4 days. The buns keep at room temperature in an airtight container for 1 week. Get dipping!

MAKES 9 BUNS

In a small bowl, dissolve your yeast in the warm water.

In a stand mixer fitted with the dough hook attachment, combine the flours, brown sugar, salt, and chili powder. Next, add vanilla bean paste, the starter mixture, eggs, and milk and mix on medium speed for 10 minutes. Cover the bowl and let rest 15 minutes.

On medium speed, add the butter slowly until fully incorporated. Then, beat for another 2 minutes for extra strength.

Clear the dough from the hook and tuck the edges of the dough against the inside of the bowl. Cover with a damp, clean kitchen towel or plastic wrap and let rise until double in volume, 2 hours for yeast-only or the hybrid method, 6 to 8 hours for sourdough.

Divide the dough in nine portions of about 85 g each. Use your hand to cup each ball of dough, keeping the edges of your hand tight to your work service and your palm vaulted over the dough, moving your hand in large circles to tighten the dough underneath. Or moving clockwise, tuck the outside edges to the center of the dough on top, stretching slightly as you go until you have a ball. Place the dough balls, seam side down, 2 to 3 inches apart on lightly sprayed parchment-lined sheet trays to proof. Lightly spray the tops of the buns with baking spray and cover with plastic wrap. Proof until they double in volume, 1 to 2 hours for yeast-only or the hybrid method, 4 to 6 hours for sourdough.

110 g warm water (see pags 57–58)

10 g yeast

60 g quinoa flour

300 g all-purpose flour

40 g dark brown sugar

5 g salt

5 g chili powder

2 g vanilla bean paste

50 g active starter

100 g unsalted butter, at room temperature

75 g whole milk

1 large egg

Baking spray

1 egg for egg wash

Splash of milk for egg wash

Hot Chocolate Drink (page 266)

CONTINUES ▶

Preheat the oven to 350°F.

When the buns are fully proofed, make an egg wash by combining the egg with a splash of milk and beating with a fork until uniform. Use a pastry brush to lightly paint all the buns, going all the way to the parchment paper. Make sure to do so lightly, to not deflate the buns and not leave a lot of egg wash on the sheet tray.

Bake the buns for 20 to 25 minutes, until golden brown and with an internal temperature of 200°F. Pull the buns from the oven and let cool completely. Serve with Hot Chocolate Drink.

Creating surface tension is the key to consistent round fluffy buns. The fluffier they are, the more chocolate drink they can soak up!

Notes: If you use the hybrid method, dough can be made with active starter or inactive starter. Putting the dough in the fridge for 30 minutes before shaping steps will help make the dough easier to handle. You can proof overnight at either proofing stage, and bake directly from the fridge.

Quinoa Upside-Down Cake WITH PINEAPPLE & CANDIED HIBISCUS

Pineapple upside-down cake was my birthday cake for most of my childhood! When made with quinoa flour, it becomes tender and vegetal. Vanilla bean is a precious ingredient from the Americas that you'll see throughout this section. It comes from a vine in the orchid family that can grow over 60 feet long, and generally only has a couple of blossoms per plant that must be pollinated often by hand! Vanilla should be an ingredient that is allowed to shine, lending its distinctive flavor to your bakes. It is the perfect partner to the sweet, tart taste of this tropical fruit. Here, we are trading out maraschino cherries for candied hibiscus flowers. These flowers are usually used in South America to make an addictive sweetened iced tea. Boiling the flowers longer in sugar makes them chewy and supersweet, like natural gummy bears. They are great out of hand, used in decorating and baked into cakes! Candied flowers keep for 1 month in the fridge in an airtight container. This cake has a lot of moisture in it and takes a while to bake. The cake keeps for 4 days at room temperature or for 1 week in your fridge.

MAKES ONE 10-INCH CAKE

Preheat the oven to 350°F. Line a 10-inch round cake pan with parchment paper and lightly spray with baking spray. Place on a sheet tray lined with parchment paper.

Place your pineapple rounds in a bowl, cover with the candied hibiscus, and gently toss to coat in the pink syrup. Set aside.

In a stand mixer fitted with the whisk attachment, mix together the butter, brown sugar, honey, and 3 g of the salt on medium speed until combined. Scoop and spread the mixture with an offset spatula to cover the bottom of the prepared cake pan. Press the pineapple and candied hibiscus into this layer in whatever fun pattern you wish.

Whisk together the flours, sugar, remaining 3 g of salt, and the baking powder and baking soda in a large bowl. In another bowl, whisk together the oil, milk, eggs, lemon juice, and vanilla bean paste.

Pour wet ingredients into your dry ingredients and whisk until just combined.

Baking spray

1 pineapple, peeled, cored, and cut into rounds no thicker than ¼ inch

50 g Candied Hibiscus, drained (page 269)

120 g unsalted butter, at room temperature

100 g dark brown sugar

70 g honey

6 g salt

60 g quinoa flour

290 g all-purpose flour

200 g sugar

6 g salt

7 g baking powder

3 g baking soda

150 g grapeseed oil

240 g whole milk

2 large eggs

40 g freshly squeezed lemon juice

6 g vanilla bean paste

CONTINUES ▶

Gently pour the batter over the caramel and pineapple, using an offset spatula to smooth across the pan in an even layer. Bake for 45 to 50 minutes, until the cake is cooked through, pulled slightly from the edges of the pan, and deep golden. The center should spring back lightly from your touch when pressed gently. Cake pans are commonly sourced as 2 or 3 inches tall. While harder to find, the 3-inch pan is preferable. If your pan is only 2 inches tall, the cake will rise above its edge, and some caramel may spill up and over onto your lined sheet tray.

Remove the cake from the oven and let cool in the pan on a cooling rack for 10 minutes exactly. Too soon and everything will shift, too late and your cake will glue itself to the sides of your pan. Neither one is something a little rearranging of the fruit on top can't fix, but patience and precision is rewarded. Use an offset spatula to clear the sides of your cake, and in one motion, invert onto your serving platter. Let cool completely and serve.

Amaranth Marigold Buñuelos

Buñuelos are a festive dessert that comes together so quickly! Amaranth and marigold combine to make the dough golden, tart, and floral. If you can't find marigolds, use a flower of your choice. It is so fun to watch them puff and bubble in the oil. You can serve them "dry," tossed in sugar, or "wet," drenched in syrup. I like them best dry, tossed in more marigold sugar. I live for biting into them fast and hard to shatter them into a million pieces. Fry and stack them high for a showstopper presentation. Beloved by all ages, they turn any day into a party! The dough keeps for 2 days, wrapped tightly, in your fridge. Buñuelos are best eaten on the same day as they're made. They are naturally vegan.

MAKES 12 TO 18

Bring the water to a boil in a small saucepot. Place the marigold flowers in a small heatproof bowl and pour the water over the marigold flowers. Let steep for 20 minutes, then strain.

In a stand mixer fitted with the dough hook attachment, combine the strained marigold tea with the flours, baking powder, baking soda, lemon juice, and salt and mix on medium speed for 5 to 10 minutes. Cover bowl with a damp, clean towel or plastic wrap, and allow to rest for 30 minutes at room temperature.

On your work surface, use a bench scraper to portion the dough into 12 to 18 pieces about the diameter of a quarter and roll into balls. Allow

Nothing is more fun than chomping into a fresh Buñuelo! As each one shatters uniquely, it is quite the party game.

150 g water

8 g dried or fresh marigold flowers

50 g amaranth flour

220 g all-purpose flour, plus more for dusting

2 g baking powder

3 g baking soda

10 g freshly squeezed lemon juice

5 g salt

Neutral oil for bowl and frying

Marigold Sugar (page 262)

CONTINUES ▶

to rest 15 minutes at room temperature on your work bench draped with a towel or plastic wrap. Dust your work surface with a light coating of flour. Use a rolling pin to roll the balls flat into circles or organic shapes, as thinly as possible without tearing. Stack rolled-out dough with parchment paper between each circle on a sheet tray.

Heat 2 inches of oil in a large saucepot to 350°F. Place the marigold sugar in a small bowl.

Slip each dough disk, one by one, into hot oil and fry for 2 minutes on each side. Use tongs to flip and then transfer to a cooling rack set over a sheet tray.

While the buñuelos are still warm, sprinkle generously with the marigold sugar. Serve while still slightly warm.

Amaranth Cookie Sandwiches

WITH PLANTAINS, CARAMELIZED WHITE CHOCOLATE & CREMA BUTTERCREAM

Amaranth is one of the smallest grains, and because it comes from a flower, it can be grown in your garden. Its bunched seed flower clusters drape dramatically, earning it the common English name Love-lies-bleeding. It has a strong sour flavor that pairs well with strong sweet notes, such as chunks of sweet fried plantains, caramelized white chocolate, and vanilla bean. Caramelizing white chocolate is easily done in your oven. I highly recommend prepping a triple batch of caramelized white chocolate for the best result; it bakes a little more evenly in a larger batch, is less prone to burning, and keeps for months in an airtight container in your fridge. You'll love sprinkling it on everything! Once cooled, you can snap it apart for snacking or include it in tons of other bakes. Chocolate is best kept somewhere cool, especially in hot climates. Caramelized chocolate can keep for 3 months in your freezer in an airtight container. The cookie dough can be made, scooped onto a cookie sheet, wrapped tightly, and kept in the fridge for 2 weeks or in the freezer for 3 months. Once baked, these cookies soften into a cakelike consistency. Here, I take them over the top by making them into cookie sandwiches. They are best eaten the same or the next day.

MAKES 12 TO 18 COOKIES

Preheat the oven to 300°F.

Spread the white chocolate on a sheet tray lined with a silicon silpat. Bake for 3 minutes, stir gently with a spatula, incorporating the edges into the middle. Return to the oven and bake for another 3 minutes, or until lightly golden, then remove from the oven. Let cool completely, then roughly chop.

Heat a little grapeseed oil in a small saucepan over medium heat and fry the sweet plantain slices, 1 to 2 minutes on each side. Use tongs to transfer to a paper towel to cool completely.

In the bowl of a stand mixer fitted with the paddle attachment, cream together the butter and sugar on medium speed until light and fluffy. Add the eggs, one at a time, until combined.

CONTINUES ▶

200 g white chocolate discs

Grapeseed oil

300 g sliced sweet plantains, cut into 1-inch-thick rounds

370 g unsalted butter, at room temperature

420 g sugar

2 eggs

200 g amaranth flour

380 g all-purpose flour

10 g salt

5 g baking powder

3 g baking soda

5 g vanilla bean paste

Crema American Buttercream (page 282)

In a separate bowl, mix together the flours, salt, baking powder, and baking soda. On low speed, add the flour mixture to the egg mixture, along with the vanilla bean paste; mix until combined. Add the caramelized white chocolate and mix for 1 minute. Remove the bowl from the stand mixer, add the plantains and stir in with a wooden spoon until incorporated, keeping the plantains, as intact as possible. Scoop about 2 ounces of dough and place about 2 inches apart on a parchment-lined sheet tray.

Bake for 12 to 15 minutes, until the cookies are puffed and golden on the edges. Let cool completely.

Put a little buttercream on one cookie and press together to make a sandwich.

Optional: For an extra fun crunch, roll the exposed buttercream on the sides in some of your extra caramelized white chocolate crumbled into pieces. You can get a nice crumble texture for this by pulsing chocolate in a food processor until the size of pebbles.

Amaranth Squash Almond Butter Pancakes
WITH MAPLE SYRUP & ROASTED SUNFLOWER BUTTER

We served these pancakes at my first restaurant as a gluten-free option. They were inspired by my sous chef who loved the challenge of creating gluten-free items. I swapped in amaranth for the more complicated initially gluten-free blend, and it was love on a plate. The earthy tart pancake is balanced with maple syrup and a butter made from roasting sunflower centers. When choosing sunflowers to roast, make sure to source them from a trusted grower—your own garden is best or seek out a farmer at a market. Do not use grocery store or florist sunflowers that are not labeled as organic, as they have been heavily sprayed with pesticides. This butter is great on everything, and I highly recommend scaling up when you get a good bouquet of flowers. The butter keeps, in an airtight container, in the fridge for 2 weeks or the freezer for 3 months. The pancake batter can be made a day ahead. The cooked pancakes keep for 3 days in the fridge. They are naturally gluten-free and vegan.

MAKES 10 TO 12 PANCAKES

Preheat the oven to 400°F. Cut, core, and cut the squash into 1-inch cubes. Roast in the oven for 15 to 20 minutes, until tender. Pour off and discard any excess juices and use a blender to puree.

Add the almond butter, salt and eggs to the blender. Blend until smooth. Pour into a bowl and fold in the amaranth flour. Scrape the spatula against the sides of the bowl and bring through to the center of the batter until combined. Place in the fridge to set up for about 30 minutes.

Heat a little grapeseed oil in a large saucepan over medium heat. Add 2- to 3-ounce portions of batter to the pan, cooking for about 2 minutes and flipping with a fish spatula to finish cooking the other side. Keep the pancakes warm in the oven set to 100° F while you cook the remaining batter. Serve with maple syrup and a chunk of roasted sunflower butter.

500 g butternut squash

75 g almond butter

8 g salt

6 large eggs

75 g amaranth flour

20 g sugar

Grapeseed oil for frying

Pure maple syrup

Roasted Sunflower Butter
    (page 287)

Amaranth & Corn Crumble
WITH PAPAYA, RASPBERRY & LIME

Corn and amaranth play off each other well in this crumble: one sweet and one sour. Corn flour (make sure you use this, not cornstarch or cornmeal) creates the base and the whole-grain amaranth on top creates great crunch and pops with each bite. Tropical fruit is not often baked because it loses structure, and many of the delicate flavors we love about them disappear with prolonged exposure to heat. However, papaya has great structure, with a somewhat muted flavor. Combined with raspberry and lime, papaya sings and establishes a hot pink jewel-toned base for this crumble. Bake fresh or build and freeze for later. Replace the all-purpose flour with equal parts corn flour and amaranth flour for a gluten-free version.

MAKES ONE 9-INCH CRUMBLE

Preheat the oven to 350°F.

Prepare the filling: Mix together all the filling ingredients in a medium bowl, tossing thoroughly to coat everything.

Prepare the crumble: Mix together all the crumble ingredients, using your fingertips to work the butter into the dry ingredients.

Pour the filling into a 9-inch pie pan. Top generously with crumble. Place on a parchment-lined sheet tray to catch any excess juices. Bake for 30 to 40 minutes, until the juices are thick and bubbling and the crumble is golden brown.

FILLING

375 g raspberries

375 g ripe papaya, diced

1 lime, cut in half vertically and sliced very thinly horizontally, seeds discarded

120 g sugar

15 g cornstarch

Salt

CRUMBLE

100 g amaranth flour

100 g corn flour

100 g all-purpose flour

200 g dark brown sugar

200 g unsalted butter, melted

10 g baking powder

10 g salt

Corn Cookies
WITH CANDIED MANGO & PINK PEPPERCORN SUGAR

For me, a sugar cookie has never had enough to offer besides, well, sugar. Enter whole-grain corn flour. A golden, cracked, crunchy exterior and an intense butter flavor take the sugar cookie to the next level. Plain, this cookie holds its own; it's like eating pudding with crisp edges. But I love adding candied and dried fruit and switching out the usual rolling sugars for a spicy sugar. One of my all-time favorites is studding the cookie dough with chunks of candied and dried mango and adding pink peppercorns to the sugar mixture. Mango is tangy, sweet, and juicy, all highlighted by the candying process. Pink peppercorn has a subtle floral heat to it that adds depth to all the butter and sugar. Make sure to only use the pink pepper skins for the cookies, as the kernels can be very bitter. The skins and kernels will separate easily in the rolling sugar. If a kernel sticks when you are rolling the cookies, simply pull it off. Triple this recipe and have some in your freezer to bake anytime. You won't regret it.

MAKES 18 TO 20 COOKIES

Preheat the oven to 350°F. Line a sheet tray with parchment paper.

In the bowl of a stand mixer fitted with the paddle attachment, cream together the butter and granulated sugar on medium speed until light and fluffy. Add the eggs, one at a time, until combined.

Mix together the flours, salt, baking powder, and baking soda in a separate large bowl. Reduce speed to low and add the flour mixture to the egg mixture, mixing until combined. Add the mango and mix for 30 seconds. Place the pink peppercorn sugar in a bowl.

Scoop about 2-ounce portions of dough and roll on all sides in the pink peppercorn sugar, paying particular attention to attaching the pink peppercorn skins but removing the kernels. Place about 2 inches apart on the prepared sheet tray or about six to a tray.

Bake for 12 for 15 minutes, until the cookies are puffed and golden on the edges.

340 g unsalted butter, at room temperature

450 g granulated sugar

2 large eggs

170 g corn flour

400 g all-purpose flour

10 g salt

5 g baking powder

3 g baking soda

200 g chopped candied and dried mango (½-inch pieces)

Pink Peppercorn Sugar (page 264)

Sweet Corn Biscuits

WITH VANILLA MACERATED FRUIT & CULTURED MILK SOUP

This is my favorite soup to make! Made with milk, cultured yogurt, lemon, and sugar, it's sweet and tangy, and gets topped with fruit and biscuits for a complete breakfast. Inspired by Nordic flavors, we served this soup at my restaurant where it was nicknamed Princess Soup. When you eat this, you can't help but feel whimsical and a little royal. I recommend making the biscuits small, like cereal, so you can have a bunch in your soup, but if you want bigger, go for it. The biscuits are buttery and crunchy; they soak up the milk soup and add substance to the meal. The biscuits can be made ahead and kept in an airtight container for 3 months in the freezer. Bake them from frozen for best structure and layers. The soup is great scaled up and keeps for 4 days in your fridge.

MAKES 20 TO 24 MINI BISCUITS

Combine the cream, milk, and lemon juice in a small bowl. Set aside to sour.

Whisk together the flours, baking powder, baking soda, granulated sugar, and salt in a medium bowl. Toss the cold cubed butter into the flour mixture to coat. Working with your fingertips, break up butter into small pieces by placing between your thumb and other fingers and acting as if you are going to snap your fingers.

Once no butter pieces are larger than a dime, make a well in the center of the flour mixture and add the soured cream mixture, stirring with a wooden spoon until combined. Lightly flour a clean work surface and dump the dough onto it. Press it down flat to 1 inch thick and use a bench scraper to cut into three equal sections. Stack these sections on top of one another and press down again. Cut in half and stack once more. Press the dough to a 1-inch thickness and cut out 1½-inch squares or circles. Place on a parchment-lined sheet tray. You can regather the scraps, press, stack, press, and cut out once more. Place the sheet tray in the freezer for 1 hour or overnight.

Preheat the oven to 375°F. Arrange the biscuits, 1 inch apart from one another, on their prepared pan. Brush with cream and sprinkle with large-grain sugar. Bake for 12 to 15 minutes, until golden brown. Serve warm, dropped into chilled cultured milk soup along with the macerated strawberries and ground cherries.

170 g heavy whipping cream, plus more for brushing

150 g whole milk

30 g freshly squeezed lemon juice

160 g corn flour

500 g all-purpose flour, plus more for dusting

25 g baking powder

10 g baking soda

150 g granulated sugar

10 g salt

225 g unsalted butter, cold, cubed

Large-grain sugar, such as turbinado, for sprinkling

Cultured Milk Soup (page 266)

Macerated Strawberries and Ground Cherries (page 269)

Corn Crust Blueberry Pie
WITH LILAC ICE CREAM

A blueberry pie is the ultimate treat of summer. I have memories of it at parks, barbecues, even on windowsills—it is that classic. Here, I pair it with my favorite pie crust for summer produce—buttery golden corn flour. Because corn lacks gluten, which helps hold pie dough together, I add an egg and milk to the dough. The egg lends its proteins that help bind the dough; the milk adds more fat and softens the thirsty corn. (This is a great technique for any low-gluten whole-grain dough.) Cooking down the blueberry filling prior to baking makes the most of this extremely juicy berry and allows the oven to concentrate on the crust, preventing the dreaded soggy bottom. The dough and fully built pie both keep unbaked in the fridge for 1 week or in the freezer for 3 months. You will make extra pie dough, as it is easier to pull together in a larger batch. Stash this in your freezer until the next time you need pie fast. The baked pie keeps for 3 days at room temperature or for 1 week in the fridge. Serve with lilac ice cream. The color of your ice cream will depend on the depth of color in your flowers. Make sure to only use the petals and remove the bitter center of the blossom. Lilac's season is so short, ice cream is a magical way to preserve the season.

MAKES TWO 9-INCH DOUBLE CRUSTS,
OR FOUR 9-INCH SINGLE CRUSTS; FILLING MAKES 1 PIE

Make the filling: Combine all the filling ingredients in a medium bowl and toss together. Transfer to a medium saucepot and cook over medium heat until it begins to thicken. Pour onto a sheet tray and transfer to the fridge to chill.

Prepare the crust: In a small bowl, dissolve the starter into the milk. Whisk in the two eggs until the mixture looks uniform. Set aside.

Place the flours, salt, and sugar in a medium bowl. Whisk vigorously to combine and break up any lumps in the sugar. Add the butter and gently coat by tossing quickly.

Dump onto a clean work surface. Use the heel of your hand to press the butter down against the work surface and away from you, creating thin sheets. Do this to all your butter. When you've touched every piece of butter, use a bench scraper to scrape everything off the work surface and back together.

Make a well in the center and add half of the milk mixture, using your bench scraper to cut it into the flour. Add the rest of the milk mixture and continue to cut it into the dough with your bench scraper. Once you have a chunky mass, use your hands to pull the mass together. Press down flat and cut into three sections. Stack these sections on top

FILLING
800 g blueberries

220 g sugar

30 g butter, cubed

1 lemon, cut in half and sliced very thinly

30 g cornstarch

3 g salt

CRUST
40 g starter

200 g whole milk, cold

2 large eggs

380 g corn flour

730 g all-purpose flour

10 g salt

150 g sugar

600 g unsalted butter, cold, cubed

1 egg for egg wash

Splash of milk for egg wash

Large-grain sugar, such as turbinado, for sprinkling

TO SERVE
Lilac Ice Cream (page 278)

of one another and press down again. Cut in half and stack once more. Divide the dough into four portions. Wrap the doughs and place in the fridge to rest for 30 minutes or overnight.

Pull two of the doughs from the fridge and, and starting from the center, roll out each dough in all directions until it is 2 inches bigger all around than your pie pan. Use your rolling pin to gather one dough onto it like a scroll, then lift and set it into the pie pan. Prick the bottom with a fork, scoop in the filling, and add the second rolled-out dough round to the top, overhanging on all sides. Trim away any excess dough with a pizza cutter or kitchen scissors. Roll both doughs together up and toward you, working your way around to create a coil. Crimp all around.

CONTINUES ▶

Cut slits in the center. Roll out the leftover dough and cut out organic shapes for decoration. Move extra dough into the freezer for the next time a craving hits for pie.

Preheat the oven to 350°F. Make an egg wash by combining the egg with a splash of milk. Use a pastry brush to brush it all over the top crust, then sprinkle with large-grain sugar. Bake for 45 to 60 minutes, until the crust is golden brown. The juice of the filling should be thick and bubbly. Remove from the oven and let cool completely. Serve with lilac ice cream and more lilacs strewn over the plate.

You can use active or inactive starter here, as the pie dough's structure is not coming from the starter. We are adding flavor and nutrition!

Masa Corn Nasturtium Quesadilla

Making your own tortillas can be a lot of fun! Small tortillas are traditional, but I like to make mine a little bigger and to press delicious spicy nasturtium blossoms into the masa. Drying out the tortillas prior to cooking is critical to get a tortilla that has bubbles and cooks through properly. Tortillas are great eaten plain, used for tacos, or turned into my favorite—quesadillas. I live for the crispy cheese skirt you get on street food varieties. Here, mine are stuffed with a blend of cheeses and pine nut spread with more nasturtium blossoms—a super colorful meal any time of day. This is naturally gluten-free. Swap in your favorite nut-based cheeses to make vegan quesadillas.

MAKES 10 TO 12 TORTILLAS

In the bowl of a stand mixer fitted with the dough hook, combine the masa harina and salt. Add the boiling water, reserving a little. Mix on medium speed for 3 to 5 minutes, until the dough feels like Play-Doh, soft and springy. Depending on your masa, you may need to add more boiling water. Let the dough rest for 15 minutes, covered with a damp, clean kitchen towel. Portion the dough into 35-gram portions, about the size of a heaping tablespoon, rolling between your hands until round and uniform.

Place a dough ball between two pieces of parchment paper in a tortilla press. Press until it forms a 4- to 5-inch tortilla, then lift the press and add the nasturtium petals or whole flowers to the dough. Press again quickly. Remove from the press and, one by one, press all the remaining tortillas. Allow to dry out for 30 minutes uncovered; this crucial step is responsible for a bubbly dough that cooks through once you place them in your pan instead of steaming.

Heat a large saucier pan over medium heat. Cook each tortilla for 60 seconds on each side, using tongs to flip. They are ready to flip when you see the dough start to lift with small bubbles of air inside. Finish cooking on the other side. Tortillas should be light colored with golden brown spots. Transfer to a bowl lined with a clean kitchen towel; wrap the corners of the towel back over tortillas to keep them warm while you cook the remaining ones.

To make quesadillas, take two tortillas and brush the inside of the tortillas with the nasturtium pine nut spread.

240 g masa harina

5 g salt

425 g boiling water

Nasturtium blossoms

Nasturtium Pine Nut & Pumpkin Seed Spread (page 287)

Unsalted butter for pan

Queso fresco

Mozzarella

CONTINUES ▶

To the same pan used to cook the tortillas, add a little knob of butter and let it melt. Take one of the brushed tortillas and place, dry side down, into the pan. Sprinkle liberally and slightly beyond the borders of quesadilla with equal parts queso fresco and mozzarella. Top with the second tortilla, brushed side down, and press down gently. Cook for 3 minutes on medium-high heat, then flip with a fish spatula and cook the paired tortillas for 3 minutes on the other side. Serve immediately.

Press any kind of edible flower into tortillas for garden vibes. I especially love using multiple colors!

Corn Tres Leches Honeysuckle Cake

A tres leches cake is a classic dessert in South and Central America. Soaked cakes go back centuries; they stay fresh longer because of the liquids added to them. I think it also makes cake super moist and provides another opportunity to add flavor to your cake. This update includes corn flour for a golden cake. The honeysuckle flowers are delicate, sweet, and juicy. Infused into the soak, they make this cake subtle and irresistible. Be sure to paint on the soak slowly so the cake can absorb the maximum amount; pouring it on will only make it run off the cake, spilling over your work surface. I like to punch up the flowers' flavor with honey in the cream topping, which keeps for 2 to 3 days in the fridge. A great casual weekday dinner dessert, this cake is also wonderful for celebrations.

MAKES ONE 8-INCH CAKE

Make the soak: Combine all the soak ingredients in a small saucepot and heat gently over medium heat to infuse the honeysuckle. Remove from the heat when you see small bubbles around the edges, then use an immersion blender to blend the honeysuckle into the cream. Let cool completely. Strain and set aside.

Make the cake: Preheat the oven to 350°F. Line three 8-inch round cake pans with parchment paper and spray with baking spray. Set aside.

In a stand mixer fitted with the whisk attachment, beat the egg whites with half (100 g) of the sugar until soft peaks form. Place all the remaining cake ingredients, including the egg yolks and the remaining 100 g of sugar, in a separate bowl. Use a whisk to mix until just combined.

Use a spatula to very gently fold egg whites into the flour mixture until incorporated. Scrape the spatula against the sides of the bowl and bring through to the center of the batter. Continue until the mixture is uniform, careful to maintain as much air as possible.

Pour the batter into the prepared pan. Bake for 30 to 35 minutes; the center should be puffed and lightly golden. Remove from the oven and run an offset spatula along the edges to release the cake. Let cool completely in the pan before turning out onto cooling rack.

Place a serving dish with a small lip upside down over the cake pan and flip the cake onto it. Use a fork to poke holes all over the top of the cake. Use a pastry brush to paint one-third of the soak mixture over the top of the cake. Let rest for 30 minutes. Paint another third of the soak mixture over the top. Let rest for 30 minutes. Reserve the remaining soak mixture for slicing and serving.

HONEYSUCKLE SOAK

5 g honeysuckle flowers

500 g heavy whipping cream

300 g evaporated milk

300 g sweetened condensed milk

CAKE

5 large eggs, separated

200 g sugar

30 g corn flour

130 g all-purpose flour

10 g baking powder

3 g salt

80 g whole milk

HONEY CREAM

500 g heavy whipping cream

60 g honey

2 g salt

CONTINUES ▶

Make the honey cream: In a stand mixer fitted with the whisk attachment, combine the honey cream ingredients and whip on medium-high speed until medium peaks form.

Transfer the whipped cream mixture onto the cake and use an offset spatula to smooth a thick layer on top of the cake all the way to the edges. Place the cake and reserved soak mixture in the fridge and chill for 2 hours or overnight. Serve cold.

Corn Cake
WITH LEMON VERBENA CUSTARD, CORN CURD & PASSION FRUIT BUTTERCREAM

This cake is a tall, yellow dream of tropical fruits! The corn cake is moist, tender crumbed, and layered here with lemon verbena custard. Lemon verbena is one of my favorite herbs in the garden; it doesn't need a lot of space and is prolific with a little sun. It's sweet, lemony, and minty. Corn curd creates another layer. The fastest and best vegan pudding, corn when juiced and simmered sets up with its own starches into a scoopable pudding. Make sure to use a sweet yellow variety for best results and strain a couple of times through a sieve to get the smoothest custard. Finally, it's all wrapped up in passion fruit buttercream. This buttercream is superspecial; it is a Swiss meringue enriched with yolk-based passion fruit curd. The result is a pale yellow, soft yet stable buttercream that's sweet and tart. I like to finish it off by whipping fresh passion fruit into the buttercream for the dramatic black pops and crunchy seed moments. Decorate with passion fruit vines and sunflowers for presentation. I hope this becomes your ultimate cake of summer. The cake layers can be made a day ahead.

MAKES ONE 8-INCH THREE-LAYER CAKE

Preheat the oven to 350°F. Line three 8-inch round cake pans with parchment paper and spray with baking spray. Set aside.

Place the flours, half of the sugar, and the salt, baking powder, yolks, and water in a medium bowl and whisk to combine.

In the bowl of a stand mixer fitted with the whisk attachment, whip the egg whites with the remaining half of the sugar on medium-high speed until medium stiff peaks form. Use a spatula to gently fold the egg whites into the yolk batter, by scraping the sides of the bowl and bringing through the center of the batter. Continue until the batter looks uniform, being careful not to deflate in haste.

Portion into the prepared cake pans. Bake the cakes for 20 to 25 minutes, or until lightly golden and springy when touched gently in the center.

Pull the cakes from the oven and let cool completely in the pans on a cooling rack before running an offset spatula around the edges and turning upside down to release the cakes. Trim away the domed portion of the cakes until you have a level layer.

150 g all-purpose flour

225 g corn flour

263 g sugar

5 g salt

13 g baking powder

12 large eggs, separated

165 g water

150 g grapeseed oil

Lemon Verbena Custard (page 278)

Corn Curd (page 278)

Passion Fruit Buttercream (page 282)

Passion fruit and sunflowers

CONTINUES ▶

Build your cake: Put the first layer of cake on a cake board or a large plate. If you have a turntable, use it, but a cake stand will do. Load your buttercream into a piping bag and pipe a ring along the outside edge of your cake layer. Fill with a thin layer of lemon verbena custard. Place a second cake layer on top and press gently to seal the edges. Use an offset spatula to add more buttercream to seal where the cake layers join. Pipe another buttercream ring and top with the corn curd. Press the final cake on top and use an offset spatula with extra buttercream to seal. Use your offset spatula to add more buttercream to coat the cake in a thin primary layer. Place in the fridge to chill for 30 minutes, or until the buttercream is firm.

Pull the cake from the fridge and add more buttercream to create a final layer. Use a bench scraper while turning your cake stand to create smooth sides. Decorate with passion fruit and sunflowers. I love to go for drama with this one, letting the vines spill off the cake. Keep in the fridge until an hour before you want to cut and serve. See Party Time (page 55) for best cutting practices.

Serve with extra passion fruit on top for the juciest bite ever. This cake is an all-time favorite.

AFRICA

DURUM TEFF MILLET OATS

193   Durum Chocolate Chunk Cookies

194   Durum Orange Blossom Overnight Porridge with Tamarind
       Syrup & Watermelon

197   Durum Fried Cheese Pastry with Juniper Gelato

198   Teff Crackers with Rooibos Olive Oil

200   Teff Sugar Moons with Peanut Frangipane
       & Marshmallow Fluff

202   Teff Anise Custard Cake

205   Millet Drop Donuts with Jasmine Sugar & Fermented Honey

206   Millet Cream Puffs with Coffee Custard

209   Millet Fried Sage Hand Pies with Runny Egg, Sweet
       Potato & Greens

211   Oat Walnut Cake with Banana Marmalade, Rose Geranium
       Custard & Sorghum Buttercream

214   Oatmeal Chocolate Chunk Cookies

217   Baked Oatmeal with Fig Bee Pollen Jam & Fig Leaf Oil

218   Oat Spice Crumble Biscuit Rolls

The Grains of Africa

DURUM: A short, oblong grain that is golden in color. It is a member of the grass family and known for having the hardest grain among wheats. Durum is another mother wheat for many modern varietals. Also known as semolina; the golden pasta wheat, durum is very extensible and elastic. It is called bulgur when ground very coarsely so the kernels are broken only a few times. Bulgur is used as a porridge and in salad preparations.

Flavor notes: Butter, yolk, cream.

How it is sourced: Durum is found whole, cracked, or as flour.

How it is used: It is a foundational grain to cuisine in Africa, Europe, and western Asia. Used in savory and sweet applications, it is tremendously versatile, complementing a variety of flavor pairings.

TEFF: The smallest whole grain in this book. Tan or white, when whole it is the size of a pin head. In the same family as millet, teff is an ancient grain packed with nutrition, great for sweet and savory applications. It is one of the oldest domesticated crops. Teff originated in Africa, where it is still an important crop today. It is labor intensive to bring to market, due to the loss of this small grain at every step of processing. Its name derives from the Amharic word for "lost" because it is so easy to misplace.

Flavor notes: Burnt honey, hazelnut, soil, maple syrup, tree bark.

How it is sourced: Teff is usually found whole grain or as flour. The flour is available as brown or ivory. Ivory bakes up golden, whereas brown takes on deeper coloring. Brown Teff also requires more liquid or fat to fully hydrate.

How it is used: It is most famous in Ethiopia where *injera*, a sourdough crepe flatbread, is the basis of a lot of the cuisine. It can be made into a porridge as well, sweet or savory. Its applications in pastry are many due to its sweet caramel notes.

MILLET: A small, round grain, found in red and white varietals. It is an ancient grain in the grass family and originated in Africa and Asia. Millet is gluten-free and very thirsty in baking applications. It is a vitamin and mineral powerhouse. It cooks up fast into a light fluffy texture. Whole it can be tossed into crumbles or puffed for added crunch.

Flavor notes: Buttermilk, shortbread, barnyard, grass, pine nuts.

How it is sourced: Millet is found as whole grain or as flour.

How it is used: Millet has been used for bread, pastry, and brewing for thousands of years and continues to be a vital crop for the regions. It has been mainly used in porridges and flatbreads. Its buttery taste and tender texture make it great for pastry applications.

OATS: A light tan grain that can be short or long. They are an ancient member of the grass family. Oats are gluten-free, though if you have a gluten sensitivity, take care to use only certified gluten-free oats. Oats originated in Africa. Oats have been whole longer than their counterparts because we have primarily eaten them as flakes or steel-cut broken kernels of grain. They are extremely nutritious and have almost no bitter taste, unlike a lot of other whole grains.

Flavor notes: Milk, cream, earth, powdered sugar.

How it is sourced: Oats can be found whole, steel-cut, flaked, or as flour.

How it is used: Oat flour is very delicate and one of my favorites for pastry. It produces great layered cakes. Oatmeal is a breakfast standard in my house. Oats carry savory flavors as well as sweet.

The Blossoms

- Bird of paradise, daisy, violet, lily, protea
- Jasmine, Saint-John's-wort, echinacea, Queen Anne's lace
- Herb blossom, wandering Jew

Durum Chocolate Chunk Cookies

Of all the chocolate chunk cookies I have made over the years, these seem to resonate with the most people! These are very special, with a custard center and crispy edge. Durum is called semolina when it is ground. When cooked, it is very soft and buttery. It also caramelizes quickly, giving you that crunch on the edge. Make it even more dramatic by lifting and banging the sheet tray down halfway through the bake. It will make the cookie collapse into itself again, making it more custardy. I first made these as the pastry chef at Rossoblu and they continue to sell out at its downtown Los Angeles Arts District location. Scale up and freeze the dough so you have it on hand anytime a cookie craving hits you. The cookie dough lasts for 2 weeks in the fridge or for 3 months in the freezer.

MAKES 24 TO 30 LARGE COOKIES

Preheat the oven to 375°F. Line two sheet trays with parchment paper.

In a stand mixer fitted with the paddle attachment, cream the butter, sugars, and salt on medium speed until light and fluffy. You'll see the color lighten as well; this process will take 5 to 7 minutes.

Add the eggs, one at a time, scraping down the sides completely between their additions.

In a separate bowl, whisk together the flours, baking powder, and baking soda. Reduce speed to low, add the flour mixture to the butter mixture, and mix until combined.

Add the dark and milk chocolate and mix for another minute on low, letting the machine break the chocolate a little.

Scoop about 2-ounce portions of the dough, arranging 3 inches apart on the prepared sheet trays, about six cookies per tray.

Bake for 7 minutes, open the oven, and quickly lift each sheet tray 1 inch off its rack and let it drop back down. Bake for another 3 to 4 minutes, until golden brown.

500 g unsalted butter
450 g dark brown sugar
400 g granulated sugar
8 g salt
3 large eggs
300 g semolina flour
500 g all-purpose flour
12 g baking powder
8 g baking soda
200 g dark chocolate discs
200 g milk chocolate discs

Durum Orange Blossom Overnight Porridge WITH TAMARIND SYRUP & WATERMELON

Durum, when kept whole for cooking, is known as bulgur. Porridge is the oldest way to eat a grain whole. Soaking it in a flavorful liquid overnight results in a creamy meal that can be pushed sweet or savory. It's a great no-heat cook process for summer. I love this porridge with sour-sweet tamarind syrup, chunks of juicy watermelon, and mint flowers. Using almond milk and almond butter makes it hearty and delicious. Feel free to sub your choice of dairy and make it your own. The porridge keeps in the fridge for 4 days. Omit the honey for a vegan version.

MAKES 4 PORTIONS

Combine the almond butter, almond milk, orange blossom water, and honey in a blender. Blend until smooth.

Combine the bulgur and milk mixture in a medium bowl. Cover with a lid and transfer to your fridge overnight or at least 6 hours.

Pull the porridge from the fridge. If you want to adjust the texture, you can add more milk here. Gently stir it in with a spoon.

Cut the watermelon into 1-inch cubes, removing the rind and seeds. Place in a medium bowl and drizzle with a small amount of tamarind syrup, then add a pinch of salt. Add the lemon juice. Use a spoon to toss the watermelon gently until lightly coated. Let sit for 15 minutes.

Spoon the watermelon onto the porridge. Garnish with the torn mint. Enjoy with more syrup.

100 g almond butter

860 g almond milk, plus more if needed

60 g honey

20 g orange blossom water

250 g bulgur

1 small watermelon, about 2 lbs

Tamarind syrup

Pinch of salt

4 to 6 fresh mint leaves, torn and smacked

Juice of ½ lemon

Durum Fried Cheese Pastry WITH JUNIPER GELATO

These fried cheese pastry pockets, inspired by *seadas*, are a classic from the island of Sardinia, off the coasts of Tunisia and Italy. Semolina makes a thin pastry dough that, when it hits hot oil, puffs and bubbles into delicate pillows. I made this dish for a private dinner at Rossoblu. They have since become a personal favorite I have riffed on endlessly. Here is my favorite, served with honeycomb candy and juniper gelato. Seadas can be made ahead and frozen for 3 months.

MAKES 16 TO 18

Combine the semolina, oil, and warm water in a medium bowl. Transfer to a clean work surface, lightly dusted with semolina flour.

Knead the dough together by using the work surface to catch the dough as you push it away with your dominant hand and give it a quarter turn with your other hand. Repeat this pattern until a soft, elastic dough forms. Take your time.

Wrap tightly in plastic wrap and let rest at room temperature for 30 minutes or overnight.

Combine the lemon zest, cheeses, and salt in a blender or food processor. Pulse until the mixture sticks together slightly.

Use a pasta machine or rolling pin to roll out the dough as thinly as possible. Use a 4-inch biscuit cutter to stamp out circles. Pull the scraps away from the circles.

Use your fingers, dipped lightly in warm water, to dampen the rim of each circle until moist. Fill the center with about a quarter-sized amount of the cheese mixture and top tightly with a second circle. Cup the center of your hand slightly and use your fingers to seal the filled circles all around. Fill all seadas.

Heat at least 2 inches of grapeseed oil in a large saucepot to 375°F. Working in batches of 3 to 4, fry your filled circle for a total of 2 minutes, using a large spoon to gently bathe each pastry with hot oil to help it fry evenly. Use tongs to transfer them to a cooling rack. Let any excess oil drain for a few seconds, then transfer to a sheet tray and place in 200°F oven to keep warm while you finish frying the other filled circles.

Serve drenched in honey, with a scoop of juniper gelato. Sprinkle with honeycomb candy.

500 g semolina flour

70 g extra-virgin olive oil

250 g warm water, about 110°F, plus more for sealing

Zest of 6 lemons

160 g diced aged pecorino (small dice)

450 diced young pecorino (small dice)

388 g diced stracchino, Taleggio, or fontina, (small dice)

5 g salt

Grapeseed oil for frying

Honey for drizzling

Juniper Gelato (page 279)

Honeycomb Candy (page 269)

Teff Crackers
WITH ROOIBOS OLIVE OIL

Depending on whether you use ivory or brown teff flour, your bakes will color less or more. Teff, being gluten-free, is perfect for flatbreads and crackers. You will need a pasta machine for this recipe, which will yield six extra-large crackers that you break up into organic shapes, perfect for snacking. Rooibos is traditionally consumed as a tea and has nutty qualities similar to teff's. Infusing it in olive oil makes for a tasty oil that can be used in vinaigrettes, pastas, and soups. These crackers benefit from brushing with the rooibos-infused oil and sprinkling with large-grain salt for an addictive snack. The oil keeps for 3 weeks in an airtight container at room temperature. The crackers keep for 1 week in an airtight container.

MAKES 6 EXTRA-LARGE CRACKERS

Preheat the oven to 450°F.

Combine the flours, water, salt, and olive oil in a medium bowl and mix with your hands until the mixture forms a shaggy dough. Transfer to a clean work surface and knead for 5 to 10 minutes, until you have an elastic dough. Let rest for 15 minutes. Divide the dough into six equal pieces. Run through a pasta machine until you finish with the thinnest setting. Prick all over with a fork.

Lay the dough pieces on a parchment-lined sheet tray. Bake for 5 to 6 minutes. Remove from the oven, brush with the rooibos-infused olive oil, and sprinkle with sea salt. Cool, snap in pieces, and serve.

40 g teff flour

120 g all-purpose flour

85 g water

3 g salt

25 g extra-virgin olive oil

Rooibos Olive Oil for brushing (page 289)

Flaky sea salt for sprinkling

Teff Sugar Moons

WITH PEANUT FRANGIPANE & MARSHMALLOW FLUFF

These cookies were born of my love for fluffernutter sandwiches. Teff's nutty flavor is deepened by the peanut butter frangipane, and it is so fun dipping the edges of the moons into the marshmallow fluff. This cookie dough benefits from a brief rest before cutting. The downtime will make it crack less as you fill, fold, and shape into moons. They can also be rolled into logs. Bake them very lightly, or else the dough will dry out. Unbaked stuffed cookies keep in the fridge for 3 days or in the freezer for 2 months. Baked cookies keep for 1 week in an airtight container on your countertop.

MAKES 24 TO 30

In a stand mixer fitted with the paddle attachment, cream the butter, sugar, and salt on medium speed until light and fluffy. You'll see the color lighten as well; this process will take 5 to 7 minutes. Scrape down the sides occasionally to make sure ingredients are mixed well.

Continuing to mix on medium speed, add the eggs. Continue to mix until combined, about 2 minutes.

In a separate bowl, whisk together the flours. On low speed, add the flour mixture to the butter mixture and beat until just combined. Scrape down the sides and bottom of the bowl and beat for 30 more seconds.

Dump the dough onto a sheet of parchment paper and top with another piece of parchment. Use a rolling pin to roll out the dough into a ⅛-inch-thick rectangle. Transfer (on its parchment) to a sheet tray and place in the fridge to chill completely.

Preheat the oven to 325°F. Line a sheet tray with parchment paper.

Pull the dough from the fridge and use a ruler and a wheel cutter to cut 3-inch squares. Pipe a tablespoon of peanut frangipane in a diagonal line across the center of each square. Wait 1 minute for the dough to soften, then fold the dough over diagonally, pressing together to seal. Tuck the center point of the triangle underneath and curve the far ends so the folded dough looks like a crescent moon. Chill in the fridge for 30 minutes to an hour.

Make an egg wash by whisking together one egg and a splash of whole milk until uniform. Pull cookies from the fridge and place 1 inch apart, on the prepared sheet tray. Use a pastry brush to lightly brush cookies with egg wash over the tops and sides; be careful not to leave any extra on the parchment. Sprinkle generously with the large-grain sugar. Bake for 15 to 20 minutes, until golden brown on the edges. Serve with marshmallow fluff for dipping.

350 g unsalted butter, at room temperature

120 g granulated sugar

8 g salt

2 large eggs

120 g ivory teff flour

480 g all-purpose flour

1 egg for egg wash

Spalsh of whole milk

Large-grain sugar for sprinkling

Peanut Frangipane (page 283)

Marshmallow Fluff (page 283)

Teff Anise Custard Cake

This recipe is based on a Malva pudding cake, a version of an African soaked cake that gets baked twice. The double bake makes it very custardy, but also means that, for the best experience, these should be eaten warm right out of the oven. It may seem like a lot of custard, but you want the cake to overflow and caramelize outside the liner, creating the addictive crunchy sugar foot at the base of the cake. Anise tastes of floral licorice and is delicious in this custard preparation. The cakes keep for 2 to 3 days in airtight container at room temperature. Best reheated a little before serving.

MAKES 12 MINIATURE CAKES

Preheat the oven to 375°F. Prepare a sheet tray with parchment plus 12 paper muffin cups or use a 12-well muffin tray lined with high-sided cupcake wrappers.

Make the cake: Stir together the flours, baking powder, and baking soda in a medium bowl. In a stand mixer fitted with the paddle attachment, combine the sugar, eggs, and salt and beat on medium-high speed until light and fluffy. Add the melted butter and cider vinegar and continue to beat for another minute. Alternate adding the milk and the flour mixture to the egg mixture in three rounds until combined. Divide the batter equally among the molds. Sprinkle with a heavy rain of sugar. Bake 35 to 40 minutes, until the cakes are deeply browned.

While the cakes are in the oven, combine all the custard ingredients in a small saucepot. Bring to a gentle simmer over medium heat, whisking occasionally. Turn off the heat and use an immersion blender to blend the aniseeds into the mixture.

When the cakes come out of the oven, use a knife to poke them a couple of times, then pour the custard onto the cakes, soaking each. Once all have been soaked, add another round of custard to fully soak. Place back in the oven for another 5 minutes. Serve immediately with tea.

TEFF CAKE

40 g teff flour

170 g all-purpose flour

6 g baking powder

4 g baking soda

210 g sugar, plus more for sprinkling

3 large eggs

5 g salt

30 g unsalted butter, melted

5 g apple cider vinegar

360 g whole milk

CUSTARD

240 g heavy whipping cream

5 g aniseeds

240 g sugar

140 g unsalted butter, melted

70 g water

Millet Drop Donuts WITH JASMINE SUGAR & FERMENTED HONEY

Millet is another small grain that packs a ton of taste and nutrition. Mixing it with all-purpose flour creates a structured dough that is also incredibly tender. Millet is subtly sweet and a little funky tasting. I love it with jasmine sugar and fermented honey. The flower adds beautiful aroma to the donuts. If you can't find jasmine flowers, use a flower sugar of your choice. The fermented honey mimics the sweet funk of the grain. Fermented honey can be used for a variety of purposes, and I recommend doubling its recipe so you have a jar on hand for whatever inspires you or just mixing into a tea. The unfried donut dough can be kept in the fridge for 3 days or in the freezer for 1 month, wrapped tightly in plastic wrap. The fried donuts are best on the same day.

MAKES 36 TO 40

Whisk together the flours, baking powder, and salt in a medium bowl.

In a stand mixer fitted with the paddle attachment, beat together the butter and sugar on medium speed for 2 minutes, or until combined. Add the yolks and mix to combine.

Turn off the mixer, scrape down all the sides, and turn the mixer back on to low speed. Add the vinegar and yogurt, then mix until combined.

Add the flour mixture slowly and mix until just combined, still on low.

Line a sheet tray with parchment paper and dust lightly with flour. Dump the dough onto the prepared sheet tray and press down to an inch thick. Lightly dust the top with flour and wrap with plastic wrap. Place the dough in the fridge to chill for 1 hour or overnight.

Heat 2 inches of oil in a large saucepot to 350°F. Use a small scoop to cut off golf ball–size bits of dough. Working in batches of 5 to 6, slip them into the hot oil and fry for 3 to 4 minutes, using tongs or a spider to turn the dough to get it browned on all sides. Transfer to a cooling rack set over a sheet tray.

Fry all the donuts. Toss in the jasmine sugar while still warm. Serve with fermented honey for dipping.

220 g millet flour

455 g all-purpose flour plus more for dusting

15 g baking powder

5 g salt

40 g unsalted butter, at room temperature

240 g sugar

6 large egg yolks

15 g cider vinegar

400 g thick yogurt

Neutral oil for frying

Jasmine Sugar (page 264)

Fermented Honey (page 289)

Millet Cream Puffs
WITH COFFEE CUSTARD

Cream puffs are so rewarding to make: a few ingredients transform into pillowy pastry clouds that can be stuffed with a variety of fillings. Millet makes these puffs so golden, they seem to glow. The coffee custard tastes like my favorite latte at the corner coffee shop. For a delicious variation, source Cascara, the fruit of the coffee berry. It makes a great lower-caffeine tea drink, and when infused into the custard, highlights these fruity nuances often lost in roasted coffee beans. Unfilled puffs keep for 2 days in an airtight container at room temperature. Custard keeps for a week in your fridge or can be frozen for 3 months. Thaw and stir to reconstitute. Filled puffs are best eaten on the same day.

MAKES 18 TO 24 SMALL PUFFS OR 12 LARGE PUFFS

Preheat the oven to 375°F. Line a sheet tray with parchment paper.

Combine the flours in a medium bowl. Set aside.

Bring the water, butter, sugar, and salt to a simmer in a medium saucepan, gently stirring together with a wooden spoon. Add the flour mixture and continue to stir vigorously, scraping the bottom as you go, for another 2 minutes, or until a thin skin forms on the bottom of the pot.

Dump the dough into the bowl of a stand mixer fitted with the paddle attachment. Beat on medium-high speed until the bowl has cooled completely.

Crack six of your eggs into a small bowl, without beating them. With the mixer still running, tilt your egg bowl to slip one egg at a time into your dough, allowing each egg to fully incorporate before you add another.

Check the consistency: Stop the machine and pull the paddle from the dough. The dough should break in a smooth consistency with a pointed end. If the dough is dry, add the seventh egg. If the dough is good, don't.

Transfer the dough to a piping bag fitted with a round tip. Pipe quarter-size or larger rounds, 2 inches apart, on the prepared sheet tray. Alternatively you can use a small scoop to portion golf ball–sized puffs directly onto the parchment-lined sheet tray. Bake for 30 to 35 minutes, until golden and hollow sounding when you tap on the bottom of them.

90 g (millet flour
220 g all-purpose flour
340 g water
170 g unsalted butter
20 g granulated sugar
8 g salt
7 large eggs
Coffee Custard (page 279)
Powdered sugar

Remove from the oven and let cool. Once cool, cut off the tops about a quarter of the way from the top of the baked puff. Fill the puff with coffee custard. Place the tops back on and sprinkle with powdered sugar. Serve chilled.

Millet Fried Sage Hand Pies
WITH RUNNY EGG, SWEET POTATO & GREENS

A lot of my memories of college involve Hot Pockets from the Wawa across the street from the College of William and Mary. This is my upgrade to that classic, further inspired by a Tunisian preparation called a *brik*, which involves a soft-baked egg in the center. I swap traditional phyllo-style dough for a thicker handmade pastry dough. And I fry it instead of bake it to mimic the crisp texture of the original and still get a runny golden yolk. The millet creates a tender pastry dough. I have found over the years that adding an egg to doughs lower in gluten adds the binding protein necessary to get a classic pie dough, and whole grains love the additional tenderizing fat of milk in place of water. I love laminating fried and fresh herbs, seeds, and spices into pastry dough. It is a largely overlooked technique whereby a ton of flavor can be built! Here, we fold fried sage into the pastry before it's wrapped around roasted sweet potatoes and a yolk. If you have access to sweet potato greens, they are delicious sautéed and stuffed into these pockets as well. The pockets can be filled and frozen for 3 months in an airtight container.

MAKES TWO 13-BY-18-INCH CRUSTS, 12 HAND PIES

Begin the dough: Heat 1 inch of grapeseed oil to 350°F in a saucepan. Drop in the sage leaves and fry for 30 seconds. Transfer to paper towel–lined plate to drain any excess oil. Sprinkle with salt. Set aside.

Make the filling: Preheat the oven to 400°F. Poke the sweet potatoes all over with a fork, wrap tightly in foil, and roast whole on a sheet tray for 20 to 30 minutes, until easily pierced with a fork. Remove from the oven and set aside to cool.

Place the caraway and cumin seeds in a dry saucepan over medium-high heat. Toast, stirring frequently, for 1 minute, or until very fragrant. Remove from the heat and transfer to a blender. Add the garlic powder, parsley, and cheeses and blend to a paste. Set aside.

Continue with making the dough: In a small bowl, dissolve the starter in the milk. Whisk in the eggs until the mixture looks uniform. Set aside.

Combine the flours and sugar in a medium bowl. Whisk vigorously to break up any lumps in the sugar. Add the butter and gently coat by tossing quickly.

Dump onto a clean work surface. Use the heel of your hand to press the butter down against the work surface and away from you, creating thin sheets. Do this to all your butter. When you've touched every piece of butter, use a bench scraper to scrape everything off the work surface and back together.

HAND PIES
Grapeseed oil for frying
Leaves from 2 bunches sage
5 g salt for sprinkling
300 g whole milk, cold
40 g active starter
310 g millet flour
2 large eggs
800 all-purpose flour
60 g sugar
450 g unsalted butter, cold, cubed

FILLING
2 sweet potatoes
8 g caraway seeds
8 g cumin seeds
5 g garlic powder
Leaves from 1 bunch parsley
250 g feta
250 g ricotta
4 g salt
Extra-virgin olive oil
12 large yolks
1 egg for egg wash
Splash of milk

CONTINUES ▶

Make a well in the center and add half of the starter mixture, using your bench scraper to cut it into the flour. Add the rest of the starter mixture and continue to cut it into the dough with your bench scraper. Once you have a chunky mass, use your hands to pull the mass together. Press down flat and cut into three sections. Sprinkle with half of the fried sage. Stack these sections on top of one another and press down again. Sprinkle with the remaining fried sage. Cut in half and stack once more. Press down with your hand. Divide the dough into two portions. Wrap portions in plastic wrap and place in the fridge to rest for 30 minutes or overnight.

Pull both dough portions from the fridge and, starting from the center, roll out each dough in all directions until it is a 13-by-18-inch rectangle. Cut in half lengthwise and then cut into thirds widthwise. Trim the outside edges to make clean lines and open up the lamination. Make an egg wash by combining the egg with a splash of milk. Use a pastry brush to brush all over the dough.

Smear some of the filling on one short side of each rectangle, then build a circular wall of sweet potato mash on the filling. Slip an egg yolk into the sweet potato well, being careful not to break it. Use a fork to prick the other side of the rectangle. Fold that side over the other, sealing all the edges. Transfer to the freezer to chill for 1 hour.

Heat 2 inches of grapeseed oil in a large, wide pot to 350°F. Working in batches of 2 to 3, fry for 7 to 8 minutes for a runny yolk; fry longer if you want your yolk cooked through. Serve immediately with an herb salad on the side for a great meal anytime of day.

Oat Walnut Cake WITH BANANA MARMALADE, ROSE GERANIUM CUSTARD & SORGHUM BUTTERCREAM

Baking spray

8 large eggs, separated

320 g sugar

120 g whole milk

50 g extra-virgin olive oil

60 g oat flour

210 g all-purpose flour

12 g baking powder

6 g salt

12 g walnuts, chopped finely

Sorghum Soak (page 280)

Sorghum Buttercream
   (page 283)

Banana Marmalade (page 273)

Rose Geranium Custard
   (page 279)

Queen Anne's lace and
   coneflowers

This cake has one of my favorite styles of decorating. It requires a good crumb coat; you later use a large piping tip to create ribbons that make the whole cake look like a present! The oat walnut chiffon is light and has chunks of nuts, calling to mind a dacquoise without all the fuss. Banana marmalade is one of my favorite examples of a tropical fruit turned into preserves, not often seen. It borrows pectin from the lemons to get a delicious marmalade great on toast or scooped into yogurt. Rose geranium has a powerful nose of roses with an herbaceous back end; I love to use the leaves and the blossoms paired with fruit and custard. Sorghum is a prized ingredient that can be found commercially as syrup and flour. It is intensely caramel in flavor and, as a syrup, runs like molasses. Added to buttercream, it is addictive. The cake layers can be made a day ahead. The built cake keeps for 3 days in your fridge.

MAKES ONE 8-INCH THREE-LAYER CAKE

Preheat the oven to 350°F. Line three 8-inch round cake pans with parchment paper and spray with baking spray.

Whisk together the egg yolks, half of the sugar, and the milk, olive oil, flours, baking powder, and salt in a medium bowl.

In the bowl of a stand mixer fitted with the whisk attachment, whisk the egg whites and remaining sugar on high speed until you achieve medium peaks. Use a spatula to fold the egg whites into the flour mixture. Working slowly to scrape the bowl, pull the flour mixture through the center of the egg whites and fold under. Continue doing this until the mixture looks uniform, being careful not to deflate.

Portion the cake batter equally into the prepared cake pans. Bake for 20 to 25 minutes, until puffed and slightly golden brown. Remove from the oven and let cool completely in the pans on a cooling rack. When completely cooled, use an offset spatula to disconnect cake from the edges of the pan and turn out onto the cooling rack.

Build your cake: Put first layer of cake on a cake board or a large plate. If you have a turntable, use it, but a cake stand will do. Paint your first layer with the sorghum soak; do a couple of passes to hydrate the cake. Load your buttercream into a piping bag and pipe a ring along the outside edge of your cake layer. Fill with a thin layer of banana marmalade. Place a second cake layer on top and press gently to seal the edges. Use an offset spatula to add more buttercream to seal where the cake layers join. Paint your second layer with the sorghum soak; do a

CONTINUES ▶

couple of passes to hydrate the cake. Pipe another buttercream ring and fill with rose geranium custard. Press the final cake layer on top and use an offset spatula with extra buttercream to seal. Paint your third layer with the sorghum soak; do a couple of passes to hydrate the cake. Use your offset spatula to add more buttercream to coat the cake completely in a thin primary layer. Place in the fridge to chill for 30 minutes, or until the buttercream is firm.

Pull the cake from the fridge and use an XL Ateco #789 ribbed ribbon piping tip to pipe large, flat ribbons from the bottom of the cake up the sides and halfway across the top. Continue this around the cake with the ribbons overlapping until the whole cake looks like a present. You can also get it smooth on all sides and then run a grooved cake scraper up all sides of the cake to create a similar effect. Decorate with Queen Anne's lace and coneflowers. Keep in the fridge until an hour before you want to cut and serve. See Party Time (page 55) for best cutting practices.

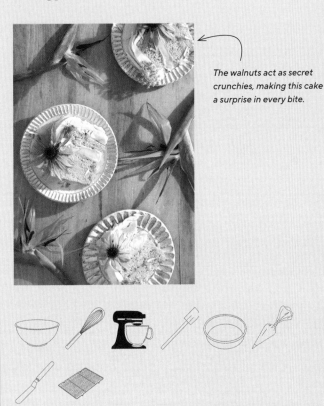

The walnuts act as secret crunchies, making this cake a surprise in every bite.

Oatmeal Chocolate Chunk Cookies

This is the first chocolate chunk cookie I ever made for Red Bread. Oatmeal cookies never felt hearty enough; usually it was a dough with a few scattered oats across the surface of the cookie. I wanted to maximize the oats and to honor California's native walnuts. I started making these in 2011—they were voted the Best Cookie in Los Angeles three years in a row, and when we would bring 800 to the Wednesday Santa Monica Farmers Market every week, they would sell out in two hours. Later, I found out that they were being used as currency by the farmers in an elaborate backdoor barter system. It is thick with oats, more akin to a granola bar. It's a treat and a meal. You can make this recipe gluten-free by replacing the all-purpose flour with oat flour (make sure your oats are certified gluten-free in this case); the cookies will spread a little more and have crispier edges. Raising the baking temperature to 375°F for the gluten-free version will give you a more cakelike cookie. The dough can be scooped and kept, in an airtight container, in the fridge for a week or in the freezer for 3 months. I hope it becomes one of your favorite go-to cookies!

MAKES 18 TO 24 LARGE COOKIES

Preheat the oven to 350°F. Line two sheet trays with parchment paper.

In a stand mixer fitted with the paddle attachment, cream the butter, sugar, and salt on medium speed until light and fluffy. You'll see the color lighten as well; this process will take 5 to 7 minutes.

Add the eggs, one at a time, scraping down the sides completely between their additions.

In a separate bowl, whisk together the flours, cinnamon, and baking soda. Reduce speed to low and add the flour mixture to the butter mixture and mix until combined.

Add the oats and mix for another minute. Add the chocolate and the walnuts and mix for another minute.

Scoop about a 2 oz portion of the dough. Flatten each with your palm to ½ inch thick. Sprinkle with large-grain sugar and sea salt. Transfer the disks to the prepared sheet trays, placing them 3 inches apart, about six total per tray. Bake for 14 to 17 minutes, until golden brown on the edges.

380 g unsalted butter, at room temperature

430 g granulated sugar

6 g salt

2 large eggs

40 g oat flour

180 g all-purpose flour

10 g ground cinnamon

8 g baking soda

600 g oats

200 g dark chocolate discs

150 g walnuts, toasted

Large-grain sugar, such as turbinado, for sprinkling

Flaky sea salt for sprinkling

Baked Oatmeal
WITH FIG BEE POLLEN JAM & FIG LEAF OIL

This was a beloved recipe at Red Bread, served warm with cold milk or cold with hot milk; everyone picked a team. We made it throughout the year with different fruits and flowers. My favorite was when the figs came in late July and early August with the building heat and the tree was flush with emerald leaves. Paired with fig leaf oil, this breakfast is nourishing, tasty, and very colorful. The oil can be scaled up and kept in the fridge for 3 months. This emerald-colored oil is delicious folded into buttercreams or used in vinaigrettes or over pasta. If figs aren't in season, switch it up with your favorite fruit or jam. Any soft leaf from an edible fruit can be used to make the leaf oil. Bee pollen provides amazing nutrients, texture, and a light honey flavor. The baked oatmeal keeps, wrapped tightly, in the fridge for a week. It is naturally gluten-free, but make sure the oats are certified gluten-free if someone has sensitivities. Replace the butter with extra-virgin olive oil or vegan butter to make this vegan.

MAKES ONE 10-INCH ROUND

Preheat the oven to 400°F. Spray a 10-inch round cake pan with baking spray. Spread the oats in the prepared pan.

Whisk together cinnamon, nutmeg, salt, baking powder, milk, melted butter, sugar, and eggs in a medium bowl. Pour over the oats and stir to combine, then allow to sit for 30 minutes to soak it up.

Right before baking, swirl the fig jam into the oatmeal with a spoon. Bake for 20 to 25 minutes, until golden brown.

Serve warm, scooped alongside cold sweet cream, drizzled with fig leaf oil, and garnished with extra figs and a sprinkle of more bee pollen.

Baking spray

300 g rolled oats

5 g ground cinnamon

2 g ground nutmeg

3 g salt

225 g whole milk

115 g unsalted butter, melted

150 g sugar

2 large eggs

8 g baking powder

120 g Fig Bee Pollen Jam
(page 273)

Sweet Cream (page 276)

Fig Leaf Oil (page 289)

Figs

Bee pollen for sprinkling

Oat Spice Crumble Biscuit Rolls

Sometimes, your cinnamon rolls don't need frosting. Stay with me on this! Topped with buttery crumbly oats, they are sublime, a sleeper hit that proves brown is beautiful. Feel free to top with as much or as little crumble as you like! The crumble is great on pies, cakes, and pastries. The crumble keeps for 3 months in the freezer. The buns can be made a day in advance and kept in your fridge or freezer before baking. If storing in the freezer, allow to thaw out a little until it can take the imprint of a finger when pressed gently. The baked buns keep for 3 days at room temperature.

MAKES 12 BISCUIT ROLLS

Prepare the crumble topping: Combine all the topping ingredients in a medium bowl and smoosh together with your fingers until crumbly. Set aside.

Prepare the filling: Combine all the filling ingredients in a medium bowl, whisking together until combined, then set aside.

Prepare the crumble biscuits: Combine the milk and lemon juice in a small bowl and set aside to sour.

Combine the flours, baking powder, baking soda, and salt in a medium bowl and whisk together. Toss the cold cubed butter into the flour mixture to coat. Working with your fingertips, break up the butter into small pieces, by placing between your thumb and other fingers and acting as if you are going to snap your fingers. Once no butter pieces are larger than a dime, make a well in the center of your bowl and add the soured milk, then stir with a wooden spoon until combined.

Lightly flour a clean work surface and dump the dough onto it. Press down flat to 1 inch thick and cut into three sections. Stack these sections on top of one another and press down again. Cut in half and stack once more. Roll out the dough to a 13-by-18-inch rectangle, about a ½ inch thick, then use an offset spatula to spread the filling all over, making sure to get the edges. Roll up the dough lengthwise into a spiral and cut into 12 equal portions, sliding the loose ends of each spiral underneath it to secure. Place on a parchment-lined sheet tray, spiral side up, snuggled close to one another. Sprinkle the crumble very generously all over the spirals. Place in the freezer to chill for 1 to 2 hours.

Preheat the oven to 375°F. Bake the biscuits for 25 to 30 minutes, until golden brown. Serve immediately.

CRUMBLE TOPPING

250 g dark brown sugar

120 g all-purpose flour

120 g rolled oats

3 g salt

160 g unsalted butter

FILLING

200 g unsalted butter, at room temperature

250 g dark brown sugar

12 g ground cinnamon

4 g ground cardamom

2 g freshly ground black pepper

3 g salt

CRUMBLE BISCUITS

340 g whole milk

10 g freshly squeezed lemon juice

110 g oat flour

510 g all-purpose flour, plus more for dusting

15 g baking powder

6 g baking soda

4 g salt

235 g unsalted butter, cold

NORTH AFRICA

SPELT   KHORASAN   EINKORN

224   Spelt Mahleb Chocolate Chunk Cookies

226   Spelt Almond Rosewater Tea Cake

228   Spelt Morning Buns with Apricot Jam & Sumac Sugar

231   Spelt Khachapuri with Dandy Green Eggs

233   Khorasan Apple Halva Lattice Sheet Pie with Halva Custard

236   Khorasan Tahini Birdseed Muffins

239   Khorasan Grape Za'atar Sugar Buns

241   Khorasan Nigella Malawach with Nettle Dip

244   Einkorn Saffron Cookies with Pepper Sugar

247   Einkorn Blondies with Brown Butter Dates

248   Einkorn Labneh Dinner Rolls with Aleppo Butter

251   Einkorn Roasted Garlic and Leek Challah

254   Einkorn Bagels with Crispy Broccoli Rabe Borage
        Cream Cheese

257   Einkorn Olive Oil Cake with Roasted Quince in Rose Hip
        Custard, Poppy Seed Cream, Pistachio Buttercream &
        Pistachio Grass

The Grains of Western Asia and North Africa

SPELT: A light brown oblong grain. It is an ancient hybrid between emmer and wild goat grass that occurred naturally more than 10,000 years ago. This makes spelt one of the oldest members in the grass/wheat family. Historically, the grain can be found throughout Europe and Asia. It first arrived in the United States in the early 1900s. Spelt is very extensible and very elastic. It also is naturally high in fiber and was once referred to as the "marching grain" by the Romans because of its high nutrition.

Flavor notes: Malted ice cream, roasted corn, fermented hay, brown butter, light caramel, almond.

How it is sourced: Spelt is found as a whole grain or as flour.

How it is used: It is a very thirsty grain, so be prepared to hydrate with water or fats. Spelt grain makes an excellent porridge or tossed into a salad. Spelt flour is another great pastry flour swap at 1:1 for your favorite all-purpose, but unlike other pastry-appropriate grains, it has the strength for bread as well.

KHORASAN: A long, plump grain that is white and golden. It is part of the grass/wheat family and an ancient grain. Originating in western Asia and North Africa, it is beloved in the cuisines of the regions. It was extremely important to early Egyptians, making up a large part of their diet. It found its way to the United States in the mid-1900s where it was branded as Kamut. Its texture, when ground, is sandy, and it is a very extensible grain.

Flavor notes: Sandy, toffee, chai, clarified butter.

How it is sourced: Khorasan is found whole or as flour.

How it is used: Although sandy in texture, Khorasan flour binds with itself well. It produces a tender crumbly bake that is excellent in any pairing with butter. Its long grains, whole, are great for use in pilafs alongside roast chicken; it will sop up any juices you serve with it.

EINKORN: A small, tan, thin, oblong grain. It is the first ancient grain cultivated by humanity and is considered another "mother wheat." Einkorn is a member of the grass family. High in protein and nutrition, it was first domesticated in what is now modern-day Turkey, but was found across North Africa, Asia, and southern Europe. It grows wild in all kinds of soil of varying quality.

Flavor notes: Malted milk, cardamom, toasted hay.

How it is sourced: Einkorn is found whole or as flour.

How it is used: As a whole grain, einkorn keeps its shape and makes for an excellent salad addition or for dropping into soups. As flour, it expresses itself best in pastry, being tender and light. In bread, it is not very elastic but is very extensible, like rye. It needs a lot of agitation to build up gluten.

The Blossoms

- Roses, lotus, jasmine, anemone
- Dandelion, apple blossoms, saffron
- Nettles, borage, poppies

Spelt Mahleb Chocolate Chunk Cookies

I first made these cookies in Lebanon in February 2019. I went to train bakers at Mavia Bakery and to learn about the grains growing there under the stewardship of Brant Stewart. Working with his team of Syrian refugee women, we made some recipes together for the bakery they were expanding from Tripoli into the capital, Beirut. These were an instant hit. A more cake-textured cookie with great height, it gets a strong nutty flavor from *mahleb* powder. Mahleb is a staple spice of the region made from the inside kernel of a specific cherry's pit and is packed with flavor; a little goes a long way. Collected, soaked, roasted, and powdered, it is reminiscent of bitter almonds and floral vanilla. A perfect addition for anyone who loves nuts but has an allergy. Baking these at a lower temperature allows them to spread more, but if you want a taller cookie, bake at 350°F. The cookie dough keeps in the fridge for 2 weeks or for 3 months in the freezer.

MAKES 18 TO 24 LARGE COOKIES

Preheat the oven to 325°F. Line two sheet trays with parchment paper.

In a stand mixer fitted with the paddle attachment, cream the butter, sugar, and salt on medium speed until light and fluffy. You'll see the color lighten as well; this process will take 5 to 7 minutes.

Add the eggs, one at a time, scraping down the sides completely between their additions.

In a separate bowl, whisk together the flour, spelt, mahleb, baking soda, and baking powder. Add the flour mixture to the butter mixture and mix at low speed until combined.

Add the dark and milk chocolate and mix for another minute, letting the machine break the chocolate a little.

Scoop about 2-ounce portions of the dough to form cookies. Place cookies 3 inches apart, on the prepared sheet trays, about six total per sheet tray. Bake for 10 minutes, open the oven, and quickly lift each sheet tray 1 inch off its rack and let it drop back down. Bake for another 3 to 4 minutes, until golden brown.

280 g unsalted butter, at room temperature

465 g sugar

10 g salt

2 large eggs

245 g all-purpose flour

225 g spelt

25 g mahleb

5 g baking soda

6 g baking powder

300 g dark chocolate discs

170 g milk chocolate discs

Spelt Almond Rosewater Tea Cake

A tender tea cake made with classic regional ingredients—almonds and rosewater—this cake is enriched with cream cheese for a dense but delicate crumb that melts in your mouth. The rosewater provides an unmistakable aroma; the nutty almonds highlight the spelt. The long bake is required to make sure the cake is cooked through entirely; keep an eye on it near the end and reduce the temperature if your oven is browning the edges too fast. Serve with fresh whipped cream and crystalized roses. Crystallized roses are easy to make, elevate any dish they are added to, and are an addictive sweet chip to snack on. Enjoy with tea or coffee after dinner or for a light breakfast. The baked cake keeps, tightly wrapped, at room temperature for 2 to 3 days or in your fridge for 1 week.

MAKES 2 LOAF CAKES, 8-BY-4-INCH LOAF PAN

In the bowl of a stand mixer fitted with the paddle attachment, beat together the butter, cream cheese, rosewater, and sugar on medium speed until light and fluffy, 3 to 5 minutes.

Combine the three flours, baking powder, and salt in a medium bowl. Crack all the eggs into a separate bowl, without beating them. With the stand mixer on low speed, add half of the flour mixture and continue to mix on low speed until incorporated. Slip four of the eggs into the bowl and continue to mix until integrated. Repeat with the remaining flour mixture and the remaining three eggs until the batter is homogenous. Remove the bowl from the mixer and use a spatula to scrape the bottom, then fold the mixture together a few times to make sure everything is incorporated.

340 g unsalted butter, at room temperature

225 g cream cheese

10 g rosewater

600 g sugar, plus more for sprinkling

270 g all-purpose flour

50 g almond flour

130 g spelt flour

9 g baking powder

5 g salt

7 large eggs

Baking spray

Fresh whipped cream for serving

Crystalized Roses (page 264)

Letting the cake cool completely before slicing helps it cut smoothly and cleanly for serving.

Line two 8-by-4-inch loaf pans with parchment long enough to overhang two opposite sides, then spray with baking spray. Divide the batter equally between the loaf pans, then chill in the fridge for 2 hours or overnight.

Preheat the oven to 350°F. Sprinkle the top of the batter generously with sugar. Bake for 25 minutes, then reduce the oven temperature to 325°F and bake for another 25 to 30 minutes, until deeply golden. Remove from the oven, let cool completely, then lift from the pans using the parchment sling.

Slice thick and serve with fresh whipped cream and crystalized roses.

Spelt Morning Buns WITH APRICOT JAM & SUMAC SUGAR

Morning buns are a classic at California bakeries and are starting to show up across the country. My favorite is brioche based, stuffed with jam and rolled in sugar. These were inspired by an incredible sorbet I had on a magical morning in Tripoli, Lebanon: smooth, honey-sweet, and sunshine-colored apricot-based, studded with toasted pine nuts. I immediately turned it into a jam when I was back home stateside. Stuffed inside these butter buns, and rolled in punchy sumac sugar, it's as if that morning never ended. The dough has a high percentage of starter and yeast because it has so much fat that will slow fermentation down. It can be made up to 5 days before rolling and baking. It is best stashed, wrapped tightly, in the freezer if you don't plan to bake immediately. If making the same day, putting the dough in the fridge for 30 minutes before the shaping steps will make the dough easier to handle in hot climates. The dough can also proof overnight at either the bulk proofing stage or the final proofing stage, whichever is convenient to your schedule. The buns can be baked from room temperature or cold from the fridge for a fast morning treat. Baked buns should be eaten within 1 to 2 days.

MAKES 12 LARGE BUNS

In a small bowl, dissolve your yeast in the warm water for a couple of minutes.

In a stand mixer fitted with the dough hook attachment, combine the flours, yeast mixture, sugar, and salt. Next, add the starter mixture, yolks, and milk, and mix on low speed for 10 minutes. Cover the bowl and let rest 15 minutes.

Turn the mixer on at medium speed and add the butter slowly until fully incorporated. Then, beat for another 2 minutes for extra strength.

Clear the dough from the hook and tuck the edges of the dough against the inside of the bowl. Cover with a damp, clean kitchen towel or plastic wrap and let rise until double in volume, 2 hours for yeast-only or the hybrid method, 6 to 8 hours for sourdough.

Roll out the proofed dough to a 13-by-18-inch rectangle. Spread the apricot jam in a thin layer across the dough, roll up lengthwise, and use a sharp knife to cut into 12 portions. Roll each portion into a spiral. Tuck the loose ends of the spiral underneath the roll to secure. Spray a 12-well muffin tray completely with baking spray. Place each roll into a prepared muffin well. Proof for 1 to 2 hours.

2%	12 g yeast
6%	37 g warm water (see pages 57–58)
39%	240 g spelt flour
61%	375 g all-purpose flour
49%	300 g active starter
10%	60 g sugar
3%	20 g salt
15%	90 g egg yolks
31%	190 g whole milk
60%	375 g unsalted butter, at room temperature

Total Formula: 273%

Baking spray

1 egg for egg wash

Splash of milk for egg wash

Apricot Pine Nut Jam (page 274)

50 g unsalted butter, melted

Sumac Sugar (page 264)

Preheat the oven to 350°F. Bake the buns for 25 to 30 minutes, until golden brown and with an internal temperature of 200°F. Pull the buns from the oven, let cool slightly, then pop from the muffin tray. Brush lightly with melted butter and roll in sumac sugar.

Note: If you use the hybrid method, dough can be made with active starter or inactive starter.

Spelt Khachapuri
WITH DANDY GREEN EGGS

3%	10 g yeast
21%	80 g starter
77%	300 g whole milk
3%	10 g pomegranate molasses
13%	50 g extra-virgin olive oil
36%	140 g spelt flour
64%	250 g all-purpose flour
3%	10 g salt

Baking spray

Total Formula: 220%

1 egg for egg wash

Splash of milk for egg wash

Sesame seeds

FILLING

350 g mozzarella

250 g ricotta

70 g goat cheese

2 large eggs

10 g spelt flour

5 g salt

3 g freshly ground black pepper

60 g minced fresh parsley

100 g de-ribbed and minced dandelion greens

Zest and juice of 1 lemon

4 large egg yolks for serving

Unsalted butter for serving

Dandelion or calendula flowers for garnish

Flaky sea salt

Khachapuri is a classic Georgian dish similar to another bread from the region—Turkish pide. I couldn't get enough of these boat-shaped breads when I visited Istanbul in 2019, the tall fluffy sides wrapped around a shallow cavity of cheese and egg. Each restaurant had their own take on this staple. I love adding dandelion greens, a dark bitter green that helps cut the fattening dairy and lifts the flavor of the whole dish. Khachapuri is fun for children, who love to tear off the sides and dip them into the delicious gooey middle. It is also a great prep for a large party; I like to make miniatures and stash them in the freezer for a crowd-pleaser at brunch parties. Khachapuri can be scaled up, shaped, filled, fully proofed, and frozen for 1 month prior to baking. Baking from frozen will add a few minutes to the bake time. Brush with egg wash and sprinkle with sesame seeds and flaky sea salt right before baking.

MAKES 4 OR 8 MINIATURES

In the bowl of a stand mixer fitted with a dough hook, mix together the yeast, starter, milk, pomegranate molasses, and olive oil on low speed to combine a little.

Combine the flours and salt in a medium bowl. Add the flour mixture to the milk mixture and mix on low speed for 10 minutes. Turn the speed to medium and mix for another 5 minutes for extra strength.

Clear the dough from the hook and tuck the edges of the dough against the inside of the bowl. Cover with a damp, clean kitchen towel or plastic wrap and let it rise until double in volume, 1 to 2 hours for yeast-only or the hybrid method, 6 to 8 hours for sourdough.

Make the filling: Place all the filling ingredients in a bowl and mix by hand. Set aside.

Line two sheet trays with parchment paper and spray lightly with baking spray.

Divide the dough into four equal portions, about 210 g each. Use a rolling pin to roll out each dough portion into a 6-by-10-inch oval. Place two on one prepared sheet tray, and the other two on the other prepared sheet tray with about 3 inches between the ovals. Let rest for 15 to 20 minutes. Spoon about 200 g of the filling into the center of each dough oval and spread out to 1 inch short of the edges. Roll the edges upward around the filling, twisting together clockwise at the ends to form a boat shape. Divide any extra filling between the boats. Proof

CONTINUES ▸

until they double in volume, 1 to 2 hours for yeast-only or the hybrid method, 2 to 4 hours for sourdough.

Preheat the oven to 375°F. Lightly beat a whole egg with a splash of milk to create an egg wash. Use a pastry brush to paint the bread edges with the egg wash. Make sure to do so lightly, to not deflate the bread and to avoid brushing the cheesy center. Bake for 20 to 30 minutes, until the bread registers 200°F, is golden brown, and the cheese is bubbly. Remove from the oven and slide an egg yolk into the center of each bread. Add a pat of butter. Sprinkle with dandelion or calendula flowers and more flaky sea salt. Serve immediately.

Note: If you use the hybrid method, dough can be made with active starter or inactive starter.

Khorasan Apple Halva Lattice Sheet Pie WITH HALVA CUSTARD

A sheet or slab pie is a statement piece no matter the occasion. I love them for big family picnics, a dinner party with friends, or a bake sale. A slap pie capitalizes on the crust-to-filling ratio being equal. People can pick between an edge slice and a center slice. And something about cutting big, fat square slices gets me every time! Khorasan makes this all-butter crust sing even more and flake beautifully on your fork. Halva is a candy made from sesame seeds, spun with sugar, and packed into a block. Traditionally you cut off sweet crumbling pieces to eat with cheese and fruit with tea for dessert. You can find it in lots of flavors, but classic plain is my favorite to use here. I love to snack on halva with apples, so this pie pairing was natural. Serve with more halva custard to make this flavor really pop. The pie can be made ahead, frozen, and baked from cold. The baked pie keeps for 3 days at room temperature or for a week in the fridge.

MAKES TWO HALF-SHEET CRUSTS; FILLING MAKES 1 PIE

Combine all the filling ingredients, except the halva, in a large saucepan. Cook over medium heat, stirring constantly, until the apples soften and the juices thicken. Remove from the heat and set aside.

Prepare the crust: In a small bowl, dissolve the starter in the cold water. Set aside.

Combine the flours, salt, and brown sugar in a large bowl. Whisk vigorously to mix and break up any lumps in the sugar. Add the butter and gently coat by tossing quickly.

Dump onto a clean work surface. Use the heel of your hand to press the butter down against the work surface and away from you, creating thin sheets. Do this to all your butter. When you've touched every piece of butter, use a bench scraper to scrape everything off the work surface and back together.

Make a well in the center and add half of the starter mixture, using your bench scraper to cut it into the flour. Add the rest of the starter mixture and continue to cut it into the dough with your bench scraper. Once you have a chunky mass, use your hands to pull the mass together. Press down flat and cut into three sections. Stack these sections on top of one another and press down again. Cut in half and stack once more. Divide the dough into two equal portions. Wrap in plastic wrap and place in the fridge to rest for 30 minutes or overnight.

FILLING

12 to 14 apples, cut in half and sliced thinly about ¼ inch

2 lemons, cut in half and sliced thinly

200 g brown sugar

25 g cornstarch

5 g salt

100 g unsalted butter

100 g halva

CRUST

30 g starter

300 g cold water

380 g Khorasan flour

700 g all-purpose flour

5 g salt

150 g brown sugar

600 g unsalted butter, cold, cubed

1 egg for egg wash

Splash of milk for egg wash

Large-grain sugar, such as turbinado, for sprinkling

Halva Custard (page 280)

CONTINUES ▶

Pull one dough from the fridge and, starting from the center, roll out the dough in all directions until it is a 15-by-19-inch rectangle that is ⅛ inch thick. Use your rolling pin to gather the dough onto it like a scroll, then lift and set it onto a sheet tray. Unroll it. Use a fork to prick the entire rectangle of dough. Top completely with the apple mixture and drop the halva all over. Divide second dough in half. Roll out one of the halves into a 7-by-19-inch rectangle. Cut into six thick strips lengthwise. Roll out the other dough half into a 9-by-15-inch rectangle. Cut into six thick strips lengthwise. Weave the strips of dough in an open weave across the filling. Where the dough meets the edges, overlap and crimp with a fork pressed all around. Chill for 1 hour or overnight in the freezer.

Preheat the oven to 350°F. Make an egg wash by combining the egg and a splash of milk. Use a pastry brush to brush the egg wash lightly over all the dough. Sprinkle generously with large-grain sugar. Bake for 40 to 45 minutes, until deeply golden brown. Place sheet tray on cooling rack to cool before slicing and serving.

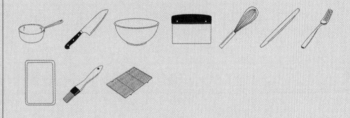

Khorasan Tahini Birdseed Muffins

These muffins are inspired by my favorite breakfast treat that Sasha Piligian made while helming the pastry kitchen at Sqirl. It was a dense muffin covered generously with mixed seeds, simple and perfect. This is my homage to that, not too sweet and extra heavy on the seeds. My base is a tahini Khorasan batter I first developed for a Lebanese restaurant I helped open. I love this batter for its buttery flavor and tender crumb due to the sandy nature of the grain. The muffin tins get sprayed and covered with a nutrient-dense "birdseed mix"—sesame, poppy, and flax—my mother used to throw into lots of her baked goods before scooping in the batter, giving them their distinctive look. These birdseed muffins keep at room temperature for 3 to 4 days. They are excellent on their own or ripped open and loaded with good butter. I love them for a breakfast on the go that is delicious and filling. Replace the milk with your favorite nut-based milk to make a vegan version.

MAKES 12

Combine all your seeds in a medium bowl. Spray an entire 12-well muffin tray with baking spray. Generously sprinkle the muffin wells with the seed mixture, making sure they are completely coated. Set aside.

Preheat the oven to 300°F.

Mix together the flours, sugar, cinnamon, baking soda, baking powder, and salt in a medium bowl and whisk to combine. In another bowl, combine the egg, milk, lemon juice, oil, tahini, and water, using an immersion blender to mix until smooth. Pour your wet mixture into the dry and stir to combine. Portion into the muffin wells, filling each two-thirds of the way.

Bake for 25 to 30 minutes. Remove from the oven and let cool completely, then pop the muffins out of the pan.

50 g poppy seeds

50 g sesame seeds

50 g flaxseeds

Baking spray

40 g Khorasan flour

110 g all-purpose flour

175 g sugar

3 g ground cinnamon

5 g baking soda

3 g baking powder

5 g salt

1 large egg

120 g whole milk

5 g freshly squeezed lemon juice

56 g grapeseed oil

144 g tahini

89 g water

Khorasan Grape Za'atar Sugar Buns

Sugar buns are delicious any time of day. Not too sweet, they put the fruit forward. I pair mine with herbs to give them more depth of flavor. I first made these for Mavia bakery in Beirut, Lebanon. I was inspired by the markets, where grapes of every color were piled high and herbs overflowed out of handwoven baskets. Za'atar is a beloved spice blend of the region, consisting of dried oregano, thyme, marjoram, summer savory, sumac, and often toasted sesame seeds. It is an annual tradition in the spring for families to go into the mountains and harvest wild herbs to make their own za'atar. When shaping these buns, make sure to really overstuff them with grapes. This will help them stay open as they bake and guarantees a grape juice gush at the center. The dough can be made 2 days before shaping, filling, proofing, and baking. Keep it wrapped tightly in the freezer until needed. Baked buns keep in an airtight container at room temperature for 3 days or for a week in your fridge.

MAKES 12 BUNS

Place the grapes in a medium bowl and toss with a splash of olive oil and a pinch of za'atar. Set aside.

In a small bowl, dissolve the yeast in the warm water for a couple of minutes.

In a stand mixer fitted with the dough hook attachment, combine the flours, granulated sugar, and salt. Next, add the starter mixture, egg yolks, and milk, and mix on low speed for 10 minutes. Cover the bowl and let rest for 15 minutes.

Turn the mixer on to medium speed and add the butter slowly until fully incorporated. Then, beat for another 2 minutes for extra strength.

Clear the dough from the hook and tuck the edges of the dough against the inside of the bowl. Cover with a damp, clean kitchen towel or plastic wrap and let it rise until double in volume, 2 hours for yeast-only or the hybrid method, 6 to 8 hours for sourdough.

Divide the dough into 12 portions, about 80 g each. Use your hand to cup each ball of dough, keeping the edges of your hand tight to the work service and your palm vaulted over the dough, moving your hand in large circles to tighten the dough underneath. Or moving clockwise, tuck the outside edges to the center of the dough on top, stretching slightly as you go until you have a ball. Line three sheet trays with parchment paper and baking spray. Divide the dough balls among

Ingredients

24 to 30 grapes, cut in half

Extra-virgin olive oil

Za'atar (page 290)

2%	8 g yeast	
7%	25 g warm water (see pages 57–58)	
37%	130 g Khorasan flour	
63%	220 g all-purpose flour	
23%	80 g granulated sugar	
4%	15 g salt	
57%	200 g active starter	
15%	54 g (3 large) egg yolks	
26%	90 g whole milk	
57%	200 g unsalted butter, at room temperature	

Total Formula: 291%

Baking spray

1 egg for egg wash

Splash of milk for egg wash

Large-grain sugar, such as turbinado for sprinkling

CONTINUES ▶

the prepared pans, placing them, seam side down, 2 to 3 inches apart. Rest the dough for 15 minutes, then use your thumbs to press down the center of each ball working outward until you have a flat area of about 2 inches in diameter in each bun. Fill the center with the grapes that had been tossed in olive oil and za'atar, 12 to 14 grape halves per bun. Lightly spray the tops of the buns with baking spray and cover with plastic wrap. Proof until they double in volume, 1 to 2 hours for yeast-only or the hybrid method, 4 to 6 hours for sourdough.

Preheat the oven to 350°F.

When buns are fully proofed, make an egg wash by combining the egg in a small bowl with a splash of milk and beating with a fork until uniform. Use a pastry brush to lightly paint all the buns, going all the way to the parchment paper. Sprinkle the buns with more za'atar and large-grain sugar.

Bake the buns for 25 to 30 minutes, until golden brown with an internal temperature of 200°F. Pull the buns from the oven and let cool completely.

Notes: Putting the dough in the fridge for 30 minutes before the shaping steps will help make the dough easier to handle. You can also proof overnight at either proofing stage, and bake directly from the fridge. If you use the hybrid method, dough can be made with active starter or inactive starter.

Khorasan Nigella Malawach
WITH NETTLE DIP

Malawach is a Yemenite Jewish flatbread or pancake that is eaten with almost everything you can imagine, sweet or savory. It's very popular among children for being delicious and buttery, but also for how fun it is to pull it apart by its long, stretchy, and flaky layers. The ultimate dipping bread, my rendition includes an herb-heavy stinging nettle sauce that is vibrant with greens and bright with acid. Make sure to use gloves when handling nettles; they sting like their name suggests, causing itching and tingles. Blanching nettles removes this component, rendering them tender, delicious, and nutrient-dense. Nigella is in the onion family and a great addition for pops of color and intense savory flavor, but the malawach are incredible with it omitted as well. These flatbreads are best cooked from frozen, allowing for the laminated layers to puff slightly and separate in your pan. This also makes it a great recipe to scale up and have a bunch rolled out in your freezer for fast lunch sandwiches and dinner accompaniment. The flatbreads keep between sheets of parchment paper, and tightly wrapped in plastic wrap, in the freezer for 3 months.

MAKES 8 TO 10

Whisk together the flours, sugar, baking powder, and salt in a large bowl. Make a well in the center and add all the warm water; use your hand to work the mixture together until it forms a shaggy dough. Transfer the dough to a smooth, clean work surface and knead until smooth and bouncy, 5 to 10 minutes. Cover and let rest for 30 minutes.

Cut into eight equal pieces and use your hand to roll them into balls. Cover and let rest for another 30 minutes.

Butter a sheet tray and line another sheet pan with parchment paper. I like to keep extra butter in a corner of the sheet pan for easy application. Place one of your dough balls on the buttered sheet tray and pat down into an oval. Add more butter on top, press, and slide until you have a thin rectangle 10 inches long or roughly the size of your sheet tray. The dough will be very thin, and it is okay if it tears a little. Smear with another thin layer of butter. Sprinkle with nigella seeds and roll up lengthwise to a 1-inch rope. Coil the rope and place on the parchment-lined sheet tray. Stretch in the butter, roll, and coil all the remaining dough balls and place them on the parchment-lined sheet tray. Place in the fridge and chill for 30 minutes to 1 hour.

160 g Khorasan flour

360 g all-purpose flour

20 g sugar

6 g baking powder

10 g salt

345 g warm water, about 115°F

240 g unsalted butter, at room temperature

40 g nigella seeds (optional)

Nettle Dip (page 289)

Yogurt

Soft-boiled eggs

CONTINUES ▶

Working one at a time, place each dough coil between two parchment papers and use a rolling pin to roll into an 8-inch rustic oval. Transfer the dough ovals, still between their parchment sheets, to the freezer for at least 2 hours, or until stiff.

Heat a large saucepan over medium high heat. Peeling off its parchment paper, add a dough oval straight from the freezer and cook for 2 minutes on each side until golden brown all over. Repeat with the remaining dough ovals. Serve immediately with nettle dip, yogurt, and soft-boiled eggs.

Einkorn Saffron Cookies WITH PEPPER SUGAR

Sugar cookies don't get enough time in the spotlight! I am an avid dough lover, so they are a perfect cookie for me—it's all about great dough! Einkorn is my favorite pick because it has savory and sour notes that balance with the sugar beautifully. I also add saffron and pepper sugar to make this an unforgettable cookie that lingers in your memory. Saffron is one of the world's most precious spices. The fragrant, colorful, and flavorful stigma at the center of the flower must be harvested by hand, using tweezers. It is a foundational spice for many cultures. Saffron is available online at far better prices than at your grocery store. But the cookies are fantastic without it as well. My favorite pepper to use is grains of paradise, which is fruity, spicy, and nutty, but even regular black pepper produces a great bite. Make this cookie dough ahead and freeze to bake as the cravings hit you. Use it as the base for endless additions and the base for cookie creations of your own. Scooped into balls, the cookie dough keeps, wrapped tightly, in the freezer for 3 months.

MAKES 20 TO 24 COOKIES

Preheat the oven to 350°F. Line two sheet trays with parchment paper.

Place the saffron threads in a spice grinder and grind to a fine powder. Set aside.

In the bowl of a stand mixer fitted with the paddle attachment, cream the butter and sugar together on medium speed until light and fluffy. Carefully scrape all your saffron powder into the butter base. Add the eggs, one at a time, until combined.

In a separate bowl, whisk together the flours, salt, baking powder, and baking soda. Add the flour mixture to the egg mixture and mix on low speed until combined.

Scoop about 2-ounce portions into the pepper sugar, coating all sides. Place about 2 inches apart on the prepared sheet tray.

Bake for 14 to 16 minutes, until the cookies are puffed and golden on the edges.

20 saffron threads

340 g unsalted butter, at room temperature

450 g sugar

2 large eggs

210 g einkorn flour

370 g all-purpose flour

5 g salt

5 g baking powder

3 g baking soda

Pepper Sugar (page 264)

Einkorn Blondies
WITH BROWN BUTTER DATES

People take sides over brownies or blondies. If there must be one, I go blondies hard. Butter and sugar caramelizing around flour tastes like butterscotch. Even if you aren't on team blondies, these will convince you to join the party! They are packed with brown butter–soaked dates and have a shiny crackled crust that is irresistible. I like to use date varieties that are softer and honey flavored, so when using them whole, the texture blends in with the blondie. Or swap in another fruit for endless variations! The blondies should be mixed and baked the same day. Keep in an airtight container for 1 week at room temperature or for 1 month in the freezer.

MAKES 15 (A SHEET TRAY)

Preheat the oven to 325°F. Line a sheet tray with parchment paper and spray with baking spray.

Pit and chop the dates in half and place them in a medium heatproof bowl. Melt the butter in a saucepan over medium-high heat; continue to cook until the butter begins to brown. Turn off the heat and pour 100 g of the brown butter over the dates. Set the dates aside.

In a stand mixer fitted with the whisk attachment, whip together the brown sugar and eggs on high speed until light and fluffy, about 5 minutes. Reduce speed to medium and pour in the remaining 564 g of brown butter in a slow, steady stream until incorporated.

In a separate bowl, combine the einkorn flour, all-purpose flour, salt, and baking powder. Fold the einkorn mixture gently into the egg mixture until just incorporated. Remove dates from the brown butter to a small plate; pour any remaining butter into the batter and fold into batter. Pour the batter onto the prepared sheet tray. Press the dates into the batter.

Bake for 25 to 30 minutes, until the blondies are cracked and puffed. Remove from the oven and sprinkle with flaky sea salt. Let cool completely, then portion by cutting it into three widthwise and five lengthwise.

Baking spray
300 g dates
664 g unsalted butter
961 g dark brown sugar
5 large eggs
150 g einkorn flour
500 g all-purpose flour
13 g salt
12 g baking powder
Flaky sea salt for sprinkling

Einkorn Labneh Dinner Rolls
WITH ALEPPO BUTTER

2%	20 g yeast
21%	200 g starter
41%	386 g whole milk
28%	270 g yogurt
6%	60 g sugar
11%	100 g (2 large) eggs
24%	230 g einkorn flour
76%	720 g all-purpose flour
2%	20 g salt
18%	170 g unsalted butter, at room temperature

Total Formula: 229%

Baking spray

1 egg for egg wash

Splash of milk for egg wash

Aleppo Butter (page 290)

The sight of dinner rolls on the table instantly makes my mind flood with memories. I swap out some of the butter found in traditional rolls with yogurt. I first did this in Lebanon upon discovering *kashk*, a sun-dried yogurt powder that was rehydrated for a variety of purposes from seasoning other dishes to eating on its own. Rehydrated into the buns gives it a unique and addictive tang. This tang can be reproduced with a good thick yogurt, such as labneh or Greek yogurt, in the absence of kashk. This dough tends to move faster than others because of the added fermentation of the yogurt, so be sure to have an eye on them in the final proof. Serve them warm with a generous spread of Aleppo butter. Aleppo is a smoky and fruity pepper with a subtle, building heat. The butter can be made ahead and keeps for 2 weeks in an airtight container in the fridge. The dough can be made up to 2 days ahead; once shaped, they should be baked on the same day. The baked buns keep for 3 days in an airtight container at room temperature.

MAKES 1 SHEET TRAY

In the bowl of a stand mixer fitted with the dough hook, combine the yeast, starter, milk, yogurt, sugar, and eggs. Mix briefly on low speed.

Combine the flours and salt in a medium bowl. Add the flour mixture to the milk mixture and mix at low speed for 10 minutes. Turn off the mixer and let rest for 10 minutes. Turn the mixer on to medium speed and add the butter slowly until fully incorporated. Then, beat for another 2 minutes for extra strength.

Clear the dough from the hook and tuck the edges of the dough against the inside of the bowl. Cover with a damp, clean kitchen towel or plastic wrap and let rise until double in volume, 2 hours for yeast-only or the hybrid method, 6 to 8 hours for sourdough.

Divide the dough into 24 portions, about 85 g each. Use your hand to cup each ball of dough, keeping the edges of your hand tight to the work service and your palm vaulted over the dough, moving your hand in large circles to tighten the dough underneath. Or moving clockwise, tuck the outside edges to the center of the dough on top, stretching slightly as you go until you have a round ball. Place the dough balls, seam side down, 1 inch apart on a parchment-lined sheet tray to proof. Lightly spray tops of buns with baking spray and cover with plastic wrap. Proof until they double in volume, 1 to 2 hours for yeast-only or the hybrid method, 4 to 6 hours for sourdough.

CONTINUES ▶

Preheat the oven to 350°F.

When the buns are fully proofed, make an egg wash by combining the egg in a bowl with a splash of milk and beating with a fork until uniform. Use a pastry brush to lightly paint all the buns; go all the way to the parchment paper. Make sure to do so lightly, to not deflate the buns and to not leave a lot of egg wash on the sheet tray.

Bake the buns for 15 to 20 minutes, until golden brown and with an internal temperature of 200°F. Pull the buns from the oven. Serve warm or cooled with slathers of Aleppo butter.

Note: If you use the hybrid method, dough can be made with active starter or inactive starter.

Einkorn Roasted Garlic and Leek Challah

One of the first breads I became obsessed with making was challah. Challah is integral to Jewish cultural, marking weekly Shabbat dinners and high holidays. It is also superversatile, from making French toast and Bostock showstoppers to great grilled cheese and savory bread puddings. These secondary preparations made me think of stuffing the challah before baking. So, this roasted leek challah was born! I wanted to make every bread eat like a meal. I love onions and garlic, so savory and comforting. The roasted garlic and braided leeks make this a decidedly savory bread. I love it for sandwiches, alongside fall vegetables, or the breakfast classic—egg in a basket or toad in a hole. Feel free to swap in other alliums, such as scallions and chives, for different results throughout the year. If you want to push this dough sweet, omit the garlic and play with braiding in rose petals or stuffing with frangipane. Try different shapes by connecting the ends together to form a crown for celebratory occasions. The baked bread keeps for 4 days, tightly wrapped, at room temperature or in the freezer for 3 months.

MAKES 2 MEDIUM LOAVES OR 4 MINI LOAVES

Preheat the oven to 325°F.

Prepare the filling by washing the leeks well and cutting in thirds lengthwise. You should have three long strips of each leek. Set aside. Put the garlic cloves in a small baking dish and add enough olive oil to cover completely. Cover with foil and bake for 40 minutes. Remove the garlic confit from the oven and let cool. Brush the leeks with the garlic oil until saturated. Bake for 15 minutes at 325°F until softened but still maintaining structure. Remove from the oven and let cool completely.

Prepare the dough by combining the yeast, starter, water, honey, olive oil, yolks, eggs, and 12 to 14 cloves of the garlic confit in the bowl of a stand mixer fitted with a dough hook. (Reserve the remaining garlic oil for later use.) Mix on low speed to combine a little.

Combine the flours and salt in a medium bowl. Add the flour mixture to the egg mixture on low speed for about 3 minutes, then increase the speed to medium and mix for 10 minutes.

Clear the dough from the hook and tuck the edges of the dough against the inside of the bowl. Cover with a damp, clean kitchen towel or plastic wrap and let it rise until double in volume, 1 to 2 hours for yeast-only or the hybrid method, 6 to 8 hours for sourdough.

FILLING

3 leeks, split in half

20 to 24 garlic cloves

Olive oil, enough to cover the garlic cloves

CHALLAH

11%	100 g garlic confit
2%	15 g yeast
11%	100 g starter
34%	300 g water
8%	70 g honey
34%	300 g extra-virgin olive oil, plus more as needed
6%	54 g (3 large) egg yolks
23%	200 g (4 large) eggs
20%	180 g einkorn flour
80%	700 g all-purpose flour
2%	15 g salt

Total Formula: 213%

2 egg whites for egg wash

Garlic flowers

CONTINUES ▶

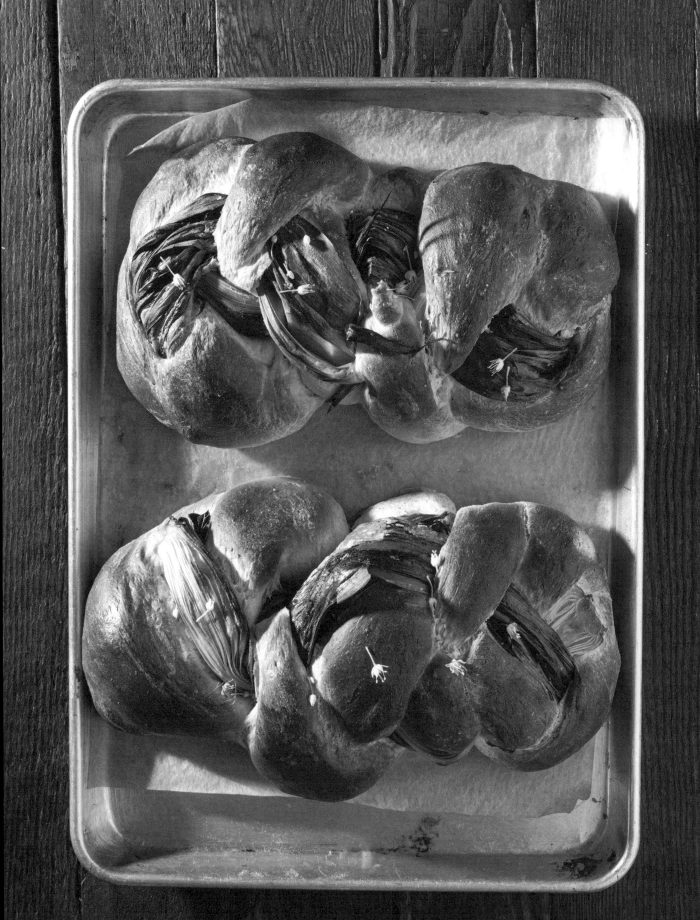

Divide the dough into two equal portions. Cut each portion into three pieces and roll each piece into a log at least 10 inches long. Connect the tips of three strands of dough by pinching them lightly together between your thumb and index finger; line up each of the thirds of roasted leeks with each strand of dough. You will braid as if the leek and its dough are one piece.

Braid gently by overlapping the strands, pinching the ends together, and tucking under at the bottom. Go back to the top, tighten the braid if necessary, and tuck the ends under. Cupping the top and the bottom with your hands, lift and transfer to a parchment-lined sheet tray. Do the same with the second loaf. Proof until they double in volume, 1 to 2 hours for yeast-only or the hybrid method, 4 to 6 hours for sourdough.

Preheat the oven to 375°F. Beat the egg whites to break up the albumen. Use a pastry brush to paint the challah with a thin layer of beaten egg white, going all the way to the parchment paper. Make sure to do so gently, to not deflate the challah.

Bake the loaves for 25 to 30 minutes, until golden brown and with an internal temperature of 200°F. Remove from the oven and let cool completely. Sprinkle with garlic flowers. Serve with reserved roasted garlic oil for dipping.

Note: If you use the hybrid method, dough can be made with active starter or inactive starter.

Braiding Challah with produce comes with practice. Master three strands before attempting more complicated plaiting.

Einkorn Bagels
WITH CRISPY BROCCOLI RABE BORAGE CREAM CHEESE

These bagels are whole-grain, sourdough leavened, and poached in molasses. The high sourdough amount makes these ferment a little faster and gives them a distinctive tang. The result is a chewy bagel with a crispy browned skin. These were voted the second-best bagel in Los Angeles in 2014, and I've been making them for hungry mouths since. I believe in loading up the seeds for maximum coverage. When shaping these, overextend the center hole and fill with seeds; this will help it stay open as the bagel expands in the oven. The dough can be made 2 days ahead, but bagels should be shaped, boiled, and baked the same day. Everyone has their ideal bagel schmear, and one of mine is this crispy broccoli and borage cream cheese spread. It's like a bowl of broccoli and cheese soup in a spread! Baked bagels keep in an airtight container for 4 to 5 days on your counter or can be frozen for up to 3 months wrapped tightly in plastic wrap. Bagels are naturally vegan. Serve with a nut butter spread to make the whole dish vegan!

MAKES 16 BAGELS

Combine the water and starter in a large bowl; agitate with your hands to break up and hydrate. In another large bowl, whisk together the flours.

Gently scatter the flour mixture over the surface of the starter mixture, then quickly agitate to fully combine. Cover and let sit for 30 minutes to 1 hour. Add the salt by scattering over the dough and breaking it up with your hands to incorporate until it is no longer gritty. Let rest for 30 minutes.

Starting at the edge farthest from you, stretch the dough up and away, then fold over and back toward you. Give the bowl a quarter turn and repeat. Do another quarter turn and repeat, then another quarter turn and repeat. Repeat another full cycle of quarter turns (4 more turns for a total of 8 turns). Let rest for 30 minutes.

Repeat the stretch and fold method, going twice around, for a total of 8 turns. Let rest another 30 minutes.

Repeat the stretch and fold method, going twice around, for a total of 8 turns. Rest for another 30 minutes.

Repeat stretch and fold method, going twice around, for a total of 8 turns. Let rest for 1 hour. Wrap tightly with plastic wrap and transfer the bowl to the fridge for 6 hours or overnight.

65%	650 g water
50%	500 g active starter
63%	625 g all-purpose flour
38%	375 g einkorn flour
3%	30 g salt

Total Formula: 219%

300 g carob molasses

Sesame or poppy seeds for sprinkling

Cornmeal for sprinkling pan

Flaky sea salt

Crispy Broccoli Rabe Borage Cream Cheese (page 290) for serving

CONTINUES ▶

First shaping: Line a sheet tray with parchment paper and flour generously. Divide the dough into 16 equal portions, about 120 g each. Use your hand to cup each ball of dough, keeping the edges of your hand tight to the work service and your palm vaulted over the dough, moving your hand in large circles to tighten the dough underneath. Or moving clockwise, tuck the outside edges to the center of the dough on top, stretching slightly as you go until you have a ball. Place the dough balls, seam side down, 1 to 2 inches apart, on the prepared sheet tray to proof. Let rest for 15 minutes.

Final shaping: Use your fingers to punch a hole through the center of each dough ball. Working slowly and gently around the hole, stretch out each bagel until you have an opening 2 to 3 inches wide. Place back on the sheet tray and proof for another 15 minutes or overnight in the fridge.

Preheat the oven to 450°F.

Set aside medium bowls filled with poppy seeds, sesame seeds, or any other topping you like.

Prepare the poaching liquid: Combine the carob molasses with 1.9 liters of water in a large, wide-mouth stockpot and bring to a gentle boil. Skim off the froth to produce a clear liquid. Working in batches of three to four, poach the bagels for 2 minutes, flipping halfway through until they are plump and have a nice glossy color. Be careful to not overcrowd the bagels in your pot or you will snag the dough as you try to move them. Transfer to a cooling rack set over a baking sheet to drain slightly, about 1 minute or when it is cool enough to have in your hands comfortably.

Place bagel in toppings bowl and sprinkle more to coat all sides. Prepare two sheet trays with parchment paper and a light dusting of cornmeal; set the poached bagels on it about 2 inches apart. Be careful to not overcrowd the bagels. Bake for 30 to 40 minutes, or until a rich golden brown and springy. Remove from the oven and allow to cool for 15 to 30 minutes before eating. Serve with broccoli rabe borage cream cheese.

Einkorn Olive Oil Cake WITH ROASTED QUINCE IN ROSE HIP CUSTARD, POPPY SEED CREAM, PISTACHIO BUTTERCREAM & PISTACHIO GRASS

Baking spray

100 g einkorn flour

320 g all-purpose flour

468 g sugar

12 g salt

3 g baking powder

12 g baking soda

400 g extra-virgin olive oil

412 g whole milk

4 large eggs

80 g freshly squeezed lemon juice

Pistachio Buttercream (page 283)

Rose Hip Custard (page 280)

Bay Leaf Roasted Quince (page 279)

Poppy Seed Cream (page 280)

Pistachios, ground finely

3 to 7 unsprayed long-stemmed roses

Oil-based cakes are some of the oldest recipes in baking, and an olive oil cake is my absolute favorite kind of cake. This cake is infinitely variable with the addition of citrus zest, herbs, or cocoa. It is moist, rich, tender, and light. As a one layer, it makes for a fantastic breakfast slice. Here as a showstopper, layered with quince, rose hip custard, poppy seed cream, and pistachio buttercream, it serves to elevate all those flavors. Quince takes some time to coax out its coral color and signature sweetness. If you can't find it, use pears or apples; the cook time for those will be significantly shorter. When making the custard, use dried rose hips only, as fresh ones have an enzyme that will curdle your dairy as it heats up. This cake takes a little patience in decorating with the pistachio grass, but is so worth it for the vibrant color and lovely texture. This is the cake I make for my favorite people on their birthdays; it's nothing but love. Serve with tea and lots of joy. The cake layers can be made a day ahead.

MAKES ONE 8-INCH THREE-LAYER CAKE

Preheat the oven to 325°F. Line three 8-inch round cake pans with parchment paper and spray with baking spray.

Whisk together the flours, sugar, salt, baking powder, and baking soda in a large bowl. Make a well in center and add the olive oil, milk, eggs, and lemon juice. Whisk together until all is combined. Divide evenly among the three pans. Bake for 30 minutes, or until the top is springy to the touch.

Pull the cakes from the oven and let cool completely in the pans on a rack before running an offset spatula around the edges and turning upside down to release the cakes. Trim away the domed portion of the cakes until you have a level layer.

Build your cake: Put one layer of cake on a cake board or a large plate. If you have a turntable, use it, but a cake stand will do. Load your buttercream into a piping bag and pipe a ring along the outside edge of your cake layer. Fill with a thin layer of rose hip custard. Cut the quince into cubes and scatter throughout the custard. Place another cake layer on top and press gently to seal the edges. Use an offset spatula to add more buttercream to seal where the cake layers join. Pipe another buttercream ring and fill with poppy seed cream. Press the final cake layer on top and use an offset spatula with extra buttercream to seal. Use your offset spatula to add more buttercream to coat the cake in a thin primary layer. Place in the fridge to chill for 30 minutes, or until the buttercream is firm.

CONTINUES ▶

Pull the cake from the fridge and add more buttercream to create the final layer. Use a bench scraper while turning your cake stand to create smooth sides. Chill for 2 hours, or until the outside is hardened slightly. Spread a layer of finely ground pistachios on a sheet tray. Use a knife or long offset spatula run under hot water, and wiped off, to cut your cake clear of the cake board. With gloved hands, turn the cake on its side and roll in the pistachios all around its circumference. Use your hands to gently press the ground pistachios into the cake, covering any bald spots. Turn the cake right side up and place gently on a cake board. Use excess ground pistachios to cover the top, gently pressing into the buttercream.

Use long-stemmed cut roses to decorate: Poke one long-stemmed rose, in three to seven places, all over the cake to mark where to place them. Remove the rose, and in these holes, place straws cut down to the height of the cake; these will hold each rose in place and prevent their moving or tearing your cake over time. Into these straws place your roses at different heights, at odd angles, all over the cake to create festive firecracker blooms. Keep in the fridge until an hour before you want to cut and serve. See Party Time (page 55) for best cutting practices.

I serve this cake with a black tea, more poached quince on the side, and, of course, more rose petals.

BREAD

The Baker's Appendix REED

Edible Flowers Monika

THE FLAVOR BIBLE KARE AND

THE FLAVOR MAT BRIGID

the spice bible Jane La

HERBAL THE NEW AMERICAN

UNCOMMON FRUITS & A COMMONSENSE G SCHNEIDER

An Illustrated Catalog of American Fruits & Nuts

Blue Pea · Chamomile · Chrysant · Globosa · Honeysuckle · Fennel

Jamaica · Jasmine · Ro · Rosehip

Lavender · Lilac · Marigold · Osmanthus

CHAPTER 4

Pantry & Larder

Having a well-stocked pantry makes meals and baked goods come together in a snap. Mine includes dry goods, such as grains, beans, nuts, and seeds. I'm guilty of stocking up on too much tinned fish, for fast date-night dinners with any of the crunchy breads from this book. Lots of dried botanicals and spices in glass containers. The rest of the real estate is dedicated to jars and jars of different salts, sugars, preserves, pickles, oils, and ferments canned throughout the year.

My larder—what's evolved into modern fridges—reflects this with buttercreams, curds, custards, sauces, compound butters, dips, and spreads. My freezer is stocked with tightly wrapped pie doughs, pizza doughs, excess, soup bases, noodles, and ice creams. You can buy many of these items at the grocery store. But building your own collection gives you tremendous control over the flavor and quality of the food you'll reach for throughout the year.

Here, you will find all the component recipes for the previous chapter that make up a well-stocked pantry and larder. The recipes are grouped by type and technique. Each recipe is tagged with its region for ease of reference. They are organized in the order in which you encounter them in this book. Use them as paired within their regions or mix things up as you begin to be adventurous in your baking journey. I am constantly tasting and testing things together to come up with new flavor pairings. It all comes down to experimentation! Know that with repetition, your skills will build, and before long, your fridge and shelves will be stacked with delicious containers of all the fillings, toppings, and buttercreams of your dreams.

Salts and Sugars

The oldest preservation methods involved burying things in salt and sugar. These two crystals maintain their power to extend the life of delicate seasonal ingredients and to amplify their flavor. Here, you will find easy salts and sugars for use in recipes throughout this book. Salts and sugars last for years in airtight containers out of direct sunlight, unless otherwise noted. All recipes in this section are naturally gluten-free. They are also vegan, except for the crystalized roses.

Salted Cherry Blossoms (Asia)

MAKES 1 PINT

450 g tightly packed fresh cherry blossoms
30 g salt

Mix the blossoms with the salt in a stainless-steel bowl, gently pressing the salt into the centers and around every petal. Pack into an airtight container and move to your fridge. Toss gently every day for 3 days to make sure everything is coated. Keeps in the fridge for 2 years.

Bay Leaf Sugar (Asia)

MAKES 1 PINT

6 dried bay leaves
350 g sugar

Pulse the bay leaves in a spice grinder to break them down to a powder. Use a sieve to sift out large pieces, then whisk together the powdered bay leaf and the sugar in a bowl. Store in an airtight container.

Coriander Sugar (Americas)

MAKES 1 PINT

350 g sugar
20 g ground coriander

Break down the sugar slightly in a spice grinder until fine but not powdered, only two or three pulses. Transfer to a bowl, add the coriander, and whisk together. Store in an airtight container.

Marigold Sugar (Americas)

MAKES 1 PINT

20 g dried marigold flowers
400 g sugar

Pulse dried marigold flowers in a spice grinder until powdered. Sift out larger pieces and either regrind or use for something else. Transfer powdered marigolds to a bowl and whisk together with sugar. Store in an airtight container.

Pink Peppercorn Sugar (Americas)

MAKES 1 PINT

100 g pink peppercorns
400 g sugar

Combine pink peppercorns and sugar in a bowl. Rub together to release skins into the sugar. Pick out bitter pits of peppercorn and discard. Store in an airtight container.

Jasmine Sugar (Africa)

MAKES 1 PINT

15 g dried jasmine flowers
350 g sugar

Combine the jasmine and half of the sugar in a spice grinder, then blitz to break down the jasmine. Transfer to a bowl and use a whisk to combine with the remaining sugar. Store in an airtight container.

Crystalized Roses
(Western Asia & North Africa)

MAKES 1 PINT

400 g superfine sugar
20 g (1 large) egg white
6 fresh, unsprayed fresh rose petals

Place the sugar in a medium bowl. Set aside. Place a cooling rack in a sheet pan. In another medium bowl, use a whisk to beat the egg whites until you have a few bubbles throughout. You don't need volume; you just want to break up the albumen. Use a pastry brush to lightly brush a thin coat of egg white on both sides of each rose petal. Place in the bowl of sugar and use your fingers to gently toss the sugar all around each petal. Use tweezers to transfer the petals to the cooling rack and let dry at room temperature for 4 to 6 hours. Transfer to a container or a sheet tray prepared with parchment paper and wrapped tightly with plactic wrap. Keeps for 2 weeks.

Sumac Sugar
(Western Asia & North Africa)

MAKES 1 PINT

35 g sumac
350 g sugar

Whisk together the sumac and sugar in a small bowl. Store in an airtight container.

Pepper Sugar
(Western Asia & North Africa)

MAKES 1 PINT

30 g black peppercorns or grains of paradise
400 g sugar

Grind the pepper to a powder. Transfer to a bowl and whisk in the sugar. Store in an airtight container.

Glazes, Sauces, Soups, and Drinks

It's all about the drip! Use these recipes for sipping, slurping, glazing, dunking, and swirling. These build on techniques of infusing flavors into liquids and concentrating them through exposure to heat or cold. Swap these around to make your favorite combinations come alive. These recipes should be kept in airtight containers in your fridge once prepared. Most recipes last for a week in your fridge, unless otherwise noted. All recipes in this section are gluten-free.

Genmaicha Glaze (Asia)

MAKES 1 PINT

  15 g genmaicha dried tea
  5 g matcha powder (optional)
  200 g whole milk
  550 g powdered sugar, sifted

Combine the tea(s) and milk in a small saucepot and bring to a gentle simmer. Turn off the heat and allow to steep and cool for 10 minutes. Some of the liquid may be absorbed or evaporate. Place the sifted powdered sugar in a medium bowl. Pour the milk tea over the sugar and whisk until combined. You may need to add more powdered sugar to reach your desired consistency; it should coat the back of a spoon but hold the shape of a valley when you run your finger through it. Pour through a sieve into another bowl to remove any lumps. Store in an airtight container. Use with donuts, cookies, or hand pies.

Lemongrass Glaze (Asia)

MAKES 1 PINT

  30 g minced fresh lemongrass
  200 g whole milk
  550 g powdered sugar, sifted

Combine the lemongrass and milk in a small saucepot and bring to a gentle simmer. Turn off the heat and allow to steep and cool for 10 minutes. Strain. Place the sifted powdered sugar in a medium bowl. Pour the milk tea over the sugar and whisk until combined. Pour through a sieve into another bowl to remove any lumps. Store in an airtight container. Use with donuts, cookies, or hand pies.

Carrot Sauce (Asia)

MAKES 1 CUP

  250 g carrot puree
  75 g sugar
  100 g water
  3 g salt
  15 g tapioca powder

Combine everything in a small pot. Bring to a gentle simmer, stirring constantly until thickened. The mixture should lightly coat the back of a spoon but hold the shape of a valley when you run your finger through it. Store in an airtight container. Use with cake, pie, or biscuits. This sauce is naturally vegan.

Chocolate Sauce (Americas)

MAKES 1 QUART

  530 g sugar
  140 g unsweetened cocoa powder
  25 g cornstarch
  3 g salt
  400 g whole milk
  400 g coconut milk

Combine all the ingredients in a small saucepan. Bring to a simmer over medium-high heat. Cook for 5 minutes, stirring with a wooden spoon, until thickened slightly. The sauce is done when it coats the back of the spoon but holds the shape of a valley when you run your finger through it. Serve warm. Store in an airtight container. Keeps in the fridge for 1 month. Use with ice cream, cakes, and donuts.

Hot Chocolate Drink (America)

<u>MAKES 1 QUART</u>

- 180 g dark chocolate discs
- 700 g whole milk
- 230 g water
- 30 g sugar
- 5 g salt
- 4 to 8 rosemary sprigs

Heat the milk in a large saucepan over medium heat until you see bubbles on the edges; do not boil. Whisk in all the remaining ingredients, except the rosemary. Continue to stir and heat over medium-low heat until almost at a light simmer. Pull from the heat. Portion into cups. Add one rosemary sprig per cup for serving. Keeps, stored in an airtight container, for 3 to 5 days in the fridge.

Cultured Milk Soup (Americas)

<u>MAKES 1 QUART</u>

- 450 g whole milk
- 25 g freshly squeezed lemon juice
- 3 large egg yolks
- 30 g sugar
- 5 g vanilla bean paste
- 400 g yogurt
- 180 g heavy whipping cream
- Zest of 1 lemon

Combine the milk and lemon juice in a small non-reactive container. Set aside to sour for 15 minutes. In a stand mixer fitted with the whisk attachment, whisk together the yolks, sugar, and vanilla until light and fluffy, 5 to 7 minutes. In another bowl, whisk together the yogurt, soured milk, cream, and lemon zest. Use a spatula to fold the egg mixture very gently into yogurt mixture until incorporated. Scrape the spatula against the sides of the bowl and bring through to the center. Continue until the mixture is uniform, being careful to maintain as much air as possible. Place in the fridge and chill for 1 hour

or overnight. Portion into bowls; top with hot biscuits and berries. Stored in an airtight container, it keeps for 2 to 3 days in the fridge.

Roasted, Macerated, and Candied

These recipes feature fruit tossed in sugar, roasted in honey, or candied until they turn to jewels! Macerating fruit is a technique that uses sugar to draw out juices without exposing the fruit to heat. It is a great hack in summer when the oven can be unbearable to turn on, or you want to preserve some delicate fresh flavors of rare fruit. I adore roasting fruit for the depth of flavor it acquires as it chars slightly and swoons out thick, colorful, syrupy juices that can be saved and used for other applications. Finally, candying is one of the most stable ways we can preserve fruit long term. Much like burying it in sugar, candying envelops fruit in liquid sugar, preserving the flavor and adding a stunning shine. Again, once the fruit is preserved these liquids can be used to soak cakes and flavor drinks. Do not discard. Use these recipes for filling and topping all your creations. All recipes in this section are naturally gluten-free. They are also vegan, except for the ones that call for honey; replace with pure maple syrup to make a vegan version.

Roasted Kumquats (Asia)

<u>MAKES 1 SHEET TRAY</u>

- 28 to 30 kumquats
- 30 g grapeseed oil
- Pinch of salt
- 75 g honey

Preheat the broiler to high. Combine all the ingredients, except the honey, in a medium bowl and toss to coat. Broil for 10 minutes, or until softened and caramelized. Pull from the oven, then pour the fruit and its juices into a heatproof bowl and stir in the honey. Allow to cool to room temperature.

Store in an airtight container. Keeps for 1 week in your fridge. Use with porridge, biscuits, and cake. Or use to spike tea or your favorite cocktail.

Candied Sudachi Limes (Asia)

MAKES 1 QUART

15 to 20 Sudachi limes
460 g water
430 g sugar

Shave the limes using a mandoline, catching the rinds, flesh, and juice but discarding the seeds. Combine the water with the sugar in a small saucepan over medium heat. Bring to a boil and then lower the heat to a simmer. Simmer for 10 minutes. Add the lime rinds, flesh, and juices, lower the heat to low, and simmer very gently for 5 minutes. Turn off the heat and allow to cool completely in the syrup. Store in an airtight container. Sudachis have such a thin rind they don't require blanching before candying. If using a different varietal of citrus, first blanch the rinds in boiling water for 5 minutes before proceeding with candying. Keeps for 1 month in your fridge. Use with cake or as an accompaniment on a cheese plate. Great to spike tea or for garnishing your favorite cocktail.

Blood Orange Caramel (Asia)

MAKES 1 QUART

450 g brown sugar
200 g blood orange juice
110 g unsalted butter
110 g heavy whipping cream
10 g salt

Stir together the sugar and juice in a small saucepot. Place over medium heat and let cook undisturbed, gently moving the pot around in circles to agitate the sugar and prevent it from burning. When the sugar is very bubbly and almost smells burnt, remove from the heat, add the butter, and stir together with a whisk. Place back over medium

heat, cook for another 30 seconds, then add the cream. Cook for another minute, or until slightly thickened. Pull from the heat and let cool completely. In an airtight container, keeps at room temperature for 1 week. Use with cookies and cake. Or on top of toast.

Tarragon Poached Pears (Europe)

MAKES 2 QUARTS

1 kg water
600 g sugar
Peel of 1 lemon
4 to 6 pears, peeled and halved, seeds removed
6 to 8 tarragon sprigs

Combine the water and sugar in a medium saucepan and bring to a boil over medium-high heat. Lower the heat to a simmer and cook for 10 minutes. Add the pears and tarragon. Poach for 10 to 15 minutes, until a pear is pierced easily with a sharp knife. The pears will continue to cook as they cool, and you want some texture. Remove from the heat and chill overnight in their own syrup. Store in an airtight container keeps for 1 month in the fridge.

Blistered Berries (Europe)

MAKES 1 QUART

500 g blackberries
2 g dried lavender
20 g sugar
5 g extra-virgin olive oil

Preheat the broiler to high.

Place the dried lavender in a spice grinder and pulse until powdered. Combine the blackberries and sugar in a medium bowl and toss with the lavender powder. Transfer to a sheet tray prepared with parchment paper. Broil for 1 to 2 minutes, until the berries have blistered and released a little juice. Remove from the heat and let cool. Store in an airtight container; keeps for 1 week in the fridge.

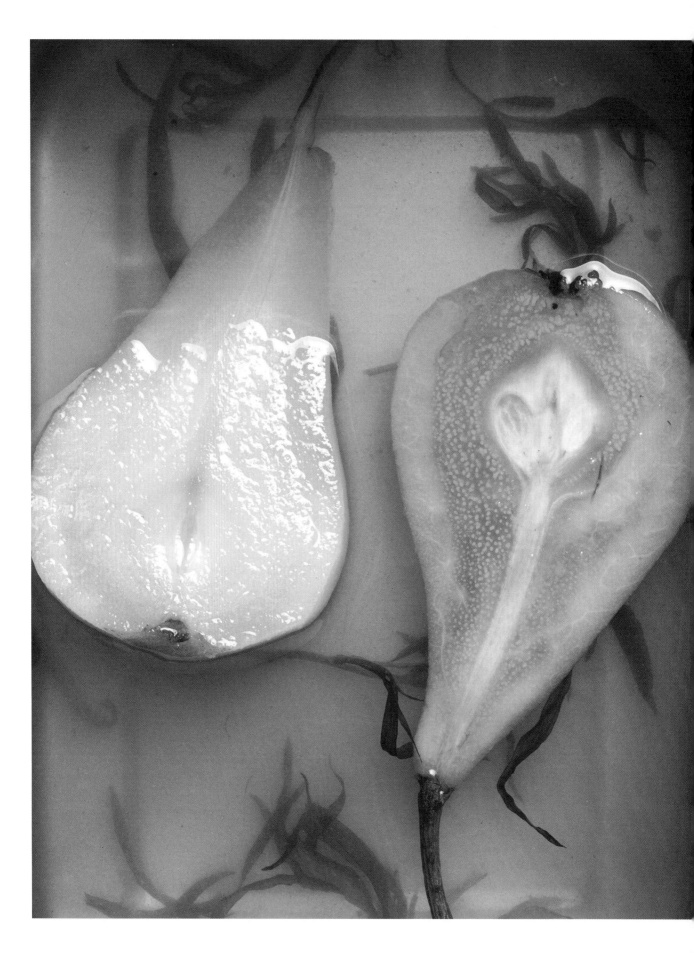

Candied Hibiscus (Americas)

<u>MAKES 2 QUARTS</u>

> 1 kg water
> 1 kg sugar
> 300 g dried hibiscus flowers

Place all the ingredients in a small saucepot and bring to a boil, then lower the heat to a simmer. Simmer for 30 to 45 minutes, until the syrup thickens. The flowers should be soft, sweet, and slightly chewy. Turn off the heat. Allow to cool completely in their syrup, then transfer the mixture to an airtight container and place in the fridge. Will keep in the fridge in its own syrup for 2 months.

Macerated Strawberries and Ground Cherries (Americas)

<u>MAKES 1 QUART</u>

> 8 strawberries, hulled and cut in half
> 10 ground cherries, cut in half
> Zest of 1 lemon
> Juice of ½ lemon
> 20 g sugar
> 3 g pure vanilla extract

Toss all the ingredients together in a bowl. Set aside for 1 hour in the fridge. Keeps for 2 days stored in an airtight container in the fridge.

Honeycomb Candy (Africa)

<u>MAKES 1 SHEET TRAY</u>

> Baking spray
> 175 g honey
> 325 g sugar
> 60 g water
> 15 g baking soda

Line a sheet tray with a silicone mat or parchment paper and spray evenly with baking spray. Gently whisk together all the ingredients, except the baking soda, in a medium pot with high sides. Then, allowing mixture to cook undisturbed, bring to a simmer over medium heat. When it deepens in color to dark amber and you smell deep caramel, almost burnt aromas, add the baking soda and whisk vigorously for 3 to 5 seconds. The candy will rush up the sides of the pot. Pour slowly and steadily onto your prepared sheet tray, being careful not to spill any on yourself. Allow to cool completely. Break apart. Keeps in an airtight container for 1 week at room temperature, out of direct sunshine and away from any heating source.

Bay Leaf Roasted Quince (Western Asia & North Africa)

<u>MAKES 2 QUARTS</u>

> 4 to 5 quinces, peeled, cored, and cut into eighths
> 400 g water, plus more as needed
> 100 g honey
> 2 to 3 fresh bay leaves

Preheat the oven to 400°F. Place the quince pieces in a single layer in a baking pan with 2- to 3-inch-high walls. Heat the water, honey, and bay leaves together in a small saucepan over medium heat until it simmers. Pour over the quince. Add more water to make sure they float freely. Wrap tightly with foil. Bake until dark pink and soft, about 2½ hours. Remove from the oven, remove foil, let cool, transfer to an airtight container, then chill completely in its syrup. Keeps in an airtight container in the fridge for 1 month.

Jams and Marmalades

This section contains techniques and recipes for the long-term preservation of seasonal fruit, via small-batch production of low-sugar, high-acid, no-commercial-pectin jams that focus on layering flavors with blossoms, herbs, spices, and the occasional booze.

Sugar is defined as a percentage against the total weight of fruit. As in how baker's math uses water against the total weight of flour! You will find preserves here ranging from 30 to 60 percent by weight of sugar. The marmalades, because they contain citrus, have an additional amount of sugar to balance the increased acid, and come in around 70 to 80 percent by weight of sugar. If this sounds like a lot, remember we eat only a small amount of jam at a time, and this is the total sugar in batches, yielding multiple jars. Also, by contrast, most commercial jams are 100 to 150 percent by weight of sugar. I use high acid to naturally activate the pectin in each fruit. Turns out, all fruit contains pectin in varying

percentages that can be coaxed out of the fruit with the right amount of acid and the proper tools and technique. It is an elegant coincidence that the very climates that required preservation for humans to be able to continue eating through winter are those in which pectin-heavy fruit thrived.

The exception is tropical fruit, which lacks pectin. I solve this by pairing my tropical fruits with citrus or using apple cores and skins wrapped in cheesecloth. This allows me to directly borrow high-pectin fruits' setting power for low- or no-pectin fruits. I do not recommend adding commercial pectin. Store-bought commercial powdered pectin may come from a "natural source," but its carbon footprint is massive. Adding extra pectin to your recipe also disrupts your jam's natural set point, allowing excess water to remain in the final product, which makes your jam very tempting to bacteria. Using a fruits-natural pectin or borrowing from a direct source creates the ideal high-acid environment to preserve your jewel-toned fruit for years.

Jam making is sugar work. In sugar work, you always want to be stirring steadily through the process. Picking a pattern for how you stir will ensure that nothing burns on the bottom. I like to run my spatula along the edges and then up and down through the center. Repeating this steadily will ensure a great-textured jam.

When you start cooking, you will see some classic signs of sugar work. First, there will be foam. A lot of people will stress constantly about removing this foam. This is completely unnecessary, and you will lose a lot of jam in the process. Most fruit will reabsorb the foam in the next step, the sugar rush. The exception is stone fruit, which will always have an initial thick layer of yellow foam that is easy to skim off the top with a spoon. This foam, when cooked into the jam, turns it brown so it is best removed.

Next, in the sugar rush, your jam will double in volume and begin to bubble wildly. After cooking for some time, the jam will fall down and the bub-

Wrinkle test. Once you've reached the large-bubble stage as just described, turn off your heat source and stop stirring. Set a timer for 4 minutes. After 4 minutes, dip your spatula into the top ¼ inch of jam at the center of your pot. Push your spatula gently toward the right or left and observe whether a wrinkle forms on the "skin" of the jam. If it does, your jam is set and ready for canning. If you don't see a wrinkle on the surface, check the edges by repeating the test there. If the edges are set, you likely need to cook the jam for only another 4 to 5 minutes and then test again. If no wrinkle is observed near the edges, cook for another 10 minutes and repeat the test.

bles will become bigger and fewer, almost fighting to pop through the surface. Continue to cook until about one and a half the original volume. Now, you can do your wrinkle test.

ADDITIONS. To layer flavor into your jams, you can add flowers, nuts, herbs, liquor, and liqueurs.

I add flowers, nuts, and whole soft herbs, such as basil and tarragon, after the jam has passed the wrinkle test. Stirring it in and letting it steep with the heat turned off is enough to infuse the jam with the added flavor of flowers or herbs without overcooking it. Simply pull the flowers or herbs from the jam and then proceed with canning. When working with flowers, sometimes I leave the petals in the final jam; it's just so dreamy and a fun additional texture. With hard herbs, such as bay leaf and rosemary, it's best to add at the beginning of cooking and let the flavor blossom throughout the process. Hard herbs need time to hydrate and mellow. Any liquor or liqueurs should be added in the last 5 minutes of cooking to allow time for the alcohol to evaporate but leave its delicate aromas and flavors behind.

OVEN CANNING. This is a process for canning using your oven, to both sterilize your jars and to can your preserves for long-term shelf-stable storage. At 250°F, all bacteria, including the dreaded botulism, are truly and effectively killed off. Water bath canning is an outdated process that wastes one of our most precious resources—water. It is also limited by its boiling point (212°F), which is not effective at killing all bacteria. Using oven canning, you can also scale up your recipes and get yields beyond the limitation of your pot size. Instead, you can fill up all the racks of your oven!

Oven canning is straightforward with a few rules. The largest jar you should use should hold 16 ounces (1 pint). When selecting jars for canning, make sure they are heat-tolerant glass, without any bubbles, cracks, or warped areas. Glass jars can be used repeatedly with an average life span of 11 years. Jar rings, lids, or single-component lids should be used only once.

First, rinse your jars with clean water and air dry. Then, bake your jars at 250°F for 15 minutes to sterilize them. Using oven gloves or hand towels (because your baked jars will be very, very hot), fill the jars, one by one with your jam, leaving

¼ to ½ inch of headspace between the jam and the jar rim. Wipe the lids with a damp towel to make sure their rim is clean. Place your lid and ring if using a two-component lid on top of each jar. Tent your hand over the top of the jam jar and use your fingertips to spin the lids until they just close—we call this fingertip tight. Do not over-tighten lids. Bake for another 15 minutes. Pull from the oven and allow to cool completely. Any jars whose lids don't pop and seal should be moved to your fridge and eaten first. Sealed jams on your shelf last for 2 years at room temperature and for 6 months in your fridge.

An easy alternative to canning: If you don't want to can, simply pack the jam, once cooled, into airtight containers and store in the fridge for up to 6 months.

The recipes here can be swapped out for similar fruit to make jam throughout the year with anything in season in your region! When working with new fruit, do a small batch first. Work with the starting ratio of roughly 40 percent sugar to 100 percent fruit, and 1 oz (about 30 g) of lemon juice per pound (455 g). Taste for flavor and acid. Explore and play!

All the recipes are naturally gluten-free and vegan.

Peach Jam (Asia)

MAKES 5 TO 6 PINTS

- 1.8 kg peaches, pitted and chopped into 1- to 2-inch pieces
- 800 g sugar
- 200 g freshly squeezed lemon juice

Toss together the peaches with the sugar and lemon juice in a large nonreactive bowl. Then, allow to sit out 8 hours or overnight at room temperature to extract the juices from the peaches. Pour the mixture into a large, wide nonreactive pot. Bring to a boil over medium-high heat. Simmer the fruit for 10 to 15 minutes, stirring constantly. The mixture will rush up the pot, producing a thick yellow foam. Remove and discard this foam. Cook, stirring constantly, for another 15 to 20 minutes. The jam will rush again in bubbles beforing sinking down. Continue to cook until the mixture slowly condenses into a thick, jewel-toned jam. Turn off the heat, allow the jam to sit undisturbed for 4 minutes, then do the wrinkle test (see page 271). If it passes, transfer to a heat-proof nonreactive container to cool; if not, turn heat back on and cook for another 5 minutes. Do the test again until the jam passes. Oven can, or store in an airtight container in the fridge. Use with porridge, biscuits, and cake. Or use to spike tea or your favorite cocktail.

Red Currant Violet Jam (Europe)

- 2.2 kg red currants
- 1.2 kg g sugar
- 150 g freshly squeezed lemon juice
- 20 to 30 g violet flowers

Combine all the ingredients, except the violets, in a large, wide nonreactive pot over medium-high heat. Cook, stirring constantly, for 20 to 25 minutes. The jam will rush in bubbles and then sink down and thicken. Turn off the heat. Set a timer for 4 minutes and leave the jam undisturbed. After 4 minutes, put a spatula straight down vertically into the top ¼ inch of jam in the middle of the pot and push the jam an inch to the left. If you see a wrinkle form on the skin of the jam, the jam is ready. If no wrinkle, turn the heat back on, cook the jam for 5 more minutes, and test again. Sink the violets into the jam. Oven can, or store in an airtight container in the fridge.

Greengage Jam (Europe)

- 2.2 kg greengage plums, pitted and halved
- 900 g sugar
- 130 g freshly squeezed lemon juice

Toss together the halved plums, sugar, and lemon juice in a large nonreactive bowl. Allow to sit out for 8 hours or overnight at room temperature to extract the juices from the plums. Heat the plum mixture in a large, wide nonreactive pot over medium-high heat. Cook the jam, stirring constantly, for 20 to 25 minutes. The mixture will rush up the pot, producing a thick yellow foam. Remove and discard this foam. Cook, stirring constantly, for another 15 to 20 minutes. The jam will rush again in bubbles before sinking down. Continue to cook until the mixture slowly condenses into a thick, jewel-toned jam. Set a timer for 4 minutes and leave the jam undisturbed. After 4 minutes,

put a spatula straight down vertically into the top ¼ inch of jam in the middle of the pot and push the jam an inch to the left. If you see a wrinkle form on the skin of the jam, the jam is ready. If no wrinkle, turn the heat back on, cook the jam for 5 more minutes, and test again. Oven can, or store in an airtight container in the fridge.

Fig Bee Pollen Jam (Africa)

- 2.2 kg figs
- 1.2 kg sugar
- 150 g freshly squeezed lemon juice
- 15 g bee pollen

Combine all the ingredients in a large, wide nonreactive pot over medium-high heat. Cook the jam, stirring constantly, for 30 to 35 minutes. The jam will rush in bubbles and then sink down and thicken. Turn off the heat. Set a timer for 4 minutes and leave the jam undisturbed. After 4 minutes, put a spatula straight down vertically into the top ¼ inch of jam in the middle of the pot and push the jam an inch to the left. If you see a wrinkle form on the skin of the jam, the jam is ready. If no wrinkle, turn the heat back on, cook the jam for 5 more minutes, and test again. Oven can, or store in an airtight container in the fridge.

Banana Marmalade (Africa)

- 6 lemons, halved and sliced horizontally
- 1.59 kg bananas
- 3 lemons, crushed and placed in cheesecloth
- 1.2 kg sugar
- 200 g freshly squeezed lemon juice

Blanch the lemon slices in a nonreactive stockpot of boiling water for 10 minutes. Pour out the water, reserving the lemon slices. Mash the bananas in a large, wide nonreactive pot. Add the blanched lemon slices, cheesecloth of lemons, sugar, and lemon juice. Cook over medium-high heat for 15 to 20 minutes, stirring constantly. Turn off the heat. Set a timer for 4 minutes and leave the jam undisturbed. After 4 minutes, put a spatula straight down vertically into the top ¼ inch of jam in the middle of the pot and push the jam an inch to the left. If you see a wrinkle form on the skin of the jam, the jam is ready. If no wrinkle, turn the heat back on, cook the jam for 5 more minutes, and test again. Oven can, or store in an airtight container in the fridge.

Apricot Pine Nut Jam (Western Asia & North Africa)

MAKES 5 TO 6 PINTS

- 100 g pine nuts
- 2.2 kg apricots, pitted and halved
- 1 kg sugar
- 150 g freshly squeezed lemon juice

Toast the pine nuts on a sheet tray in a 350°F oven for 5 to 7 minutes, until golden and fragrant. Set aside. Toss together the apricots, sugar, and lemon juice in a large nonreactive bowl. Allow to sit out overnight at room temperature to extract the juices from the apricots. Combine the all ingredients, except the pine nuts, in a large, wide nonreactive pot over medium-high heat. Cook the jam, stirring constantly, for 30 to 35 minutes. The mixture will rush up the pot, producing a thick yellow foam. Remove and discard this foam. Cook, stirring constantly, for another 15 to 20 minutes. The jam will rush again in bubbles before sinking down. Continue to cook until the mixture slowly condenses into a thick, jewel-toned jam. Turn off the heat. Set a timer for 4 minutes and leave the jam undisturbed. After 4 minutes, put a spatula straight down vertically into the top ¼ inch of jam in the middle of the pot and push the jam an inch to the left. If you see a wrinkle form on the skin of the jam, the jam is ready. If no wrinkle, turn the heat back on, cook the jam for 5 more minutes, and test again.

Stir in the toasted pine nuts. Oven can, or store in an airtight container in the fridge.

Soaks, Creams, Curds, Custards, and Ice Creams

The star of these recipes is dairy. Dairy is a delicate protein, such that when heat is applied, it unravels and recombines in new delicious ways! Add eggs and the delicate factor goes up. All these recipes are best made over medium heat or medium-low heat and involve slow, meditative stirring. Visual cues of tracks and texture changes you can feel are your guide as you build your skills. These recipes can be used to soak, decorate, serve alongside, or enjoy on their own. Adding them lifts any dish out of the ordinary and makes it feel like more of a party! Swap them around to your heart's content.

Save all your separated whites in an airtight container for up to 2 weeks in your fridge. Use whites to make meringues and buttercreams in the next section. Curds, custards, and ice creams can be scaled up and kept in the fridge or frozen for later use and consumption. Soaks and creams are best used within a few days. All the recipes in this section are naturally gluten-free.

Clotted Cream (Asia)

MAKES 1 PINT

- 400 g heavy whipping cream
- 15 g freshly squeezed lemon juice
- 20 g powdered sugar

Combine all the ingredients in a small nonreactive container and stir together gently. Cover with a lid and leave out at room temperature for 24 to 36 hours, until the cream has thickened slightly. Transfer to the fridge. Keeps for 2 weeks in an airtight container. Use with porridge, biscuits, and cake.

Chrysanthemum Custard (Asia)

<u>MAKES 1 QUART</u>

- 20 g dried chrysanthemum flowers
- 6 large egg yolks
- 25 g cornstarch
- 140 g sugar
- 6 g salt
- 345 g whole milk
- 200 g unsalted butter

Pulse the chrysanthemum flowers into a powder in a spice grinder. Set aside. Skip this step if subbing fresh flowers. Infuse fresh flowers directly into milk and strain out before you pour into your yolk mixture. Whisk together the egg yolks, cornstarch, sugar, and salt in a medium bowl, then set aside. Heat the milk and chrysanthemum powder in a small saucier pot over medium heat until it reaches a light simmer. Remove from the heat and slowly pour into the yolk mixture while stirring. Pour the mixture back into the pot and return to medium heat. Whisk until the mixture thickens; you'll feel the texture change as well as being able to observe the tracks of the whisk in the custard when it is ready. Remove from the heat. Pass the custard through a sieve into another bowl to remove any large particles. Add the butter, using an immersion blender to combine. Press plastic wrap directly onto the surface of the custard. Transfer to the fridge to cool completely. Keeps in an airtight container in the fridge for 1 to 2 weeks or in the freezer for 3 months. Use with rice balls, pie, donuts, and cake.

LÉGÈRE VARIATION:

<u>MAKES 1 PINT</u>

- 200 g heavy whipping cream
- 300 g prepared custard

In a stand mixer fitted with the whisk attachment, whip the cream until soft peaks form. Add the custard and whip until medium peaks form. Serve immediately. Keeps in an airtight container for 1 to 3 days in the fridge. Rewhip as necessary. Use with rice balls, pie, and cake.

Buckwheat Milk Soak (Asia)

<u>MAKES 1 PINT</u>

- 300 g whole milk
- 30 g buckwheat grouts, toasted
- 150 g sweetened condensed milk

Heat the milk and buckwheat together in a small pot over medium heat until simmering. Turn off the heat and let infuse for 15 minutes. Strain out and discard the buckwheat groats. Whisk the condensed milk into the infused milk and cool completely. Keeps in an airtight container for 1 to 2 weeks in the fridge. Use in cake or enjoy in tea.

Coconut Custard (Asia)

<u>MAKES 1 QUART</u>

- 60 g sweetened unsweetened shredded coconut
- 100 g coconut cream
- 6 large egg yolks
- 25 g cornstarch
- 140 g sugar
- 6 g salt
- 360 g whole milk
- 200 g unsalted butter

Combine the shredded coconut and coconut cream in a bowl. Set aside to absorb. Whisk together the egg yolks, cornstarch, sugar, and salt in a medium bowl, then set aside. Heat the milk in a small saucier pot over medium heat until it reaches a light simmer. Remove from the heat and slowly pour in the yolk mixture while stirring. Pour the mixture back into pot and return to medium heat. Whisk until the mixture thickens; you'll feel the texture change as well as being able to observe the tracks of the whisk in the custard. Remove from the heat. Pass the custard through a sieve into another bowl to remove any large particles. Add the butter, using an immersion blender to combine. Stir in the plumped shredded coconut and remaining coconut cream if any. Press plastic wrap directly onto the surface of the custard. Transfer to the fridge to cool completely. Keeps in an airtight container for 1 to 2 weeks in the fridge. Use in cake, donuts, and pie.

Yuzu Curd (Asia)

MAKES 1 QUART

- 4 large egg yolks
- 3 large eggs
- 170 g sugar
- 3 g salt
- Zest of 2 yuzu
- 180 ml freshly squeezed yuzu juice
- 150 g unsalted butter

Combine all the ingredients, except the butter, in a medium heatproof bowl. Place the bowl atop a saucier pan that is filled with 2 inches of water to create a double boiler. Cook over medium heat, whisking constantly until thickened or a thermometer reads 180°F. Remove from the heat and strain. Add the butter, using an immersion blender. Keeps in an airtight container for 1 to 2 weeks in the fridge or for 3 months in the freezer. Substitute yuzu with any citrus you like as it comes into season. When working with citrus like oranges, I like to do half lemon juice to maintain the punch of acid we want from a good curd. Use in cake, donuts, and pie.

Salty Honey Custard (Europe)

MAKES 1 QUART

- 225 g whole milk
- 80 g honey
- 6 g salt
- 4 large egg yolks
- 110 g sugar
- 40 g cornstarch
- 200 g unsalted butter

Heat the milk, honey, and salt in a small saucepan over medium heat until it simmers on the edges. Combine the yolks, sugar, and cornstarch in a medium bowl. Pour half of the hot milk mixture into the egg mixture, whisking constantly. Add this mixture back into the pan, whisking constantly. Return the pan to the heat and continue to cook, whisking constantly, until thickened. Pass through a strainer. Add the butter, using an immersion blender, until smooth. Transfer to a container, press plastic wrap directly onto the top of the custard, and chill completely in the fridge. Keeps in an airtight container for 1 to 2 weeks in the fridge or for 3 months in the freezer. Use in cakes or eat straight like a pudding cup.

Sweet Cream (Europe & Africa)

MAKES 1 QUART

- 700 g heavy whipping cream
- 85 g sugar
- Zest of 1 lemon
- 3 g salt

In a stand mixer fitted with the whisk attachment, beat all the ingredients together until medium peaks form. Fill a pastry bag with the sweet cream and set aside in the fridge to chill. Keeps for 1 to 2 days in the fridge. Rewhip as necessary. Serve alongside cakes and pies.

Hazelnut Chocolate Custard (Europe)

MAKES 1 QUART

- 150 g unsalted butter
- 100 g dark chocolate discs
- 6 large yolks
- 20 g cornstarch
- 140 g sugar
- 6 g salt
- 360 g whole milk
- 70 g hazelnuts, toasted and chopped

Add butter and chocolate to a bowl with a sieve over the top. Set aside. Whisk together the egg yolks, cornstarch, sugar, and salt in a medium bowl, then set aside. Heat milk in a small saucier pot over medium heat until it reaches a light simmer. Remove from the heat and slowly pour into the yolk mixture while stirring. Pour the mixture back into the pot and return to medium heat. Whisk until the mixture thickens; you'll feel the texture change as well as being able to observe the tracks of the whisk in the custard. Remove from the heat. Pass the custard through a sieve into your bowl to remove any large particles. Let sit for 1 minute to melt chocolate, then use an immersion blender to combine. Stir in the hazelnuts. Press plastic wrap directly onto the surface of the custard. Transfer to the fridge to cool completely. Keeps in an airtight container for 1 to 2 weeks in the fridge or for 3 months in the freezer. Use in cakes or eat straight like a pudding cup.

Sweet Woodruff Cocoa Nib Cream (Europe)

MAKES 1 PINT

- 350 g heavy whipping cream
- 15 g sweet woodruff
- 60 g sugar
- 30 g cocoa nibs, chopped

Add the sweet woodruff to the cream in a saucepan. Heat until just warmed through and turn off the heat. Infuse and chill overnight. Strain and discard the woodruff. Whip the infused cream with the sugar on medium-high until you have medium peaks. Fold in the cocoa nibs. Keeps in an airtight container for 2 to 3 days in the fridge. Rewhip as necessary. Use in cakes or serve alongside pies.

Chicory Cream (Europe)

MAKES 1 PINT

- 350 g heavy whipping cream
- 60 g sugar
- 3 g salt
- 15 g chicory, ground

In a stand mixer fitted with the whisk attachment, beat together all the ingredients, except the chicory, until it reaches medium peaks. Fold in the ground chicory. Transfer to the fridge to chill. Keeps in an airtight container for 2 to 3 days in the fridge. Rewhip as necessary. Serve with cakes and pies.

Whipped Cheesecake (Europe)

MAKES 1 QUART

- 450 g cream cheese
- 200 g heavy whipping cream
- 120 g sugar
- Zest of 3 lemons

In a stand mixer fitted with the whisk attachment, whip cream cheese with sugar until fluffy, about 5 minutes. Add the cream and zest to the bowl and whip to combine. Keeps in an airtight container for 2 to 3 days in the fridge. Rewhip as necessary. Use with cakes.

Lilac Ice Cream (Americas)

<u>MAKES 2 QUARTS</u>

- 720 g whole milk
- 20 g lilac flowers, blossoms only
- 6 large egg yolks
- 200 g sugar
- 600 g heavy whipping cream
- 10 g vanilla bean paste

Heat the milk and lilac flowers gently in a small saucepot over low heat until small bubbles appear on the edges. Turn off the heat and let infuse for 15 minutes. Strain. You can substitute dried lilacs. Place the yolks and sugar in a medium bowl and whisk to combine. Set aside. Bring the cooled lilac milk, cream, and vanilla to a simmer over medium heat. Remove the mixture from the heat and slowly whisk into the yolk mixture. Return the mixture to the pot and place back over low heat. Cook for another minute, stirring constantly with a whisk, until thickened slightly. Remove from the heat, strain, and place in the fridge to chill for 4 hours or overnight. Use an immersion blender to remix prior to churning. Follow your ice cream maker's instructions. Pack into pint- or quart-size containers. Keeps for 3 months in the freezer. Serve with pie and cake.

Lemon Verbena Custard (Americas)

<u>MAKES 1 QUART</u>

- 6 large egg yolks
- 25 g cornstarch
- 140 g sugar
- 4 g salt
- 360 g whole milk
- 2 or 3 lemon verbena sprigs
- 200 g unsalted butter

Combine the egg yolks, cornstarch, sugar, and salt in a medium bowl. Whisk together and set aside. Heat the milk and lemon verbena in a small saucier pot over medium heat until it reaches a light simmer.

Remove from the heat, then strain out the lemon verbena and slowly pour into the yolk mixture while stirring. Pour the mixture back into the pot and return to the heat. Whisk until the mixture thickens; you'll feel the texture change as well as being able to observe the tracks of the whisk in the custard. Remove from the heat. Pass the custard through a sieve into another bowl to remove any large particles. Add the butter, using an immersion blender to combine. Press plastic wrap directly onto the surface of the custard. Place in the fridge to cool completely. Keeps in an airtight container for 1 to 2 weeks in the fridge or for 3 months in the freezer. Use in cakes or eat straight like a pudding cup.

Corn Curd (Americas)

<u>MAKES 1 PINT</u>

- Kernels from 8 to 12 ears yellow sweet corn
- 70 g sugar

Place the kernels in a blender and process until a juice. Strain, discarding the solids. Strain again. Heat the corn juice in a saucepan until thickened, 5 to 8 minutes. Strain again and transfer to a bowl. Cover with plastic wrap and chill. Keeps in an airtight container for 1 week in the fridge. This recipe is naturally vegan.

Passion Fruit Curd (Americas)

<u>MAKES 1 QUART</u>

- 4 large egg yolks
- 3 large eggs
- 170 g sugar
- Salt
- Zest of 2 lemons
- 120 g passion fruit juice
- 60 g freshly squeezed lemon juice
- 150 g unsalted butter
- 2 passion fruit

Combine all the ingredients, except the butter, in a medium heatproof bowl set over a saucier pan filled with 2 inches of water. Heat over medium heat until thickened, whisking constantly. Strain. Add the butter, using an immersion blender. Cut open the passion fruit and scoop out the flesh. Stir into curd. Keeps in an airtight container for 1 to 2 weeks in the fridge or for 3 months in the freezer. Use in cake, donuts, and pie.

Juniper Gelato (Africa)

MAKES 2 QUARTS

  1.67 kg whole milk

  50 g juniper berries

  112 g milk powder

  450 g sugar

  7 g guar gum or locust bean gum

  3 g salt

  700 g heavy whipping cream

Heat the juniper berries with half the milk (835g) in a medium saucepot over medium heat until it reaches a light simmer. Remove from the heat and set aside. Whisk together the milk powder, sugar, and guar gum to create your dry mixture. Place the remaining milk in a large bowl. Use an immersion blender to blend the milk as you add the dry mixture. Strain the juniper mixture, discarding the juniper. Continue to blend as you add the juniper-infused milk and the cream. Transfer to the fridge for 4 hours or overnight. Use an immersion blender to remix prior to churning. Follow your ice cream machine's instructions. Pack into pint- or quart-size containers. Keeps for 3 months in the freezer.

Coffee Custard (Africa)

MAKES 1 QUART

  6 large egg yolks

  25 g cornstarch

  140 g sugar

  6 g salt

  30 g ground coffee

  345 g whole milk

  200 g unsalted butter

Whisk together the egg yolks, cornstarch, sugar, and salt in a medium bowl, then set aside. Heat the milk and coffee grounds in a small saucier pot over medium heat until it reaches a light simmer. Remove from the heat, and slowly pour into the yolk mixture while stirring. Pour the mixture back into the pot and return to the heat. Whisk until the mixture thickens; you'll feel the texture change as well as being able to observe the tracks of the whisk in the custard. Remove from the heat. Pass the custard through a sieve into another bowl to remove any large particles. Add the butter, using an immersion blender to combine. Press plastic wrap directly onto the surface of the custard. Transfer to the fridge to cool completely. Keeps in an airtight container for 1 to 2 weeks in the fridge or for 3 months in the freezer.

LÉGÈRE VARIATION:

MAKES 1 PINT

  200 g heavy whipping cream

  300 g prepared custard

Whip the cream in a medium bowl until medium peaks form. Add the custard and whip until medium peaks form again. Serve immediately. Keeps in an airtight container for 1 to 3 days in the fridge. Rewhip as necessary.

Rose Geranium Custard (Africa)

MAKES 1 QUART

  6 large egg yolks

  25 g cornstarch

  140 g sugar

  4 g salt

  360 g whole milk

  200 g unsalted butter

  10 g rose geranium leaves and blossoms

Whisk together the egg yolks, cornstarch, sugar, and salt in a medium bowl, then set aside. Heat the milk and rose geranium in a small saucier pot over medium heat until it reaches a light simmer. Remove from the heat, strain, and slowly pour in the yolk mixture while stirring. Pour the mixture back into the pot and return to the heat. Whisk until the mixture thickens; you'll feel the texture change as well as being able to observe the tracks of the whisk in the custard. Remove from the heat. Pass the custard through a sieve into another bowl to remove any large particles. Add the butter, using an immersion blender to combine. Press plastic wrap directly onto the surface of the custard. Transfer to the fridge to cool completely. Keeps in an airtight container for 1 to 2 weeks in the fridge or for 3 months in the freezer. Serve with cakes and pies.

Sorghum Soak (Africa)

MAKES 1 PINT

> 200 g sorghum syrup
> 200 g water

Combine the sorghum syrup and water in a small saucepan over medium heat and bring to a simmer. Simmer for 5 minutes, then turn off the heat. Keeps in an airtight container for a week in the fridge.

Halva Custard
(Western Asia & North Africa)

MAKES 1 QUART

> 300 g whole milk
> 312 g heavy cream
> 65 g halva
> 8 large egg yolks
> 200 g sugar

Combine the milk, cream, and halva in a medium saucier pan. Use an immersion blender to make smooth. Heat until there are bubbles on the edges. Whisk together the yolks and sugar in a medium bowl. Pour the hot milk mixture into the egg mixture, whisking constantly. Return to the heat and

cook until slightly thickened or 180°F. Strain and chill. Keeps in an airtight container for 1 to 2 weeks in the fridge or for 3 months in the freezer.

Rose Hip Custard
(Western Asia & North Africa)

MAKES 1 QUART

> 6 large egg yolks
> 25 g cornstarch
> 140 g sugar
> 4 g salt
> 360 g whole milk
> 200 g unsalted butter
> 20 g dried rose hips

Combine the yolks, cornstarch, sugar, and salt in a medium bowl. Whisk together, then set aside. Heat the milk and rose hips in a small saucier pot over medium heat until it reaches a light simmer. Remove from the heat, strain, and slowly pour into the yolk mixture while stirring. Pour the mixture back into the pot and return to the heat. Whisk until the mixture thickens; you'll feel the texture change as well as being able to observe the tracks of the whisk in the custard. Remove from the heat. Pass the custard through a sieve into another bowl to remove any large particles. Add the butter, using an immersion blender to combine. Press plastic wrap directly onto the surface of the custard. Transfer to the fridge to cool completely. Keeps in an airtight container for 1 to 2 weeks in the fridge or for 3 months in the freezer. Do *not* substitute fresh rose hips. Use with cakes and pies.

Poppy Seed Cream (Western Asia & North Africa)

MAKES 1 PINT

> 350 g heavy whipping cream
> 15 g poppy seeds
> 60 g sugar

Add the poppy seeds to the cream. Infuse and chill overnight in the fridge. Whip with sugar until combined. Rewhip as necessary. Keeps in an airtight container for 2 to 3 days in the fridge.

Meringues, Marshmallow Fluff, and Buttercreams

This section has all the finishing touches, the things that, as a kid, I always remembered after a party—the big swoops and clouds of meringues and buttercreams! You'll find lots of different approaches to buttercream based on which region it hails from; each has their merits and strengths for expressing flavor. I have a slight bias for Swiss-style meringue-based buttercreams. I encourage you to play with all of them and find your favorites. Save all your separated yolks in an airtight container for up to 1 week in your fridge. Use yolks to make custards and curds in the previous section. Except for meringue, which should be used immediately, these recipes keep for months in your fridge in an airtight container. I love having a few on hand to make quick snacking cakes for guests and to mix and match flavors if I ever need inspiration. All recipes in this section are naturally gluten-free.

Torched Meringue (Asia)

MAKES 2 QUARTS

    366 g egg whites (about 8 large eggs)
    570 g sugar

Create a double boiler by adding 2 inches of water to a small saucepot and placing the bowl of a stand mixer on top of it, over medium heat. Whisk the egg whites and sugar together in the mixer bowl. Continue to whisk until the mixture is very runny, the sugar has dissolved, and the mixture has reached a temperature of 161°F. Transfer the bowl to the stand mixer fitted with the whisk attachment. Whip until the bowl is cool to the touch and the meringue has tripled in volume. The meringue should be white, light, and fluffy. Use immediately, spreading over cake or topping pies. Use a kitchen torch to char deeply.

German Chocolate Buttercream (Europe)

MAKES 2 QUARTS

    4 large egg yolks
    25 g cornstarch
    150 g sugar
    5 g salt
    480 g whole milk
    100 g unsweetened cocoa powder
    50 g unsalted butter, at room temperature
    200 g dark chocolate discs
    550 g unsalted butter, at room temperature
    150 g powdered sugar (optional)

Whisk together the yolks, cornstarch, sugar, and salt in a medium bowl, then set aside. Heat the milk over medium heat until it reaches a light simmer. Remove from the heat and slowly pour into the yolk mixture while stirring. Pour the mixture back into the pot and return to the heat. Whisk until the mixture thickens; you'll feel the texture change as well as being able to observe the tracks of the whisk in the custard. Remove from the heat. Whisk in the cocoa powder. Pass the custard through a sieve into another bowl to remove any large particles. Add the 50 g of butter and all of the chocolate, wait 1 minute, then use an immersion blender to combine. Press plastic wrap directly onto the surface of the custard. Transfer to the fridge to cool completely. Transfer the custard to a stand mixer fitted with the whisk attachment. On medium high, add in the remaining butter a little at a time until fluffy. Taste and add powdered sugar to your desired sweetness (if using). Whip to combine. Keeps in an airtight container for 6 months in the fridge.

Smoky Honey Swiss Buttercream (Europe)

<u>MAKES 4 QUARTS</u>

- 244 g egg whites (8 large eggs)
- 380 g sugar
- 1.35 kg unsalted butter, at room temperature
- 60 g honey
- 8 g Maldon smoked sea salt
- 5 g liquid smoke (optional)

Heat the honey in a saucepan over medium-high heat until it bubbles and smells almost burnt. Remove from the heat and let cool completely. Create a double boiler by adding 2 inches of water to a small saucepot and placing the bowl of a stand mixer on top of it, over medium heat. Whisk together the egg whites and sugar in the mixer bowl. Continue to whisk until the mixture becomes very runny, the sugar has dissolved, and the mixture has reached a temperature of 161°F. Pull the bowl from the heat and transfer to the stand mixer fitted with the whisk attachment. Whip on high speed until the bowl is cool to the touch and the meringue has tripled in volume. Reduce speed to medium-high, adding in the butter a little at a time, until smooth. Add the honey and smoked sea salt and whip to combine. Keeps in an airtight container for 6 months in the fridge.

Crema American Buttercream (Americas)

<u>MAKES 1 QUART</u>

- 225 g unsalted butter, at room temperature
- 100 g crema
- 450 g powdered sugar
- 5 g salt
- 5 g freshly squeezed lemon juice
- Zest of 1 lemon
- 3 g vanilla bean paste

In the bowl of stand mixer fitted with the whisk attachment, combine the butter, crema, and half (225 g) of the powdered sugar. Beat on low speed until combined, then turn up speed to medium-high for 10 minutes. Add half of the remaining powdered sugar, salt, lemon zest, lemon juice, and vanilla bean paste; beat for another 10 minutes on medium-high. Add the rest of the powdered sugar on low speed until combined, raise speed to medium-high, and beat until light and fluffy, about 10 more minutes. Keeps in an airtight container for 6 months in the fridge.

Passion Fruit Buttercream (Americas)

<u>MAKES 4 QUARTS</u>

- 244 g egg whites (8 large eggs)
- 380 g sugar
- 1350 g unsalted butter, at room temperature
- 5 g salt
- 4 passion fruits
- Passion Fruit Curd (page 278)

Create a double boiler by adding 2 inches of water to a small saucepot and placing the bowl of a stand mixer on top of it, over medium heat. Whisk together the egg whites and sugar in the mixer bowl. Continue to whisk until the mixture becomes very runny, the sugar has dissolved, and the mixture has reached a temperature of 161°F. Pull the bowl from the heat and transfer to the stand mixer fitted with a whisk attachment. Whip on high speed until the bowl is cool to the touch and the meringue has tripled in volume. Mix in the butter a little at a time on medium-high. Season with salt and whip another 2 minutes. Add the passion fruit curd to taste, maximum amount of 350 g. Cut open fresh passion fruit. Whip the fresh passion fruit into the buttercream until smooth. Keeps in an airtight container for 6 months in the fridge.

Peanut Frangipane (Africa)

MAKES 1 PINT

- 160 g unsalted butter, at room temperature
- 200 g dark brown sugar
- 160 g smooth peanut butter
- 2 large eggs
- Pinch of salt

In a stand mixer fitted with the whisk attachment, combine all the ingredients. Beat on medium speed until smooth. Transfer the frangipane to a piping bag and set aside. Keeps for 2 to 3 days in the fridge. Use in cookies and pies.

Marshmallow Fluff (Africa)

MAKES 2 QUARTS

- 300 g sugar
- 300 g honey
- 120 g water
- 6 g salt
- 4 large egg whites
- Pinch of cream of tartar

Combine the sugar, honey, water, and salt in a small saucepot and gently swirl the pan to agitate and move ingredients around; bring to a boil or until the mixture reaches 240°F. Remove from the heat. In the bowl of a stand mixer fitted with the whisk attachment, whip egg whites on medium speed. Once you see bubbles throughout, add the cream of tartar and continue to whisk until you have medium peaks. Reduce the speed to low and slowly drizzle in a small amount of the sugar syrup while you continue to whisk. Increase the speed to medium and drizzle in the remaining syrup in a slow steady stream until combined. Increase the speed to high and continue to whip until thick and glossy. Use immediately or place in an airtight container and transfer to the fridge. Keeps for 2 weeks in the fridge. Use in cookies, marshmallow and peanut butter sandwiches, ice creams, pies, or eat straight with a spoon.

Sorghum Buttercream (Africa)

MAKES 4 QUARTS

- 244 g egg whites (8 large eggs)
- 380 g sugar
- 1.35 kg unsalted butter, at room temperasture
- 80 g sorghum syrup
- 5 g ground grains of paradise
- 5 g salt

Create a double boiler by adding 2 inches of water to a small saucepot and placing the bowl of a stand mixer on top of it, over medium heat. Whisk together the egg whites and sugar in the mixer bowl. Continue to whisk until the mixture becomes very runny, the sugar has dissolved, and the mixture has reached a temperature of 161°F. Pull the bowl from the heat and transfer to the stand mixer fitted with the whisk attachment. Whip on high speed until the bowl is cool to the touch and the meringue has tripled in volume. Add the butter a little at a time on medium-high speed. Add the sorghum, grains of paradise, and salt; whip to combine. Keeps in an airtight container for 6 months in the fridge.

Pistachio Buttercream (Western Asia & North Africa)

MAKES 4 QUARTS

- 200 g pistachios
- 60 g extra-virgin olive oil
- 244 g egg whites (8 large eggs)
- 380 g sugar
- 1.35 kg unsalted butter, at room temperature
- 5 g salt

Combine the pistachios and olive oil in a blender. Blend until a smooth paste. Set the pistachio butter aside. Create a double boiler by adding 2 inches of water to a small saucepot and placing the bowl of a stand mixer on top of it, over medium heat. Whisk together the egg whites and sugar in the mixer bowl. Continue to whisk until the mixture becomes very runny, the sugar has dissolved, and the mixture has reached a temperature of 161°F. Pull the bowl from the heat and transfer to stand mixer fitted with the whisk attachment. Whip until the bowl is cool to the touch and the meringue has tripled in volume. Add the butter a little at a time on medium-high speed. Add the pistachio butter and salt and whip until combined. Keeps in an airtight container for 6 months in the fridge.

Ferments, Spreads, Butters, Oils, and Spice Mixes

This section is focused on the ferments, fats, and spices that give the recipes throughout this book their kick and will eventually fill your shelves. The preservation here depends on salt in brines or fat as protection for long-term storage. Review Prepping for Fermenting and Troubleshooting (see below) before you begin. You can control how bright, spicy, or seasoned things are, making your pantry unique to your tastes. Taste each ferment often as it ferments to see when it is fermented to your liking. There is no wrong answer! Once they reach your ideal flavor, these ferments should be moved for long-term storage to your fridge and enjoyed with all meals. All recipes in this section are naturally gluten-free. Most are also vegan, except for the cured egg yolks, nasturtium pumpkin seed spread, fermented honey, and the butters.

Prepping for Fermenting and Troubleshooting

In fermentation, your prep work is the most important part you will do. Before you begin any ferment, you must make sure you have clean tools and fermenting vessels. You can ferment in glass, ceramic, or plastic if it is all you have available. Prepare your vessels and tools by washing them with hot water and soap and allowing them to air dry at room temperature. I am often impatient, and I like to pop mine on a sheet tray in the oven at 200°F for 10 minutes to dry faster. If you do that,

remove hot jars carefully to cool to room temperature. You do not want to use any antibacterial or scented detergents as these will indiscriminately kill both bad and good bacteria. We want good bacteria to flourish! Likewise, make sure you are washing your hands frequently throughout the process, with only hot water and soap. Your skin has a lot of the good bacteria to help your ferments along! It is the first step of symbiosis with your imaginary friends in your environment!

Fermentation is one of the oldest techniques humans have used to process food. Given the right environment, it wants to happen! Its results are the many nutrient-rich, safe, and delicious foods beloved the world over. Troubleshooting fermentations is most often a simple fix. If your ferment has not begun to bubble after a few days, do not despair. It could be that you are in a cooler environment or perhaps you have kept an immaculate house—it will take some time for good bacteria to build up! Simply continue to give your ferment a good stir or shake to oxygenate. While the fermentation cycle is anerobic—happens without oxygen present—exposure to oxygen encourages the capturing and proliferation of bacteria. You can also inoculate most sluggish ferments by adding a splash of Bragg Apple Cider Vinegar—the one with the living mother.

If you see what looks like a mold growing on your ferment, isolate the ferment and identify the color of the mold. White or green molds are harmless—in fact, they are the molds we want when doing a special ferment we call cheese. They are just out of place. Simply scrape them off the top of your ferment, replace any lost liquid or mass with brine or salt, and return your ferment to its spot on your shelf or in your fridge. If, however, you see a yellow, orange, or black mold growing on your ferment, throw out the entire ferment and thoroughly sterilize the vessel. Do not try to cut away the parts with the mold and use what's left. There is probably more mold that you can't see: this kind of mold in fact invades the entire ferment. These molds are highly

toxic. Should this rare occurrence happen to you, carefully examine the place where you are storing your ferments and consider cleaning the whole area with white vinegar or another stronger substance (www.healthline.com/health/does-vinegar-kill-mold#where-not-to-use-vinegar). Ferments are often the canary in the coal mine for mold infestations in our homes.

Kosho Oil (Asia)

MAKES 1 CUP

Zest and juice of 8 limes
Zest and juice of 4 lemons
Zest of 1 grapefruit
5 g salt
5 g ground Sichuan pepper
300 g extra-virgin olive oil

Mix together all the zests and juice, salt, pepper, and olive oil in a medium nonreactive bowl. Keeps in an airtight nonreactive container for 1 month in the fridge.

Nukazuke Pickles (Asia)

MAKES 1 BED

800 g distilled water
100 g salt
800 g rice bran
Red pepper flakes (optional)
One 4-inch-square piece kombu seaweed
    (optional)
Vegetables of your choice

Bring the water to a boil in a large saucepot, add the salt, and stir to dissolve. Turn off the heat and let the water cool completely. Preheat the oven to 350°F. Spread the rice bran on sheet pans and roast in the oven until fragrant, 3 to 5 minutes. Remove from the oven and let cool completely. Combine rice bran and salt water in a large bowl and mix with your hands until crumbly. Pack into a container for fermentation and cover with its lid slightly ajar. Add the red pepper flakes and/or seaweed pieces (if using). This is your nukadoku pickling bed. Every day for the next 10 days, vigorously stir the bran mixture and pack it back down to encourage proper fermentation in your nukadoku bed, keeping the fermentation container in a cool, dry place, out of direct sunlight. After 10 days, the bed should smell funky and sweet. Bury your vegetable of your choice in the bed for 8 to 24 hours. Uncover, rinse off the excess pickling bran, and enjoy. Stir the bed every 3 days to maintain and reuse to ferment a variety of produce. Most produce will ferment within 30 minutes to a couple of hours for larger items. For long-term storage or a break in fermentation, transfer the pickling bed to an airtight container and keep in the fridge.

Cured Egg Yolks (Asia)

MAKES 1 SHEET TRAY

500 g salt
500 g sugar
Egg yolks

In a medium bowl, mix salt and sugar. Pour three-fourths of the mixture onto a quarter sheet tray; you want the mixture to cover the entire bottom to a depth of at least ½ inch. Use an egg to make divots about 2 inches apart. Place an egg yolk in each divot, being careful not to break them. If they break, remove the yolk and any dirtied salt-sugar mixture, then replace with more 1:1 salt-sugar mixture and continue to put your yolks into place. Once yolks are in place, bury them beneath more of the salt-sugar mixture. Cure uncovered for 2 to 3 days in the fridge. Pull the yolks from the cure, brush off any excess salt, and transfer to a cooling rack to dry out in your fridge for 24 to 48 hours. Keeps in an airtight container for 3 months in the fridge.

Roasted Sunflower Butter (Americas)

MAKES 1 PINT

- 3 to 5 sunflowers with medium heads
- 300 g unsalted butter, at room temperature
- Salt

Preheat the oven to 425°F. Remove the petals from the sunflower heads and cut away the stems. Spread a thin layer of the butter over the heads and sprinkle with salt. Put the sunflower heads on a sheet tray lined with parchment paper. Roast for 20 to 25 minutes, until the sunflowers are fragrant and browned on all edges. Remove from the oven and let cool completely. Scoop out each roasted head from the flower base and place the heads in a small bowl. Use a wooden spoon to break up the heads and then to work sunflower head puree into the remaining room-temperature butter until combined. Add salt to taste. Place the butter mixture on sheets of plastic wrap and roll up like a sausage, twisting the ends, or pack into airtight pint-size containers. Transfer to the fridge to chill. Keeps for 2 to 3 weeks in the fridge or for 3 months in the freezer.

Nasturtium Pine Nut & Pumpkin Seed Spread (Americas)

MAKES 1 PINT

- 141 g pine nuts
- 28 g pumpkin seeds
- 100 g packed nasturtium flowers
- 50 g packed nasturtium leaves
- 85 g extra-virgin olive oil, plus more
- 56 g grapeseed oil
- 100 g Cotija
- Zest of 1 lime
- 15 g freshly squeezed lime juice

Toast the pine nuts and pumpkin seeds on separate sheet trays at 350°F until lightly fragrant, 3 to 5 minutes. Place the nuts, seeds, nasturtium flowers and leaves, the grapeseed oil, Cotija, and lime zest and juice in a blender. Blend until a puree. Remove from blender to a bowl, drizzle in olive oil, and whisk to combine. Pack into an airtight container, top off with an extra ¼ inch of olive oil to protect the spread from bacteria and oxidation. Keeps in an airtight container for 2 weeks in the fridge.

Fermented Honey (Africa)

MAKES 1 QUART

700 g honey
70 g warm water, about 100°F

Combine the honey and warm water in a jar. Place an airtight lid on top and shake vigorously until well mixed. Open lid the slightly and allow to ferment at room temperature, out of direct sunlight, for 10 days. Transfer to the fridge or allow to continue fermenting at room temperature. Keeps for 6 months.

Rooibos Olive Oil (Africa)

MAKES 1 PINT

400 g extra-virgin olive oil
60 g loose-leaf rooibos tea

Heat the oil in a small saucepot over medium-low heat to 110°F. Remove from the heat and stir in the rooibos. Infuse for 24 to 48 hours at room temperature. Strain. Keeps in an airtight container for 3 weeks at room temperature.

Fig Leaf Oil (Africa)

MAKES 1 PINT

30 fig leaves
Water
Salt
500 g extra-virgin olive oil

Bring the water and salt to a boil in a small saucepot. Use enough salt to make the water just ever so slightly salty. Have a medium bowl filled with ice and a little water nearby. Drop the leaves into boiling salt water and blanch for 40 to 60 seconds. Using a sieve or tongs, remove them from the water and put in the ice water to stop cooking. Remove the leaves from the water and dry them between paper towels. Place the blanched leaves in a blender with the olive oil and blend for 2 minutes. Using a

cheesecloth-layered strainer, strain to get a clear beautiful oil. If you don't strain your oil, it will have more body and be speckled with plant matter. Both are great options depending on your intended application. Keeps in an airtight container in the fridge for 1 month.

Nettle Dip
(Western Asia & North Africa)

MAKES 1 PINT

2 bunches stinging nettles
4 garlic cloves
Leaves from 2 bunches parsley
5 g salt
5 g ground cardamom
3 g ground cumin
Zest and juice of 2 lemons
100 g extra-virgin olive oil, plus more

Fill a stockpot with water and bring to a boil. Blanch the nettles for 2 minutes, then transfer to a bowl of ice water to stop cooking. Drain. Pull the leaves off the stems. Place the nettle leaves, parsley, salt, cardamom, cumin, lemon zest and juice, and 25 g of the olive oil in a food processor. Pulse until all is mixed and very finely chopped. Keeping the food processor running, drizzle in the remaining olive oil until the mixture becomes smooth, adding the oil to your desired texture is reached and you have a vibrant green oil. Keeps in an airtight container topped off with extra olive oil for 2 months in the fridge.

Za'atar (Western Asia & North Africa)

MAKES 1 QUART

- 200 g dried sumac
- 130 g dried thyme
- 130 g dried oregano
- 130 g sesame seeds

Combine the thyme, oregano, and sumac in a medium heatproof bowl. Set aside. Heat a dry saucepan over medium heat. Add the sesame seeds and stir until toasted. Once you smell the aroma, immediately add to your bowl of herbs and toss together. Keep tossing until the herb mixture is completely cool. The heat from the sesame seeds will toast the rest of your herbs and make the blend come together. Keeps in airtight container for 1 year at room temperature.

Aleppo Butter (Western Asia & North Africa)

MAKES 1 PINT

- 750 g heavy whipping cream
- 20 g ground Aleppo pepper, or to taste
- 3 g ground cumin, or to taste
- 3 g salt, or to taste

In a stand mixer fitted with the whisk attachment, beat the cream on medium-high speed until the solids split from the liquid, about 10 minutes. Dropping a kitchen towel over the mixer will keep your kitchen from splatters. Continue to beat until the solids bunch together on the whisk and the liquid has separated. Gather the butter solids into a separate bowl. Add the pepper, cumin, and salt to taste. Use a wooden spoon to incorporate the spices and salt into the butter. Transfer the butter to sheets of plastic wrap and roll into a log, or pack into pint-size containers. Transfer to the fridge to solidify. Keeps for 2 to 3 weeks in the fridge or for 3 months in the freezer.

Crispy Broccoli Rabe Borage Cream Cheese (Western Asia & North Africa)

MAKES 1 PINT

- 1 head broccoli rabe, cut into small florets
- 3 garlic cloves, sliced ¼ inch thick
- Extra-virgin olive oil
- Freshly ground black pepper
- Salt
- 250 g cream cheese
- 100 g feta
- 30 g heavy whipping cream
- 10 to 15 borage flowers

Preheat oven to 450°F. Line a sheet tray with parchment paper. Place the broccoli rabe florets and sliced garlic in a medium bowl and sprinkle with olive oil, pepper, and salt. Spread out across the prepared sheet pan. Bake for 12 to 15 minutes, until crispy. Remove from the oven and let cool completely, then roughly chop to ¼-inch pieces. In a stand mixer fitted with the whisk attachment, combine the cream cheese, feta, and cream. Whip on medium speed, for 2 minutes, increase to high speed and whip until light and fluffy. Gently fold in the broccoli mixture and borage flowers. Keeps in an airtight container for 2 weeks in the fridge.

Staying Hungry

This book was written over the first two years of a global pandemic. While it was a frightening time, some beautiful practices emerged. Gardening in any small space was embraced by so many, to their delight, seeing that with each new plant relationship their lives were enriched with food and flora. Bread making had a huge renaissance, as more people had hours to fill and curious minds were ignited by the connection with ancient bacteria. Cakes have never been so beautiful, as they have been used as beacons of joy in dark times. Farmers and food workers were essential and venerated every day for doing the hard and integral work to keep their communities fed. We can keep these beautiful practices alive, beyond our emergency state. We can deepen our curiosity, and our connections with food and those who help bring it to the table.

Once you've worked through the flavor combinations in this book and know where food comes from, I encourage you to play! Feel free to mix and match cakes and fillings, bakes with different fruit or nuts, different sauces and spreads for different flatbreads or crackers. You get the idea! We live in a global world with established trade that allows many of us to access things year-round and far away. Let your imagination be your guide, but remember your best kitchen will be built mainly with local and in-season items and a few faraway treasures. Celebrate where you are. Everyday choices of where you source your ingredients and what makers you support make a huge impact. These daily habits begin to do the big work we need for changing systems.

And it's the global systems that need to change to become more transparent, accountable, and accessible. It is overly romantic to imagine that individual choices alone will suffice. This book has attempted to illustrate how using more whole grain strengthens agricultural diversity and supports farmers' ability to set their real cost for grain. But systems require larger steps taken by people with power in regulatory and governmental bodies. You can impact this level as well! Read up on food literature and ingredient origins to understand more deeply how we humans have formed our systems. Always look for transparency when sourcing ingredients near or far. City and state elections are a wonderful way to get involved and directly affect food policy. The Farm Bill is a federal bill that gets amended every five years and directs huge amounts of funds to food and agricultural production. Your voice and where your dollar is spent change its terms.

A lot of apps and websites are available to deepen your knowledge of plants and food systems. Volunteer at farmers' markets or research becoming a Master Food Preserve or Master Gardener under the guidance of a state land grant university in your area. Or search for similar programs at NGOs or volunteer groups. Don't be afraid to get started! To learn and try new things! Like in the kitchen, we learn the most from our failures in the garden. Share what you learn with others; this is how we build community. The following are my favorite resources; many are community specific, but most can be accessed globally. Let this be your jumping-off point for more research. Each choice is a powerful step toward the food systems we want to build for our future. Keep asking, How do we take this further? How do we have good bread and also roses?

Resources

Mills

Anson Mills

Arrowhead Mills

Authentic Foods

Barton Springs Mill

Bob's Red Mill*

Camas Country Mill

Capay Mills

Carolina Ground

Central Milling*

Hayden Flour Mills

Grist & Toll

GrowNYC Grains

Janie's Mill

King Arthur*

Maine Grains

Montana Flour & Grains

Small Valley Milling

Tehachapi Heritage Grain Project

Wade's Mill

Wild Hive Farm

* Denotes a mill that produces stone-ground and roller-milled flours.

Pantry Ingredients

Acid League. Artisan vinegars featuring garden produce.

Brightland. Wonderful California olive oil.

Burlap & Barrel. High-quality spices and spice blends.

Diaspora Co. Incredible single-origin spices.

Frontier Co-op. Resource for lots of fun baking items.

Graza olive oil. High-quality oil in a squeeze bottle.

Jacobsen Salt Co. Great sea salt on the West Coast.

Maldon Salt. Fantastic flaky sea salt in a few flavors.

Mandelin, Inc. For great almond pastes and marzipan.

Starwest Botanicals. Great resource for culinary-grade dried flowers.

Tart Vinegar. Unique small-batch vinegar flavors.

Tools

Breadtopia. Great resource for bread-specific tools.

Feast of Burdens. Incredible company making beautiful tablecloths.

GIR. Fantastic kitchen tools that are well weighted in your hand.

KitchenAid. Classic stand mixer; I recommend 5- or 8-quart.

Material Kitchen. Kitchen tools that are durable and beautiful.

Made In. Great everyday knives. Incredible pots and pans.

Shun Cutlery. Specialty knives.

WebstaurantStore. Resource for restaurant-quality storage containers and sheet trays.

Guilds and Academic Organizations

Bread Bakers Guild of America (www.bbga.org)

Oxford Symposium on Food & Cookery (oxfordsymposium.org.uk)

Slow Food USA (slowfoodusa.com)

Farmers' Markets and Gardens

Community Gardening Toolkit for starting a community garden in your area (cfnm.org/wp-content/uploads/2013/06/FINAL-HOW-TO-START-A-COMMUNITY-GARDEN-5.21.12.pdf)

National Farmers Markets Directory (nfmd.org)

Community Gardens registry (www.communitygarden.org/garden)

USDA Community Gardening guide (www.nal.usda.gov/legacy/afsic/community-gardening)

USDA Farmers Market Directory (www.usdalocalfoodportal.com)

Apps

NatureID: App for identifying plants in the wild. Safely forage with this app in hand.

VILD MAD: App with forage maps from around the world. Crowd sourced.

Gaia GPS: App for navigation when going off trail and out of service.

Acknowledgments

This book is a dream come true. After a decade celebrating whole grains and a lifetime spent traveling, I am so grateful to share my passion with you through these recipes. I am endlessly grateful for the following people who have been colleague, mentor, teacher, and dear friends:

My mother, who defined my food philosophy. She taught me to bake early, and it's a skill that's enriched my life ever since. She shared her own love of food generously with everyone at her table, old friend or new. And she introduced me to my first best friend—the garden. I wish I could place this book in your hands and throw my arms around you. I love and miss you every day.

I want to thank Guy Tabibian, who has kept our world spinning, taking care of the chickens, walking the dogs, and reminding me to eat while I sat for weeks on end throughout the last two years' writing. Who tasted everything sweet, salty, savory, and sour at every hour of the day and night by the spoonful and endured endless repetition of "What do you think?" Thank you for always telling me the truth. Thank you for being my best friend and my greatest fan. Thank you for washing so many dishes. I love you. I could not have written this book without you.

I want to thank my amazing team of photographers and co–food stylists who made this beautiful book with all my adjusting and proper changes. Rebecca Stumpf, your eye for light has enchanted me since we first met years ago. Your organization is unmatched; thank you for the magic moments. I love you. Jessica Dean, a last-minute addition to the team that made all the difference; your laughter, love of color, and thoughtfulness was a joy to collaborate with on styling. Instant best friends. Thank you to Megan Potthoff, Bronwen Wyatt, and Elisa Sunga, for all the help bringing the food to life through the weeks of shooting. Your hands throughout the book make me so happy. Thank you for sharing the laughter, the stress, and the love of this experience with me. I miss eating all the pastries at the end of each day with all of you.

I want to thank Myrita Craig for reading over sections of this book, keeping me fed in the last weeks of writing, playing with my dogs, and helping me stay sane throughout the roller coaster of creativity. Thank you for your loving support and radical honesty always.

I want to thank Mika Shannon-Link, for always being my number 1 cheerleader and confidant. Here's to always believing in all our dreams.

I want to thank Martha and Jim Desrosiers, Camila Wynn, Caroline Schiff, Lisa Beck, Jessie Sheehan, Dina Furumoto, Michelle Boulos, and my manager, Chris Billig. At different points in my life, you have been pillars of inspiration, guidance, strength, and love for me. I would have been lost without you.

I want to thank everyone who tested these recipes across the nation and sometimes internationally so that they could be as reliable and approachable as possible: Erin Sweet, Emma Hayes, Kerry Efron, Madeleine Bersin, Dominique Butler, Maria Wolter, JoMarie Ricketts, Emily Weigand, Vanessa Matins, Sofia Villain, Corie Greenberg, In Chieh Chen, Dari Matilsky, Kathryn McClelland, Alissa Rothman, Susannah Lester, Madalyn Nones, Katie Stelmanis, Scarlett Cisneros, Mia Crisostomo, Nora Loechler, Elena Screener, Sarah Pierce, and Felicity Spector. The book is better for all your attention, time, creativity, insights, and suggestions.

I want to thank Clemence Gossett, for sharing your passion for baking with me for over a decade. Thank you for giving me my first opportunity to share my knowledge through teaching at the Gourmandise School. My happiest cooking and baking memories are laughing and making food with my students at your school. I am so grateful for you and all those years.

I want to thank Nan and Chris Kohler of Grist and Toll. Thank you for being true friends in my darkest hours and always meeting me with tenderness. Thank you for all the illumination you have brought to my life through all your beautiful flours. I cannot live without them. Thank you for teaching me everything I know about milling and all the fun test bakes in the back kitchen. I admire your passion, your work ethic, and all your knowledge. The community was bolstered, and the movement thrust forward with the opening of your mill in Pasadena, California. I am so very grateful for you both.

I want to thank Sherry Mandel of the Tehachapi Heritage Grain Project for always giving me great grains from California. Your constant encouragement, words of love, and sometimes a weekly cocktail have kept me going the last several years. Seeing you every Wednesday at the Santa Monica Farmers Market is a psychic anchor I cannot live without. You are a light in the world.

I want to thank all the farmers, mills, and bakeries, in the United States and internationally, that have hosted me for popups and collaborations over the years. I have learned so much from everyone who has allowed me to stand alongside them and practice this craft. Thank you for continuing to make beautiful flour and food for people to enjoy.

I want to thank all the home bakers and home cooks, in so many different countries around the world, who generously shared their table, stories, and food practices with me over the last several decades. Every time I make food, I am transported to your loving, humble, and celebratory tables. Thank you from the bottom of my heart for sharing your passions with me.

I want to thank all the farmers at the Santa Monica Farmers Market. It has been a joy to champion your great produce for the last 12 years. And my four years as a vendor at the market were some of my favorites! Thank you to all the markets the world over I have been lucky to walk through, tasting and dreaming. Thank you to planet Earth for all the daily miracles.

I want to thank Petra Paredez, without whose encouragement I would not have taken the meetings that led to this book. Thank you for all your years of friendship since high school and years of professional cheerleading. A seat at your pie shop and a delicious slice are all I ever need when I come through New York City.

I want to thank my agent, Eryn Kalavsky, who enthusiastically championed this book and all my wild ideas for delicious slow food! Thank you for always sharing my enthusiasm! It is a gift to work with someone who gets you. Thank you for talking me through every epiphany and doubt. And for finding the perfect home for *Bread and Roses*.

I want to thank my publishing team: my editor, Ann Treistman, and designer, Allison Chi. I have appreciated every discussion and brainstorming to make this book the best it could be. Thank you for believing in my colorful botanical vision and trusting me to bring it to life. I am so grateful to have been on this journey with you. Thank you forever to Countryman Press and W. W. Norton for making this book a reality.

Index

Gluten-Free Recipes

The following recipes are gluten-free or can be made gluten-free with just a simple swap or adjustment outlined in the recipe:

73 Brown Rice Kinako Salted Cherry Blossom Cherry Crisp

80 Fried Brown Rice Pudding with Chrysanthemum Custard

82 Brown Rice Cotton Cake with Candied Sudachi Lime

93 Buckwheat Brown Sugar Crumble Carrot Peach Icebox Cake

99 Buckwheat Soba Noodles with Cured Egg, Nukazuke Pickles, Kosho Butter Chicken

151 Puffed Quinoa Brown Sugar Brownies with Persimmon

168 Amaranth Squash Almond Butter Pancakes with Maple Syrup & Roasted Sunflower Butter

171 Amaranth & Corn Crumble with Papaya, Raspberry & Lime

179 Masa Corn Nasturtium Quesadilla

214 Oatmeal Chocolate Chunk Cookies

217 Baked Oatmeal with Fig Bee Pollen Jam & Fig Leaf Oil

262 All Salts and Sugars

264 All Glazes, Sauces, Soups, and Drinks

266 All Roasted, Macerated, and Candied

270 All Jams and Marmalades

274 All Soaks, Creams, Curds, Custards, and Ice Creams

281 All Meringues, Marshmallow Fluff, and Buttercreams

284 All Ferments, Spreads, Butters, Oils, and Spice Mixes

Vegan Recipes

The following recipes are naturally vegan or can be made vegan with just a simple swap or adjustment outlined in the recipe:

84 Toasted Barley Porridge with Clotted Cream & Roasted Kumquats

117 Emmer Everything Bread: Bâtard, Boule & Grissini

120 Rye Triple Chocolate Crinkle Cookies

123 Rye Apple Onion Focaccia

125 Rye Black Bread

162 Amaranth Marigold Buñuelos

168 Amaranth Squash Almond Butter Pancakes with Maple Syrup & Roasted Sunflower Butter

179 Masa Corn Nasturtium Quesadilla

194 Durum Orange Blossom Overnight Porridge with Tamarind Syrup & Watermelon

217 Baked Oatmeal with Fig Bee Pollen Jam & Fig Leaf Oil

236 Khorasan Tahini Birdseed Muffins

254 Einkorn Bagels with Crispy Broccoli Rabe Borage Cream Cheese

262 All Salts and Sugars

265 Carrot Sauce

266 Roasted Kumquats

267 Candied Sudachi Limes

267 Tarragon Poached Pears

267 Blistered Berries

269 Candied Hibiscus

269 Macerated Strawberries and Ground Cherries

270 All Jams and Marmalades

286 Kosho Oil

286 Nukazuke Pickles

289 Rooibos Olive Oil

289 Fig Leaf Oil

289 Nettle Dip

290 Za'atar

General Index

A

Agar agar, 24
Amaranth, 149
  buñuelos, 162
  cookie sandwiches, 165
  crumble, 171
  pancakes, 168

B

Baker's math, 52
Baking powder, 57
Baking soda, 57
Barley, 69
  chocolate chunk cookies, 88
  fritter, 91
  porridge, 84
  thumbprint cookies, 87
Blossoms
  African, 191
  of the Americas, 149
  Asian, 69
  European, 107
  of western Asia and north
      Africa, 223
  See also Flowers, edible
Botanicals. *See* Edible blooms
    and herbs
Bread
  fermentation process, 40–42
  hybrid method, 42
  building and storing a liquid
      starter, 42–44
    pro tips for, 44
  building the dough, 44–49
  baking, 49–50
    pro tips for, 50, 52
  baker's math, 52
Buckwheat, 69
  cake, 101
  icebox cake, 93
  milk soak, 275
  soba noodles, 99

sugar tarts, 96
Butter
  Aleppo, 290
  roasted sunflower, 287
Butter (dairy), 24
Buttercream
  crema American, 282
  German chocolate, 281
  passion fruit, 282
  pistachio, 283
  smoky honey Swiss, 282
  sorghum, 283

C

Cake, 52–53
  baking, 53
  building, 53–54
  decorating with blooms, 54–55
  serving, 55–56
  failures with, 54
  types of, 53
Candied recipes
  blistered berries, 267
  blood orange caramel, 267
  hibiscus, 269
  honeycomb candy, 269
  Sudachi limes, 267
Cheese, 24
Chocolate, 25
  buttercream, 281
  chunk cookies, 88, 214, 224
  crinkle cookies, 120
  custard pie, 133
  hazelnut chocolate custard,
      277
  history of, 63
  hot chocolate drink, 266
  sauce, 264
Cocoa powder, 25
Commercial yeast
  as biological leavener, 56–57
  fermentation with, 41–42
  time shifting with, 56–59
Conversions between
  leaveners, 57

Cookies and tarts, about, 37–38
Corn, 149
  biscuits, 175
  blueberry pie, 176
  cake, 185
  cookies, 172
  honeysuckle cake, 182
  quesadilla, 179
Cream, 24
Creaming method, 38
Creams
  chicory, 277
  clotted, 274
  poppy seed, 280
  sweet cream, 276
  sweet woodruff cocoa nib, 277
  whipped cheesecake, 277
Curds
  corn, 278
  passion fruit, 278
  yuzu, 276
Custards
  chrysanthemum, 275
    légère variation, 275
  coconut, 275
  coffee, 279
    légère variation, 279
  halva, 280
  hazelnut chocolate, 277
  lemon verbena, 278
  peanut frangipane, 283
  rose geranium, 279
  rose hip, 280
  salty honey, 276

D

Dough
  bread, 44
    choosing a leavener, 45
    mixing the dough, 45
    adding salt, 45
    bulk ferment, stretch, and
        fold, 45–47
      methods, 45, 47
    shaping, 47

using your work surface, 47

final proof, 47, 49

poke test, 49

time shifting with, 57–59

windowpane test, 47

cookie and tart, 37

methods for, 38

resting the dough, 38

pastry, 38–40

Drink, hot chocolate, 266

Durum, 191

chocolate chunk cookies, 193

fried cheese pastry, 197

overnight porridge, 194

E

Edible blooms and herbs, 26, 29, 31

See also Flowers, edible

Egg(s), 24

yolks, cured, 286

Einkorn, 223

bagels, 254

blondies, 247

challah, 251

cookies, 244

dinner rolls, 248

olive oil cake, 257

Emmer, 107

everything bread, 117

maritozzo, 114

pear tarragon honey tart, 111

sourdough pasta, 109

Extracts and pastes, 25

F

Farmers' markets, 31–32

Fermentation process, 41–42

seed rate affecting, 59

Fermented recipes

fermented honey, 289

nukazuke pickles, 286

Float test, 43

Flour

all-purpose, 17–18

replacing, 18

families, 22–23

tasting wheel, 18–19

Flowers, edible, 26, 29, 31

decorating with, 54–55

See also Blossoms

Food map of the world, 64–65

Food regions, 62

Africa, 191

the Americas, 149

Asia, 69

Europe, 107

western Asia and north Africa, 223

Foraging basics, 32

Frissage technique, 39

G

Gardening basics, 31–32

Glazes

genmaicha, 265

lemongrass, 264

Gluten-free recipes, 299

Grains. *See* Whole grains; *specific grains*

Grains (regional). *See* Food regions

H

Herbs. *See* Edible blooms and herbs

Honey, 21

Hybrid method, 42

I

Ice cream

juniper gelato, 279

lilac ice cream, 278

Ingredients

food history related to, 62–63

measuring and weighing, 27–28

modern wheats (*see* Wheats, modern)

other types of, 21, 24–26

tasting, 18–21

whole grains (*see* Whole grains)

J

Jams and marmalades, 270

additions to, 271

apricot pine nut jam, 274

banana marmalade, 273

fig bee pollen jam, 273

greengage jam, 273

oven canning, 271

peach jam, 272

red currant violet jam, 273

K

Khorasan, 223

malawach, 241

muffins, 236

sheet pie, 233

sugar buns, 239

Kitchen rules, 26

experimenting and substitution, 29

keeping food prep area clean, 28

knowing your oven, 28

mise en place, 27

practice baking, 26

scaling up recipes, 28

taking notes, 29

using it all, 28–29

weighing and measuring ingredients, 27–28

L

Laminating technique, 39–40

Larder. *See* Pantry & Larder

Leaveners, 24

amount added (seed rate), 59

chemical *vs.* biological, 56–57

Leaveners (*continued*)
  converting between, 57
  See also Fermentation
    process
Levain/leaven defined, 41
Liquid starter, building, 42–43
  See also Sourdough starter
Liquid temperature, changing,
    57–58

M

Macerated strawberries and
    ground cherries, 269
Maple syrup, 21
Marmalade. *See* Jams and
    marmalades
Marshmallow fluff, 283
Meringue, torched, 281
Milk, 24
  alternative milks, 24
  buckwheat milk soak, 275
  cultured milk soup, 266
Millet, 191
  cream puffs, 206
  drop donuts, 205
  hand pies, 209
Molasses, 21

N

Nuts, 24–25

O

Oats, 191
  baked oatmeal, 217
  biscuit rolls, 218
  chocolate chunk cookies, 214
  walnut cake, 211
Oil(s), 25
  fig leaf, 289
  kosho, 286
  nettle dip, 289
  rooibos olive, 289
Oven canning, 271
Ovens, conduction *vs.*
    convection, 28

P

Pantry & Larder, 261–62
  ferments, spreads, butters,
    oils, and spice mixes, 284,
    286–87, 289–90
  glazes, sauces, soups, and
    drinks, 264–66
  jams and marmalades,
    270–74
  meringues, marshmallow fluff,
    and buttercreams, 281–84
  roasted, macerated, and
    candied, 266, 269
  salts and sugars, 262, 264
  soaks, creams, curds,
    custards, and ice creams,
    274–81
Pastes and extracts, 25
Pastry, about, 38–40
Percentages. *See* Baker's math
Pie. *See* Pastry
Poached fruit recipes: tarragon
    poached pears, 267
Poke test, 49
Poolish/biga defined, 41
Porridge test, 20
Produce, seasonal, 26

Q

Quinoa, 149
  biscuits, 175
  brownies, 151
  chili buns, 156
  churros, 153
  upside-down cake, 159

R

Rice, 69
  brown rice cotton cake, 82
  brown rice pudding, 80
  cherry crisp, 73
  donut bars, 74
  scallion pancake, 77
  shortbread, 70
Roasted fruit recipes

bay leaf roasted quince, 269
  roasted kumquats, 266
Rye, 107
  black bread, 125
  chocolate cake, 131
  chocolate crinkle cookies,
    120
  focaccia, 123
  malt ice cream, 128

S

Salt, 21
Salted cherry blossoms, 262
Salty honey custard, 276
Sanding method, 38
Sauces
  carrot, 264
  chocolate, 264
Scaling up recipes. *See* Baker's
    math
Seed rate, 59
Seeds, 25
Shortbread test, 20–21
Soaks
  buckwheat milk, 275
  sorghum, 280
Sonora, 107
  cheese sticks, 141
  chocolate custard pie, 133
  madeleines, 138
  pistachio linzer cookies, 136
  vegetable confetti cake, 143
Sorghum soak, 280
Soup, cultured milk, 266
Sourdough starter
  as biological leavener, 56–57
  building and storing, 42–44
  changing variables for,
    57–59
  conversion methods, 57
  dehydrating, 44
  float test for, 43
  pro tips for, 44
  terms, 41
  See also Bread

Spelt, 223
    almond rosewater tea cake,
        226
    chocolate chunk cookies,
        224
    khachapuri, 231
    morning buns, 228
Spice(s), 25–26
    history of, 63
    mix: za'atar, 290
Spreads
    crispy broccoli rabe borage
        cream cheese, 290
    nasturtium pine nut &
        pumpkin seed spread,
        287
Starter. See Sourdough starter
Substitution in recipes, 29
Sugar, 21
    types of
        bay leaf, 262
        coriander, 262
        crystallized roses, 264
        jasmine, 264
        marigold, 262

    pepper, 264
    pink peppercorn, 264
    sumac, 264
    history of, 62–63

T
Tarts and cookies, about,
    37–38
Tasting grain and ingredients,
    18–21
Techniques
    frissage, 39
    laminating, 39–40
Teff, 191
    anise custard cake, 202
    crackers, 198
    sugar moons, 200
Temperature of liquids,
    adjusting, 57–58
Time shifting, 56–59
Tongue test, 20
Tools, 36–37

V
Vegan recipes, 299

W
Wheats, modern, 17–18
    See also Durum; Emmer;
        Sonora
Whole grains, 15–17
    all-purpose flour, 17–18
    farmers' markets, 31–32
    gardening basics, 31–32
    foraging basics, 32
    impact of choosing, 18
    milling at home, 17
    modern wheats, 17
    tasting, 18–21
    terms for, 21
    See also specific grains
Wild yeast
    fermentation with, 41, 59
    as leavener, 24
Windowpane test, 47
Wrinkle test, 271

Y
Yeast. See Commercial yeast;
    Wild yeast
Yogurt, 24

About the Author

ROSE WILDE is a writer, chef, master food preserver, master gardener, and owner of Red Bread. Since 2011, Red Bread's commitment to social justice has provided for over 74,000 meals working with the Los Angles Food Bank and through bake sales with Gather for Good and Bakers Against Racism. Rose's goal is to champion good food and good people. Her work has appeared in the *Los Angeles Times*, *Washington Post*, *Wall Street Journal*, *Edible* magazine, *Cherry Bombe*, and many other publications. She has been a regular on the Food Network, Cooking Channel, Tastemade, and NPR. She lives in Los Angeles, California, with her partner, two dogs, and nine chickens. For more inspiration find her on Instagram @trosewilde.

"Rose is as technicolor and exuberant as her gorgeous cakes. But this book is so much more—it is an exhaustive and encyclopedic collection of knowledge, techniques, and recipes from someone who has made a life's work of deeply exploring flours and flowers. There is something for every baker here, from light, fresh, and simple to layered and elaborate. The baking world is lucky to have Rose, and this book." **—JENNIFER LATHAM**, author of *Baking Bread with Kids*

"Beautiful, inventive, and thoughtful recipes from a generous and kind baker. This cookbook is exactly the inspiration and inventiveness that seasoned bakers crave, with the approachable and gentle instruction that new bakers need to learn new techniques. Equal parts how-to, history, and aspirational flavors, *Bread and Roses* is a delightful pleasure-packed kitchen companion." **—BONNIE OHARA**, owner/baker of Alchemy Bread and author of *Bread Baking for Beginners* and *Let's Bake Bread!*